MANAGING
CORPORATE SOCIAL RESPONSIBILITY

W. TIMOTHY COOMBS & SHERRY J. HOLLADAY

MANAGING CORPORATE SOCIAL RESPONSIBILITY

A Communication Approach

WILEY-BLACKWELL
A John Wiley & Sons, Ltd., Publication

This edition first published 2012

Blackwell Publishing was acquired by John Wiley & Sons in February 2007. Blackwell's publishing program has been merged with Wiley's global Scientific, Technical, and Medical business to form Wiley-Blackwell.

Registered Office
John Wiley & Sons Ltd, The Atrium, Southern Gate, Chichester, West Sussex, PO19 8SQ, UK

Editorial Offices
350 Main Street, Malden, MA 02148-5020, USA
9600 Garsington Road, Oxford, OX4 2DQ, UK
The Atrium, Southern Gate, Chichester, West Sussex, PO19 8SQ, UK

For details of our global editorial offices, for customer services, and for information about how to apply for permission to reuse the copyright material in this book please see our website at www.wiley.com/wiley-blackwell.

Library of Congress Cataloging-in-Publication Data

Coombs, W. Timothy.
Managing corporate social responsibility : a communication approach / W. Timothy Coombs, Sherry J. Holladay.
p. cm.
Includes bibliographical references and index.
ISBN 978-1-4443-3629-0 (hardback) – ISBN 978-1-4443-3645-0 (paperback)
1. Social responsibility of business. 2. Business communication.
I. Holladay, Sherry J. II. Title.
HD60.C6347 2011
658.4'08–dc23

2011017060

A catalogue record for this book is available from the British Library.

This book is published in the following electronic formats: ePDFs 9781118106655; Wiley Online Library 9781118106686; ePub 9781118106662; Kindle 9781118106679

Set in 10/12 pt Sabon by Toppan Best-set Premedia Limited
Printed and bound in Malaysia by Vivar Printing Sdn Bhd

1 2012

We dedicate this book to Jeanne, Tom, and Dorothy.

We dedicate this book to Leonard Jr. and Dorothy.

Contents

Contents in Detail ix

Acknowledgments xiii

1 **Conceptualizing Corporate Social Responsibility** 1

2 **Strategic CSR** 29

3 **CSR Scanning and Monitoring** 51

4 **Formative Research** 63

5 **Create the CSR Initiative** 89

6 **Communicate the CSR Initiative** 109

7 **Evaluation and Feedback** 137

8 **CSR Issues** 153

References 165

Index 177

Contents in Detail

Acknowledgments xiii

1 Conceptualizing Corporate Social Responsibility 1

Box 1.1: The Sullivan Principles 2
Corporate Social Responsibility: Seeking Parameters 5
Defining CSR 6
Box 1.2: Definition of CSR 8
Benefits and Costs of CSR 9
Two Sides of CSR Cost-Benefit Analysis 9
CSR Costs for Corporations 10
CSR Costs for Society 12
CSR Benefits for Corporations 13
CSR Benefits for Society 14
Winning and Sustaining Support for CSR 14
Other Conceptual Questions about CSR 16
CSR: Modern or Historic? 16
Box 1.3: Forest Stewardship Council (FSC) Standards 19
Forms of CSR 20
Where Is CSR's Home? 22
Should CSR Standards Be Localized or Globalized? 24
Conclusion 27

2 Strategic CSR 29

Characteristics of the Corporation 31
Stakeholder Expectations and the Importance of Organizational Identification 32
Reputational Benefits of CSR 35

Perceived Motives for CSR Initiatives 38
General Strategic Guidance: Approaching the CSR Process as Change Management 44
Everyone Loves a Good Story 45
The CSR Process Model: A Brief Preview 47

3 CSR Scanning and Monitoring 51

Issues Management 53
Scanning and CSR 54
Prioritizing CSR Concerns 54
Monitoring and CSR 57
Scanning and Monitoring in Concert 58
Stakeholder Engagement's Role in Scanning and Monitoring 58
Conclusion and Critical Questions 60

4 Formative Research 63

Researching Stakeholder Expectations for CSR 67
Box 4.1: MyStarbucksidea CSR Suggestions 68
The Expectation Gap Approach 69
Box 4.2: IKEA Child Labour Code of Conduct 71
Origins of Expectation Gaps 73
Box 4.3: Pinkwashing Detection 75
Relevance of Operant Conditioning Theory to Stakeholder Challenges 77
The Alignment Approach 80
The Counterbalance: Corporate Concerns 85
Conclusion and Critical Questions 85

5 Create the CSR Initiative 89

Selecting the CSR Initiatives: Appreciating the Contestable Nature of CSR 90
Differing CSR Expectations among Stakeholders 90
Stakeholder Salience 91
Box 5.1: Stakeholder Salience 92
What Constitutes CSR? 92
Stakeholder Participation in Decision Making 94
Organizational Justice in the Engagement Process 96
The "Right Amount" of CSR 98

When Employees Challenge CSR: Considering Internal Stakeholders 99
Preparing for Negative Stakeholder Reactions: Message Mapping 101
Developing CSR Objectives 101
Box 5.2: Message-Mapping Template 102
Process versus Outcome Objectives 103
Conclusion and Critical Questions 105

6 Communicate the CSR Initiative 109

CSR Promotional Communication Dilemma 110
Box 6.1: Overview of Corporate-Activist Partnerships 116
Communication Channels for CSR Messaging 116
Overview of Communication Channels for CSR 117
Box 6.2: Social Media Overview 118
Employees as a Communication Channel 122
External Stakeholders as a Communication Channel 123
Strategic Application of Social Media to CSR Communication 124
The Overall CSR Promotional Communication Strategy 128
Annual Reports and CSR Communication 128
Conclusion and Critical Questions 133

7 Evaluation and Feedback 137

Evaluation 138
Assurance and CSR Evaluation 141
Stakeholder Engagement in the Evaluation Process 142
Box 7.1: Musgrave Group Assurance Statement 2006 143
Box 7.2: Basic ROI Formula 145
Considering Return on Investment 145
Feedback 146
Feedback from Stakeholders on the CSR Process 147
The Communication Audit 148
Conclusion and Critical Questions 148

8 CSR Issues 153

Overarching Concerns for CSR Initiatives 154
Responsibility for CSR Initiatives 155
Limitations from Industry, Culture, and Law 157

Industry Standards 157
The Culture and Socioeconomic Context 158
Box 8.1: Culture and Activism 160
The Legal Context 161
Beyond Limitations 161
Parting Thoughts 162

References 165

Index 177

Acknowledgments

Many individuals supported us along the way to make this text a reality, and to all we are very grateful. Most importantly, we thank Elizabeth Swayze, our editor at Wiley-Blackwell, for continuing to be an enthusiastic and responsive advocate for our work. This text, along with our previous publications with Wiley-Blackwell, has benefited from Elizabeth's encouragement and judicious feedback. Elizabeth's guidance has enabled us to pursue projects that are important to our discipline, accessible to our readers, and often enable us to push the boundaries of the status quo.

We owe thanks to our production team who worked hard to get our manuscript into shape. Matthew Brown ably supervised the process and amazingly kept everyone on a tight schedule. We acknowledge Dave Nash, who worked with permissions and images to secure visual elements we believed would enhance the book. Dave persistently sought permissions from often reluctant (and sometimes completely uncooperative) sources. We also thank Cheryl Adam, our copy-editor. Cheryl's competence undoubtedly makes us look better and adds to our readers' experiences with the material in our book.

We also thank the scholars who reviewed the early version of the manuscript and offered suggestions that enhanced the book.

W. Timothy Coombs
Sherry J. Holladay
University of Central Florida, Orlando

Home Depot, the world's largest home improvement retailer, operates in the US, Canada, Mexico, and China. Home Depot supports "Team Depot," a volunteer program led by store associates that participates in community programs. Courtesy of Volunteer Canada

1

Conceptualizing Corporate Social Responsibility

Apartheid is an historical artifact for many people reading this book rather than a current issue or reality. Apartheid was a severe, state-sanctioned racial segregation practiced in South Africa and what was then called Rhodesia (now Zimbabwe). A white minority used apartheid to oppress the indigenous black populations. In the 1970s, Dr. Leon Howard Sullivan, a US minister, plotted a corrective course of action that became known as the Sullivan Principles. The Sullivan Principles were designed to help end apartheid in South Africa by placing requirements on US corporations wanting to conduct business in South Africa. Box 1.1 lists the final seven points to the Sullivan Principles (Leon H. Sullivan Foundation, n.d.). The Sullivan Principles, along with the divestment campaign of the 1980s, did exert some pressure on the South African government. The divestment campaign worked in tandem with the Sullivan Principles. Investors were asked to divest (remove investments) from any US companies that did not adopt the Sullivan Principles. College campuses were a hotbed of activity for divestment pressures in the 1980s. Campus protests brought attention to the issue and pressured universities to cease investing in corporations doing business in South Africa. While the Sullivan Principles alone precipitated very little change, the divestment campaign is credited with having a significant effect on eradicating apartheid in South Africa.

The Sullivan Principles and related divestment efforts are indicators of corporate social responsibility (CSR) making a difference on a global scale. Fair treatment of workers and socially responsible investing are recognized today as CSR. The Sullivan Principles provide a foundation for socially

Managing Corporate Social Responsibility: A Communication Approach, First Edition.
W. Timothy Coombs, Sherry J. Holladay.

Box 1.1 The Sullivan Principles

1. Non-segregation of the races in all eating, comfort, and work facilities.
2. Equal and fair employment practices for all employees.
3. Equal pay for all employees doing equal or comparable work for the same period of time.
4. Initiation of and development of training programs that will prepare, in substantial numbers, blacks and other nonwhites for supervisory, administrative, clerical, and technical jobs.
5. Increasing the number of blacks and other nonwhites in management and supervisory positions.
6. Improving the quality of life for blacks and other nonwhites outside the work environment in such areas as housing, transportation, school, recreation, and health facilities.
7. Working to eliminate laws and customs that impede social, economic, and political justice. *(added in 1984)*

Source: Leon H. Sullivan Foundation (n.d.).

responsible investing and, therefore, comprise a form of CSR as well. The focus of the Sullivan Principles was social improvement through the elimination of apartheid. The Sullivan Principles were not the first CSR effort or the first socially responsible investing guidelines to appear in the business world. However, the anti-apartheid efforts illustrated the potential power of CSR. Corporations were pressured to change their behavior not because their actions were illegal but because their actions failed to meet expectations for responsible behavior.

On December 3, 1984, the Union Carbide India Limited facility in Bhopal, India, leaked tons of deadly methyl isocyanate (MIC) gas. Bhopal quickly became the worst industrial accident in the history of the world. Estimates place the death toll at between 3,000 and 10,000 people in the first 72 hours. One estimate places the number of those who have died since being exposed at around 15,000. Between 120,000 to 500,000 people suffered permanent medical conditions from the exposure (Amnesty, 2009). Investigative reports since the accident all noted lax safety as the cause. Union Carbide's own investigation identified procedural violations and operating errors (Diamond, 1985). Many safety systems did not function, and overall the facility was in disrepair. This created a very unsafe operating environment that led to tragic consequences for employees and those living near the facility (Bedford, 2009).

People in the United States were concerned because Union Carbide was using the same chemical at a US facility. Union Carbide reassured US citizens that the facility in the United States was safer. That led some people to question the original safety commitment in Bhopal (Diamond, 1984). Here is one description of the safety discrepancies between Bhopal and the United States.

> Carbide had dropped the safety standards at the Bhopal plant well below those it maintained at a nearly identical facility in West Virginia. It is also important to note here that Carbide was able to operate its deteriorating plant because industrial safety and environmental laws and regulations were lacking or were not strictly enforced by the state of Madhya Pradesh or the Indian government making them indirectly responsible for the tragedy at Bhopal. (Trade Environmental Database, 1997)

The US facility was slightly different as it had fewer control systems and relied more on manual rather than automatic systems (Shabecoff, 1984). In fact, Union Carbide documents released during litigation indicated the Bhopal facility was built using some untested technologies (Trade Environmental Database, 1997).

Bhopal should not be forgotten so that it is never repeated. Bhopal stands as an appalling example of the exploitation of developing countries. The same deadly chemical was present in Bhopal, India, and in the United States. In Bhopal, the safety standards were lax from the start and were allowed to deteriorate. In the United States, the safety standards were maintained to a higher standard. Why the neglect in Bhopal? The answer is financial gain. Union Carbide saved money by requiring less rigorous safety standards in India and by not investing in preventative maintenance (Bedford, 2009). We cannot assume corporations will naturally act in a responsible or even a humane manner. This is not to say that all corporations are inherently evil and callous toward constituent safety. Bhopal reminds us that CSR may not be naturally occurring within the corporate environment. The allure of profit sometimes can be deadly for constituents.

Nike remains the leader in the athletic shoe and garment market globally. The brand is widely recognized around the world and associated with winning. In the 1990s, Nike became associated with sweatshops and exploitation of workers. Many nongovernment organizations (NGOs), such as Global Exchange and Sweatshop Watch, began to complain about the treatment of workers in facilities that supplied Nike with products and materials. This mix of religious, student, and labor groups noted problems with corporal punishment, low wages, forced overtime, inhumane working conditions, and child labor (Team Sweat, 2008). An awareness campaign used public relations to inform constituents about the origin of Nike products. Combining the Internet with traditional news exposés, the NGOs were able to exercise a significant amount of pressure on Nike to reform its practices. Constituents increased public awareness of supplier practices, and this created negative publicity and pressure for Nike to change (Carty, 2002). We should note that the sweatshop issue was (and continues to be) endemic to the entire garment and shoe industry, not just Nike. Nike was targeted because activists know that confronting the market leader maximizes the attention that activists attract for their efforts.

NGOs included universities in the United States as their targets for the Nike effort. Students used various public relations tactics to pressure administrations into changing contracts if Nike did not alter its business practices. US universities have lucrative athletic shoe contracts with major shoe manufacturers such as Nike, Adidas, and Reebok. The Nike labor case illustrates how public relations becomes translated into political pressure via financial threats. Negative attention on the supply chain created policy changes (Bullert, 2000). O'Rourke (2005) notes that the NGOs used public relations and marketing campaigns to alter global production and consumption. The public relations efforts shifted demand from "problematic to improved products" (O'Rourke, 2005, p. 116). In essence, socially responsible consumption was creating more socially responsible corporate behavior – consumers were pushing for CSR.

These three vignettes are all pieces of the mosaic that comprise corporate social responsibility. They offer different insights into CSR and its transformative potential while reminding us that CSR transpires within a business landscape, not some abstract utopia. In these three cases, corporations engaged in "bad behavior" while experiencing economic success. But the public scrutiny of their actions contributed to outrage and pressure for change. As we shall see, pressure for "responsible behavior" may originate from inside the organization (e.g., it is seen as central to its mission), or they may emanate from pressures outside the organization as we saw in the three cases at the beginning of this chapter.

The challenge in discussing CSR is that it is not reducible to one simple concept. Our examples illustrate how irresponsible corporate behavior may take many forms. Similarly, *responsible behavior* is not easily defined. Nor can concerns surrounding CSR be traced to one common history. CSR is a composite of activities drawn from different academic and professional disciplines. Moreover, what constitutes CSR actions will differ from country to country. The complex nature of CSR results in a challenging first chapter that explains the conceptualization of CSR we have developed for this book, identifies costs and benefits for the corporation and society, and demonstrates the value of a communication-centered approach to CSR.

Throughout this book, we refer to stakeholders, their relationship to CSR and the corporation, and their role in the CSR process. Edward Freeman (1984) provides the classic definition of a *stakeholder* as "any group or individual who can affect or is affected by the achievement of organizational objectives" (p. 46). How the group or individual affects or is affected by the organization is the *stake* that binds them to the organization. We acknowledge that this is a broad definition and can even include nonhuman entities such as the environment. Our communication approach to CSR focuses on the importance of stakeholders and the stakeholder engagement process in conceptualizing, implementing, and evaluating CSR initiatives.

Thinking in terms of stakeholders represents a way of classifying or segmenting people – dividing people into similar groups. That is why writers often refer to types or categories of stakeholders. The *stake* is used to create the categories for segmentation. Typical stakeholder categories include employees (for whom employment is the stake), members of the community (for whom living near the organization is the stake), customers (for whom the product or service is the stake), and investors (for whom financial interest is the stake). Stakeholders also can be conceptualized in terms of CSR concerns or interests. For example, some stakeholders are especially concerned about and segmented according to environmental issues like air and water pollution, depletion of natural resources, or organizational impacts on endangered species. Their interest in environmental concerns is the stake that binds them to the organization. Other stakeholders are concerned with human rights and labor issues. They may focus on issues like child labor, the rights of workers to unionize, or workplace safety. The concerns of stakeholders can change and lead them to redefine their memberships. For example, those living near or working at Union Carbide's Bhopal facility may have thought of themselves as having an economic stake in its success. But that stake may have shifted dramatically following the Bhopal industrial accident and be broadened to include health and life-and-death concerns. Stakes also can shift when people are made aware of the relevance of the corporation to their interests. For instance, campaigns have helped to inform consumers of the conditions under which their apparel is manufactured and have led them to demand change. Stakeholders, their relationships with corporations, and communication's role in this relationship and the CSR process comprise the major theme woven throughout this book.

Corporate Social Responsibility: Seeking Parameters

When introducing a concept, it is important to define that concept and to articulate its parameters. We cannot assume everyone is working from the same conceptualization. That is especially true for CSR since it lacks one accepted definition and is a concept utilized in a variety of academic and professional disciplines. Moreover, the actions that constitute CSR can vary widely. Conceptualizing CSR is much like trying to map sand dunes in a desert. We can see the dunes, but they shift over time in both location and the grains of sand that comprise the dunes. What we can understand about dunes is that they are composed of sand and that certain forces, such as wind, serve to shape them. As we conceptualize CSR, we need to take a macro rather than a micro view to identify common elements within CSR. In a way, we are treating CSR as a *philosophy* and a *process* that anchors practices that can transform organizational behavior. We realize not everyone will agree with this approach and how we conceptualize CSR. However, we need to make a stand somewhere, and hopefully our conceptualization will stimulate discussion – even if part of that discussion targets what people feel we have failed to include.

At its most abstract, CSR is about the role of business in society. Nobel Prize-winning economist Milton Friedman (1962) is the most notable voice to claim that the primary role of business is to make money. We cannot deny this conclusion because if businesses do not make money they cease to operate, resulting in lost jobs, tax revenues, and investments. But a CSR orientation challenges the notion that the pursuit of financial concerns should be the sole or even the dominant concern of corporations. Instead, businesses are urged to consider their effects on the entire range of stakeholders connected with their operations, not just the financial stakeholders. In addition, businesses must consider their effects on the natural and social environments. The CSR philosophy encourages businesses to use their expertise and other resources to improve society.

Defining CSR

Our conceptualization of CSR is influenced by definitions that have preceded this book. For example, we appreciate Werther and Chandler's (2006, 2011) characterization of CSR as both a means and an end. They explain that CSR is a means because it "is an integral element of the firm's strategy: the way a firm goes about delivering its products or services to markets" (2006, p. 8). CSR is an end because it "is a way of maintaining the legitimacy of its actions in the larger society by bringing stakeholder concerns to the foreground" (2006, p. 8). We concur and believe that CSR is both a means and an end, a process and an outcome. Being socially responsible necessitates a focus on business practices and the outcomes associated with those practices. Those outcomes are not merely financial; rather, outcomes include sensitivity to the impacts on stakeholders. CSR can best contribute to the societal good when CSR acknowledges and incorporates the concerns of the wider society.

Along the same lines, the European Commission (EC) defines CSR as follows: "A concept whereby companies integrate social and environmental concerns in their business operations and in their interaction with their stakeholders on a voluntary basis" (European Commission, 2010). This definition also joins business practices with stakeholder concerns. As reflected in the EC's definition and Werther and Chandler's (2006, 2011) work, we endorse the idea of *strategic* corporate social responsibility. A corporation's CSR initiatives should be driven by the organization's vision and purpose. What needs does the organization seek to meet? An organization may develop a mission statement and develop strategies for pursuing the mission that include CSR objectives. As Vogel (2005) states, many corporations are "doing good to do well" (p. 19). We see CSR as complementary to, not competing with, the corporation's mission.

We also concur with the European Commission and Werther and Chandler's (2006, 2011) view that strategic CSR focuses more on voluntary ethical and discretionary concerns that lack clear mandates for performance. We do not consider behaviors that are required by law to be part of corporate social responsibility. We assume corporations must conform to legal requirements, and CSR extends beyond those legal requirements to include additional voluntary initiatives consistent with the public good. We view specific *CSR initiatives*, the enactment of particular forms or means of pursuing CSR, as *voluntary*. That is, corporations select which (if any) CSR processes and activities to engage in and how to enact those. However, as noted earlier, the expectations of relevant internal and external stakeholders, irrespective of where those stakeholders may be located, may have a strong influence on CSR strategy. For example, corporations may be pressured by stakeholders to conform to certain expectations and be rewarded for doing so (through purchase decisions, support, etc.) and be punished for violating those expectations (e.g., through boycotts, negative word of mouth, or negative media attention). In a global society filled with multinational corporations (MNCs), a macro view of CSR would hold that the larger society itself functions as a stakeholder for the corporation. Along the same lines, many people may view the environment as a stakeholder. While it may seem too broad to conclude that we are stakeholders of every corporation in our known world, we may feel that as members of humanity we have a vested interest in the operations and effects of all corporations. Later in this chapter, we explore the tension between localization and globalization in a corporation's CSR orientation.

Based on the previous discussion of central concerns, we propose this definition of CSR: *CSR is the voluntary actions that a corporation*

Box 1.2 Definition of CSR

CSR is the voluntary actions that a corporation implements as it pursues its mission and fulfills its perceived obligations to stakeholders, including employees, communities, the environment, and society as a whole.

implements as it pursues its mission and fulfills its perceived obligations to stakeholders, including employees, communities, the environment, and society as a whole.

Our definition is sensitive to the "triple bottom line": concern for people, the environment, and profit. We believe that CSR initiatives involve voluntary actions. As mentioned above, if a corporation is required by law to perform an action, it does not qualify as a CSR action. Corporations must choose to exceed the minimum legal expectations. Some readers may notice that our definition (like many others) sidesteps the issue of specific business motivations for engaging in CSR. Although we have not included motivations for pursuing CSR as part of our definition, we note that CSR actions must be consistent – or at least not inconsistent – with an organization's mission. The mission is what the organization does to provide products and services that meet others' needs.

Our definition also acknowledges the importance of stakeholder expectations in influencing CSR initiatives. Corporations have obligations to stakeholders, and these include the obligation to understand and be responsive to stakeholder expectations. The phrase *perceived obligations* is included to denote that corporations can act only on what is known and accepted as legitimate. For example, stakeholders concerned with animal rights may believe that any corporations that serve meat are irresponsible. However, the fast food industry is built around supplying meat products to consumers. The industry would not survive without serving meat products. So the expectations of serving no meat would be perceived as unrealistic and would be rejected as inconsistent with their mission. However, the industry could meet with animal rights representatives to explore ways of trying to satisfy some expectations. In fact, this is what McDonald's, Burger King, and Wendy's have done to address issues related to the humane treatment and slaughter of animals they use for meat. We will explore these and other issues implicated in our definition of CSR in more detail in chapter 2 on strategic corporate social responsibility.

Benefits and Costs of CSR

The discussion of the benefits and costs of CSR is complex and riddled with ideology. The complexity stems from two factors. First, the benefits and costs of CSR must be considered from both the corporation's perspective and society's (stakeholders') perspective. Where is there congruency and where is there conflict between the benefits and costs for a corporation and society? Moreover, as chapter 1 illustrates, CSR is not simply one thing but a wide variety of activities. Second, the same argument is often used as both a benefit and cost of CSR. For instance, CSR is said to both reduce the competitiveness of a corporation (a cost, because engaging in CSR can consume resources) and increase the competitiveness of a corporation (a benefit, because the CSR effort can attract positive attention). The interpretative frame is largely a function of ideology. Those who favor the free market and profit view of corporations may view CSR as decreasing competitiveness, while those who support the business case for CSR favor CSR as increasing competitiveness. Although there is a lack of consensus in the existing data on CSR costs and benefits, trends are emerging. This section navigates the complexities of CSR costs and benefits by reviewing the arguments that managers should consider when developing their cost-benefit analysis for CSR.

Two Sides of CSR Cost-Benefit Analysis

Managers should construct a CSR cost-benefit analysis around their own organization. How is CSR – as a process and as a general outcome or end – a benefit for their corporations, and how is it a cost? This analysis is complicated by the fact that CSR is not unidimensional. Myriad initiatives count as CSR. But we recommend that managers begin with the general idea of CSR (the philosophy) and then move to considerations of specific activities that might mesh well with the corporation's mission and stakeholder expectations (the means or process).

But that is only half of the CSR picture. Managers also must consider the effects of CSR on society. How will engaging in CSR benefit society, and how will engaging in CSR activity cost society? CSR is about infusing a variety of stakeholder interests into the corporation's thinking and strategy. Focusing solely on the corporation's concern recreates a corporate-centric perspective that marginalizes social interests while privileging financial concerns. A corporate-centric perspective not only devalues society but also may alienate nonfinancial stakeholders, lead to criticism, and make it more difficult for the corporation to operate. Therefore, management must consider the CSR costs and benefits associated with society and stakeholders. The two cost-benefit analyses are related. For instance, a failure to address CSR concerns can create stakeholder churn – where stakeholders mobilize against an organization (Marquez & Fombrun, 2005; Sethi, 1977) – and create costs for the corporation.

We have developed a summary table for the CSR cost-benefit analyses. Table 1.1 includes separate lists of primary costs and benefits for the corporation and for society. The list, though clearly not exhaustive or mutually exclusive, provides a starting point for the discussion of CSR costs and benefits.

CSR Costs for Corporations

The CSR costs for corporations often are seen as rooted in Milton Friedman's view, mentioned earlier in this chapter, that the primary purpose of a business is to make money for shareholders (Friedman, 1962, 1970). Let us reconsider that view before reviewing CSR costs. In Friedman's (1962) words,

> There is one and only one social responsibility of business – to use its resources and engage in activities designed to increase its profit so long as it stays within the rules of the game, which is to say, engages in open and free competition, without deception or fraud. (p. 133)

Friedman is advocating for the free market ideology, and that does not entirely rule out social concerns. For example, the market (stakeholders) shapes the actions of business through their investing and consumer behaviors. That means the market can demand social responsibility from businesses, thus creating a scenario where social and financial concerns become complementary if not isomorphic. The business case for CSR is tied to free market ideology as well. However, businesses are not compelled to address social and environmental concerns if strong market pressures are absent.

We have distilled our discussions of CSR costs for corporations into three major themes. First, the dominant theme associated with costs for corporations is that CSR initiatives detract from the business's focus on profits. Profits, efficiency, and competitiveness are reduced by CSR spending; customers ultimately will bear the costs of CSR; management is distracted by CSR and does not focus on strategic organizational goals; and shareholders suffer less return on their investments. From this perspective, CSR is essentially a financial burden for the corporation and its stakeholders. Moreover, managers must devote part of their time to CSR, and this detracts from profit making. The new demands of CSR become a distraction, represent a financial loss for the business, and are a time drain on management.

Table 1.1 CSR costs and benefits

CSR Costs		*CSR Benefits*	
Costs to the Corporation	*Costs to Society*	*Benefits to the corporations*	*Benefits to Society*
Businesses have a legal obligation to manage the company in the interest of shareholders – and not other stakeholders. Large capital investments (e.g., in green technology) may be difficult to justify to shareholders who invest for the short term. The pursuit of social goals dilutes businesses' primary purpose. Stock devaluation may occur if financial analysts see the CSR initiatives as too costly. The efficient use of resources will be reduced if businesses are restricted by CSR in how they can operate. Developing and implementing a CSR policy will be a complex, costly, and time-consuming activity. CSR costs will be passed on to consumers and reduce competitiveness. CSR places unwelcome responsibilities on businesses rather than on governments or individuals. Failing to meet stakeholder expectations will create churn. Stakeholders will place increasing CSR demands on organizations that commit to CSR. Employees may fear that CSR threatens their jobs.	Discourages government regulation and uniform application of rules. Stakeholders may be co-opted by the corporation. Marginalized stakeholders may remain marginalized. Environmental and social degradation may continue without CSR. Governments and social welfare organizations may allow corporations to determine what is in the public interest. CSR-related costs may simply be passed on to consumers.	CSR can help avoid excessive governmental regulation. CSR initiatives can enhance the social legitimacy of the corporation. Socially responsible actions can be profitable; CSR can create cost-saving improvements. CSR can improve the corporation's reputation. CSR initiatives will be attractive to some investors. CSR profiles will attract customers. Employee motivation and identification may be increased. CSR can enhance their identity and corporate culture through values reinforcement and an other-orientation. Discussions about CSR encourage employees to think in new ways and develop new skills. CSR initiatives may attract positive media coverage. An improved stakeholder environment will benefit the corporation by reducing churn. Partnering with other organizations and/or third parties to share ideas can enhance capabilities, credibility, visibility, and reputation.	CSR helps to correct social and environmental problems caused by business operations. CSR holds corporations accountable for their actions. CSR leads corporations to avoid externalizing costs. Dialogue and partnerships among diverse stakeholders are encouraged. CSR programs encourage corporations to see a wider range of perspectives. Successful CSR initiatives lead other corporations to imitate those initiatives. CSR contributes to social justice. CSR can supplement governmental and social welfare programs to improve social and environmental concerns.

Note: The inventories of costs and benefits presented here are not intended to be exhaustive. They represent common arguments for and against a CSR philosophy and/or initiatives.

A second major theme linked to CSR costs for corporations is that social issues are outside of the responsibility and expertise of businesses. Governments, not businesses, were designed to address social concerns. How can managers effectively identify and address social concerns? Corporations are not responsible for social concerns and lack the skills to confront them. Corporations should leave social issues to those best suited to addressing them (Friedman, 1970; McMillan, 2007).

The final theme is the corporation's loss of power and control. At various points throughout this book, we address how corporations' use of collaborative decision making requires sharing power and control over decisions with stakeholders. Also, simply adjusting business policies to accommodate stakeholder complaints cedes some power to stakeholders. Some critics of CSR consider power sharing a dangerous proposition because it represents a concession to stakeholders. They see concessions as signs of weakness that will encourage other stakeholders to make demands and push around the corporation. Corporations must be free to pursue their business operations, and accommodating stakeholders could interfere with that mandate.

CSR Costs for Society

The dominant concern surrounding CSR costs for society is that the success of CSR actually creates harm for many stakeholders. First, if CSR efforts are successful, there will be no government regulation of business. In essence, the CSR efforts become a form of industry self-regulation. Corporations favor self-regulation over government regulation because it is cheaper and corporations control the content and enforcement of the rules. Application can be spotty if the CSR is not codified into a specific set of self-regulatory guidelines. If CSR practices are assumed to be self-regulation but are not formalized, corporations are free to choose whether or not to engage in the suggested CSR practices. This includes the possibility that some corporations will simply ignore the rules in favor of operating in their own self-interest and produce negative consequences for society. CSR initiatives cannot substitute for government regulation of business. If CSR is ignored or is superficial, there will be social and environmental degradation. Society becomes a worse place due to business practices.

The second theme concerns the role of governments versus corporations in supporting social welfare and is interrelated with the first theme of self-regulation. Society may suffer if corporate efforts are expected to substitute for government efforts to address social problems. Corporations should not make decisions that previously were made by democratically elected governments and social welfare organizations. Ideally, governments should be more aware of and better suited to addressing the social concerns and problems of their people. Relying on corporations to adequately confront social problems essentially externalizes government costs to organizations. Corporate interests are relatively narrow compared to what should be the broader focus of a government designed to represent the interests of the people.

Third, the stakeholder engagement process that characterizes "best practices" in CSR has the potential to co-opt stakeholders. Stakeholders may begin to see the world from the perspective of the corporations and lose their own identity and vision for CSR. The stakeholders become part of the problem when they think they are helping to create a solution. Co-optation fears are real. This idea is elaborated in our discussion of stakeholder-corporate partnerships in chapter 6. In addition, marginalized stakeholders are likely to remain on the fringe. Their lack of power and voice makes them easy to overlook when engaging more salient stakeholders (e.g., Prieto-Carron, Lund-Thomsen, Chan, Muro, & Bhushan, 2006).

CSR Benefits for Corporations

Although there are numerous benefits for corporations that engage in CSR, we focus on two primary themes. Benefits for corporations reflect themes related to reducing business costs and enhancing reputations. Corporations are profit conscious and seek ways to minimize costs. Stakeholder support for a corporation can reduce the costs of doing business. CSR may reduce stakeholder churn, enhance the social legitimacy of the corporation, and help to avoid costly government regulation (Levine, 2008). CSR initiatives themselves may reduce costs when they focus on issues like sustainability, energy efficiency, and renewable resources.

Corporations benefit from a favorable reputation. A corporation's CSR initiatives may attract investors, employees, consumers, and positive media coverage. Socially responsible investors will be interested in corporations with a strong CSR identity. Talented potential employees (as well as current employees) could find working with a socially responsible corporation intrinsically rewarding. Aligning stakeholder interests and corporate interests builds identification with and support from stakeholders. This idea is elaborated in chapter 2's discussion of strategic CSR. In addition, consumers may be attracted to companies with a positive CSR record (Bhattacharya & Sen, 2004; Sen & Bhattacharya, 2001; Vogel, 2005). Consumers can support the corporation through purchases as well as positive word of mouth and online communication. Traditional and online media may highlight the activities of socially responsible corporations and help cultivate a positive reputation (Tench, Bowd, & Jones, 2007).

This is merely a brief inventory of positive outcomes that may derive from CSR initiatives. This book includes numerous illustrations of these benefits and offers recommendations for realistically appraising and confronting the challenges of implementing successful CSR programs.

CSR Benefits for Society

Society benefits when corporations take responsibility for their actions and impacts on society. For example, CSR initiatives can discourage corporations from externalizing their costs. *Externalized costs* are costs that are passed onto others in the environment. This includes profiting from externalities like pollution, the consumption of natural resources, and the exploitation of marginalized groups in society. Although the exploitation of shared (societal) resources can be externalized by the corporation, CSR initiatives help hold corporations accountable for these externalities. Corporations can be pressured by stakeholders to recycle, invest in more environmentally friendly technologies, and engage in labor practices that respect human rights.

Another common theme in discussions of CSR benefits to society is how recognizing shared social concerns can lead diverse corporations and groups to work together. Pursuing shared social concerns might unite corporations, including NGOs and other organizations interested in similar concerns. Partnering with other corporations can help to pool resources like expertise, financial capital, and social capital and thereby amplify the good that can accrue from these collaborations.

Imitation is not a bad thing when it comes to CSR initiatives. Corporations look to enhance their success and are quick to mimic successful businesses. If corporations see other corporations achieving positive outcomes such as increased profits, more favorable reputations, and positive media coverage when they pursue CSR initiatives, they may try to mimic the corporation, and more societal good will be done. Although criticism may arise when businesses seem to "jump on the CSR bandwagon," following the lead of other corporations with successful CSR programs could magnify positive societal outcomes.

This discussion of the costs and benefits of CSR to both corporations and society has illustrated common concerns surrounding the development of CSR programs. Issues surrounding these costs and benefits are addressed at various points throughout this book.

Winning and Sustaining Support for CSR

One reason for reviewing the corporate costs of CSR is to prepare managers for attacks on proposed CSR efforts. The corporate costs represent the likely reasons why other managers will oppose CSR efforts. Pro-CSR managers must be ready to refute these arguments against engaging in CSR. The best option is to be aggressive from the start by formulating arguments in favor of the corporation's involvement in CSR, anticipating the attacks, and developing messages designed to counter the attacks against CSR. As we know from decades of persuasive research, people who oppose an idea are unlikely to be convinced to support it. Persuasive communication is designed to reinforce positive attitudes and to win support from those who are generally undecided or neutral on the topic. Presenting the case for CSR and specific CSR efforts can be more effective when the potential attacks are anticipated and incorporated into the initial messages.

When presenting the case for CSR, managers should acknowledge the potential costs to the corporation. The technical term for this strategy is a *two-sided message*. The two sides are the benefits and the costs of CSR. Other managers are educated, and educated audiences prefer two-sided messages (e.g., presenting both costs and benefits) over one-sided messages (e.g., presenting benefits only). The next step is to include refutation in the two-sided message. A refutational message includes reasoning that explains why the opposing argument (e.g., cost) is wrong or much weaker than the primary argument (O'Keefe, 2002). The message provides reasons for rejecting the cost-based attacks on the CSR efforts.

Refutational two-sided messages are persuasive initially and in the long run, in comparison to one-sided or nonrefutational two-sided arguments (Miller, 2002; O'Keefe, 2002). The long-term effect is important in the organizational setting. We want others to remain committed to CSR. The initial push for the CSR efforts can build a base of support. That base of support can erode over time as opponents begin to argue against the CSR efforts. However, the use of refutational two-sided arguments "inoculates" supporters against later critics who oppose CSR. A persuasive message is fortified (inoculated) against those arguments designed to weaken it (Miller, 2002; Pfau, 1992). By presenting and refuting the cost arguments from the beginning, the pro-CSR managers should gain support for CSR that remains robust over time. People in the organization have the information necessary to resist the arguments offered by the opposition (Miller, 2002). Follow-up CSR messages can reinforce support as well. An initial refutational two-sided argument coupled with occasional reinforcing messages should create sustained support for CSR efforts.

To help managers craft their pro-CSR messages, we have identified possible counterarguments to the most common attacks based on the organizational costs of CSR. The most common attack may be loss of profit or lack of return on investment (ROI). True, some studies fail to demonstrate any financial benefit from CSR. However, the bulk of the studies do prove there is a financial return. Hence, CSR is not just a cost. The likelihood of a financial return is enhanced when the CSR effort is strategic and communicated effectively.

A second point of attack against CSR is that social concerns are outside of corporate responsibility and expertise. But stakeholders now expect corporations to address social issues, especially those related to their businesses. It will be costly for a corporation to ignore this societal trend. They can no longer afford to deny the responsibility. Engaging stakeholders will provide added expertise to CSR efforts and contribute to success.

Finally, there is the concern over the loss of power and control. We need to ask, "Are stakeholders enemies or allies?" and "Is it better to consider stakeholders allies rather than enemies?" The amount of power and control that is shared is relatively minimal and should be beneficial to both sides. The CSR expertise of the stakeholders will improve the quality of and the benefits derived from the co-created CSR efforts. It is better to embrace stakeholders as allies than to fear them as enemies. The shared power and control can yield valuable returns for the corporation.

Other Conceptual Questions about CSR

A precise and comprehensive history of CSR is problematic. Experts disagree as to when CSR was first used, and no single academic or professional discipline can claim it. So we are left with some important yet bewildering questions:

- Is CSR a relatively modern development or a concept that has appeared sporadically throughout history to influence businesses?
- What behaviors count as CSR?
- Is CSR's "home" located in accounting, marketing, or public relations, or should it be a separate unit unto itself?
- Should CSR standards be localized or globalized?

Addressing these questions helps us to begin setting parameters for what constitutes CSR.

CSR: Modern or Historic?

Is CSR a relatively recent phenomenon or part of a long but sporadic chain of thought in business? The answer is both. CSR can trace its roots to a number of ideas, including social investing and social audits of businesses. The concept of *noblesse oblige* originated with concerns over the proper behavior of nobles toward others. The assumption was that privilege brings with it responsibility: "nobility obligates." The concept has evolved to the idea that responsibility is commensurate with wealth, power, and prestige. It should be noted that the term has been applied in a mocking fashion to CSR. However, the phrase demonstrates the roots of concern over obligation to society and how concerns with effects on society predate modern corporations (MerriamWebster.com, n.d.).

Social investing can be traced back as far as the 1700s. The early socially responsible investing (SRI) movement had religious origins with links to the Quakers (avoiding businesses in the slave trade) and Methodism (Wesley's urging to avoid companies that caused harm to workers such as the tanning of hides). However, it would be incorrect to say SRI was widespread globally since the 1700s (L'Etang, 2006). The concept of SRI requires stakeholder knowledge of corporate actions relative to some standard of social performance, thus introducing the concepts of social accounting, social auditing, and social reporting. *Social accounting* is the collection and measurement of social performance. *Social auditing* is the assessment of a corporation's performance against some specified criteria. *Social reporting* is the dissemination of the social performance evaluation to stakeholders (Hess, 2008).

Social accounting, audits, and reporting were developed to provide a richer picture of a business' responsible and irresponsible behavior. Stanford professor Theodore Kreps used the term *social audit* in the 1930s to describe businesses reporting their social responsibility. Kreps was seeking to extend the evaluation of a corporation's societal contributions beyond financial concerns to include social concerns such as health, education, and international peace. In the 1950s, Howard Bowen sought to develop a system that auditors could employ to assess concerns such as human relations, community relations, and public relations. Kreps envisioned social auditing as an external assessment of a corporation's contribution to society. Bowen, on the other hand, conceptualized social auditing as an internal mechanism to help managers understand their corporations better (Hess, 2008). This distinction actually marked the start of the tension between the public and private applications of social auditing. While the idea of CSR existed, it was not prominent in either the academic writings or businesses practices. It was not until the 1970s that the term CSR became widely used in discussion, but it was still with limited application.

The 1970s witnessed the crude introduction of social reporting by businesses. Some annual reports began to include sections on the environment. This development corresponded with the increased societal interest in the environment. The term *crude* is used to describe the reported use of information that focused on the value of the environment without providing information about corporate performance relative to the environment. In fact, it would be safe to conclude that most of these early social reports were *greenwashing*, efforts to benefit from a corporation's green efforts without truly committing to a green agenda (Marlin & Marlin, 2003). Hess (2008) reported that, in 1974, 76% of major corporations conducted social audits. However, most were produced for internal consumption and never made public. Ben & Jerry's led the move to hire social auditors for creating social reports. They hired a social auditor in 1989 to evaluate their corporate social performance. The use of social auditors marks what can be termed the *second phase of social reporting*.

In the 1990s, social auditing (and reporting) started the movement toward normative behavior in corporations. During this time, social investors and consumers began voicing their concerns, and this led to the refinement of environmental auditing. Most importantly, the Global Reporting Initiative (GRI) began in 1997. The GRI provides guidelines for what should be included in social reports (Hess, 2008). Additional information about the GRI and ISO 26000 performance indicators is provided in chapter 6. The third phase of social reporting involved the use of third-party certification of reports and certification by groups that compare corporate performance against specific social and environmental standards. The first of the third-phase reports appeared in 1998 and were created by Social Accountability International (SAI) (Marlin & Marlin, 2003).

The new millennium witnessed a growth in both certifying bodies and corporations creating social reports. In 2000, only 50 corporations made their social reports (social audit results) publicly available. By 2007, that number had reached over 1,000 (Hess, 2008). Among the certifying bodies are FairTrade, the Forest Stewardship Council (FSC), and the International Federation of Organic Agriculture Movement (IFOAM). Box 1.3 provides a summary of the standards utilized by the FSC. The certification process includes certified auditors conducting onsite inspections. A number of the certifying bodies have united to form the International Social and Environmental Accreditation and Labeling (ISEAL). The social audit and social reporting link CSR to accounting given the connection each has to SRI.

Overall, social reporting (the results of social audits) is designed to improve a corporation's social performance by verifying that it is contributing to social betterment. To put it another way, social reporting documents changes in corporate behavior to improve social concerns. Hess (2008) distills social reporting into three pillars: (1) dialogue, (2) development, and (3) disclosure. *Dialogue* involves understanding what social concerns are important to a corporation's stakeholders so that a corporation can address shared social concerns. Chapter 2 examines this topic in more detail under the guise of engagement. *Development* is how the corporation embodies these social concerns and improves society. *Disclosure* publicly displays a corporation's behavior so that stakeholders can determine whether or not the corporation has lived up to the espoused shared social concerns. The

Box 1.3 Forest Stewardship Council (FSC) Standards

Forestry Stewardship Council Principles and Criteria

Principle 1: "compliance with all applicable laws and international treaties"

Principle 2: "demonstrated and uncontested, clearly defined, long-term land tenure and use rights"

Principle 3: "recognition and respect of indigenous peoples' rights"

Principle 4: "maintenance or enhancement of long-term social and economic well-being of forest workers and local communities and respect of worker's rights in compliance with International Labour Organisation (ILO) conventions"

Principle 5: "equitable use and sharing of benefits derived from the forest"

Principle 6: "reduction of environmental impact of logging activities and maintenance of the ecological functions and integrity of the forest"

Principle 7: "appropriate and continuously updated management plan"

Principle 8: "appropriate monitoring and assessment activities to assess the condition of the forest, management activities and their social and environmental impacts"

Principle 9: "maintenance of High Conservation Value Forests (HCVFs) defined as environmental and social values that are considered to be of outstanding significance or critical importance "

Principle 10: "in addition to compliance with all of the above, plantations must contribute to reduce the pressures on and promote the restoration and conservation of natural forests."

Source: Forest Stewardship Council (n.d.).

ideas supporting these three pillars of social reporting are significant and woven throughout this book.

From the theoretical side, Sethi (1975) is among the earliest researchers to provide a detailed discussion of CSR. He used the term *corporate social performance*. Sethi (1975) identified three levels of corporate social performance: (1) social obligation, (2) social responsibility, and (3) social responsiveness. *Social obligations* included compliance with regulations and market demands. *Social responsibility* moved beyond compliance to the need to meet societal expectations. Here we see the early recognition of the importance of stakeholder expectations on CSR activities. This also included the realization that culture shaped CSR. *Social responsiveness* is anticipatory of emerging expectations that require an understanding (engagement) of stakeholders. Chapter 2's discussion of the idea of strategic CSR reflects Sethi's social responsiveness level of corporate social performance.

Carroll (1979) extends Sethi's work to create a four-dimensional model of corporate social performance. The four dimensions are (1) *economic*, in that a business produces goods and services to make a profit; (2) *legal*, in that a business must obey societal laws and regulations; (3) ethical, which are ill defined but are the ethical norms in society that must be followed even though they are not laws or regulations; and (4) *discretionary*, which are voluntary (such as philanthropy) and represent yet another set of societal expectations that are less defined than the legal or ethical ones (Carroll, 1979). The dimensions are not mutually exclusive, can be viewed as an evolution in business thinking, and can even be at odds with one another.

In 1991, Carroll refined his CSR thinking to embody the form of a pyramid. *Economic responsibilities* (to be profitable) comprised the base of the pyramid. The next layer was *legal responsibilities* (to obey laws) followed by *ethical responsibilities* (to do what is right and avoid harm). *Philanthropic responsibilities* were situated at the pyramid's apex and involved being a good corporate citizen. Carroll's CSR conceptualization has been examined using an international collection of businesses. The results support the belief that there are four distinction dimensions, and they are valued roughly as Carroll describes with the lower levels being considered more important than the upper levels of the pyramid. The one difference was that German and Swedish managers ranked legal responsibilities as more important than economic responsibilities (Pinkston & Carroll, 1994).

Forms of CSR

Thus far, we have provided several examples of CSR activities. We described how CSR may be viewed as a mosaic composed of myriad activities directed toward multiple issues. CSR initiatives may focus on *people* (human rights, children, the immediate community, labor rights, education, and/or those with financial or medical needs) and/or the *natural environment* (waste reduction, sustainable forest harvesting, recycling, noise reduction, restoration of indigenous plant life, and/or the sustainability of a manufacturing process). CSR initiatives can impact both simultaneously. For example, a manufacturing facility's focus on emissions reduction can benefit both people and the environment.

In addition to identifying the types (contents) of social concerns or causes that may be addressed through CSR initiatives, we also should consider the scope of the initiative. We use the term *scope* to refer to the boundaries that corporations establish for their CSR initiatives. For a large pharmaceutical corporation, the scope may be very broad – international – as it has the resources to develop initiatives to address poor health care throughout developing countries. For a smaller business, the scope may be more limited. For example, a smaller business may focus on helping a nonprofit construct a local playground. The issue of scope should not negate the importance of the CSR effort. A smaller corporation may not be able to save the planet, but it may be able to offer positive contributions to the youth in the community. In sum, the range of stakeholders and issues that are served through CSR initiatives may range from broad to narrow, depending on the corporation's resources and strategic decision making about where to focus their efforts. This issue of strategy will be examined in greater detail at the end of this chapter in our discussion of local and global business strategies.

We also can identify traditional forms of CSR activities. These traditional ways of conceptualizing CSR can be enacted regardless of the specific content or scope of the initiative. For example, philanthropy can aid different types of causes. Social marketing campaigns can target a variety of problematic or risky behaviors. Employees can volunteer for numerous types of nonprofit organizations. Typical examples include the following:

- *Philanthropy:* the corporations contributes money, services, products, or the like directly to a cause or social concern.
- *Cause promotion:* the corporation contributes money or other resources to increase awareness of a cause or social concern.
- *Cause marketing:* the corporation contributes a percentage of its consumer sales of particular products or services to a cause (e.g., on a particular day 20% of the purchase amount of a particular product is donated to a charity).
- *Social marketing:* the corporation tries to influence behavior to promote a social good, such as recycling, seatbelt safety, or health.
- *Volunteering:* the corporation encourages its employees to volunteer and/or partner with specific organizations; the corporation may allow employees to volunteer during work time (e.g., Home Depot may partner with Habitat for Humanity to allow workers time off to volunteer several hours per week).

Although these forms of CSR are familiar to most people, this list of traditional CSR activities does not fully capture the range of practices associated with ethical corporate behavior and the complexities of contemporary CSR. CSR now commonly includes broader corporate initiatives designed to reduce the negative impacts of operations (e.g., the consumption of resources and production of waste) and increase the positive impacts (e.g., fair wages and working conditions, sustainability, and social justice). In this book we try to cover a breadth of activities that qualify as CSR, including management of environmental impacts, ethical investing, ethical sourcing, protecting human rights, supply chain monitoring, and sustainability initiatives.

Where Is CSR's Home?

"Where is CSR's home?" is both an academic and a practical question. Clearly CSR reflects a wide range of concerns and activities. Academics study CSR, and the research should help to advance its practice. But who should be studying CSR? Social investing creates a claim for finance and management. To benefit from CSR, managers must effectively communicate CSR initiatives to stakeholders. The discussion of CSR benefits brings marketing, public relations, corporate communication, and advertising into the discussion. CSR research lines are emerging in all of these disciplines. Each of the CSR research traditions provides value for understanding and improving CSR as a practice. Of course, where CSR is studied has implications for where it should be located in practice.

Should CSR be part of an existing organizational function or a specific function unto itself? Direct ties to public relations, corporate communication, advertising, or marketing could tarnish motives behind CSR. Links to any of these functions might create a strong impression of self-interested promotion, thereby obscuring the benefits to stakeholders. Because of the possibility of taint through association, it can be argued that CSR should be housed in its own distinct department. There is a practical reason for creating a separate CSR department as well. A specific unit would have responsibility for the strategic application of CSR. Situating CSR within its own department would facilitate the development of a consistent CSR approach. In contrast, when different departments enact CSR, this risks diverse and perhaps mixed CSR messages being delivered to stakeholders. The basic premise behind integrated marketing communication is the need for and value in creating consistent stakeholder messages (Harris, 1997). The same holds true for CSR. Inconsistent CSR messages can create more harm than good. A CSR department helps to avoid divergent CSR messaging.

While situating CSR in a separate department could create a buffer of integrity and promote consistent messaging, it could risk creating CSR initiatives that are detached from the lifeblood of the organization. CSR becomes the responsibility of "that department," not the entire corporation. As a result, CSR may not become part of the corporation's DNA but rather an entity attached to the business. CSR should be part of who the corporation is – its identity – and what it does, not some "thing" that a corporation has. Creating a separate CSR department may undermine its integration into the larger policy decisions and practices of a corporation. When CSR is infused throughout various departments, it becomes part of the corporation's culture, and ownership of CSR is advanced. CSR becomes "everyone's responsibility," thereby reinforcing its importance to the organization. Of course, the challenge of coordinating CSR to promote consistency remains. However, any manager with a communication function is aware of that concern, and savvy corporations have found ways to ensure coordination and integration of stakeholder messages across different departments. Marketing, public relations, corporate communication, and advertising departments still exist as separate units. If they were unable to coordinate messaging, most corporations would have integrated marketing departments by now.

We believe that CSR benefits from being part of a variety of academic and practical disciplines. Research from various disciplines brings multiple perspectives to bear on CSR. Managers know that decision making is enhanced when multiple points of view are considered (Kreps, 1991). The same should hold true for CSR. In addition, we can witness unique insights from each academic discipline serving to advance our understanding and practice of CSR. Review the citations for this book, and you will see the variety of fields fruitfully contributing to CSR. Similarly, CSR application should be the responsibility of various functions within an organization, not just one. All employees should feel that CSR is part of their job in some way. It should be infused throughout the corporate culture. The key is to build a coordinated system for CSR planning, execution, and communication. Often, this involves the creation of a CSR team that represents many departments and organizational functions. CSR is best served by being integrated into various departments. In that way, CSR is more likely to become part of who the organization is and what it does. The corporation's identity, processes, and outcomes reflect a CSR orientation.

For CSR to become a priority, strong visible support from the corporation's leadership is required. Leaders can create a mandate for CSR that permeates the corporation regardless of department or function. Leaders can provide a unifying vision for CSR that reflects the existing mission, values, and capabilities of the organization. Internal messaging from leaders must demonstrate that the commitment to CSR will be ongoing and not merely some management fad.

Should CSR Standards Be Localized or Globalized?

Obviously, this question is not new for managers involved in multinational corporations. All management functions have wrestled with the issue of localization or globalization (e.g., Wakefield, 2001). Prahalad and Doz (1987) were among the first to systematically examine localization and globalization's effect on international business strategy. They note that MNCs face two pressures that shape their strategy: (1) pressure for global integration and (2) pressure for local responsiveness. On one hand, managers have a need to standardize operations across their enterprise. Pressures for global integration include pressure for cost reduction, universal needs, and the importance of multinational customers. On the other hand, the pressures for local responsiveness include market structure, government demands, and adaptation. Managers must respond to the two demands as they formulate the most appropriate course of action for their international business strategy.

The two pressures have been converted into axes used to create a 2 × 2 integration-responsiveness grid (I-R grid). Figure 1.1 illustrates the I-R grid and its four international business strategies. When both global integration and local responsiveness are low, managers can use an international strat-

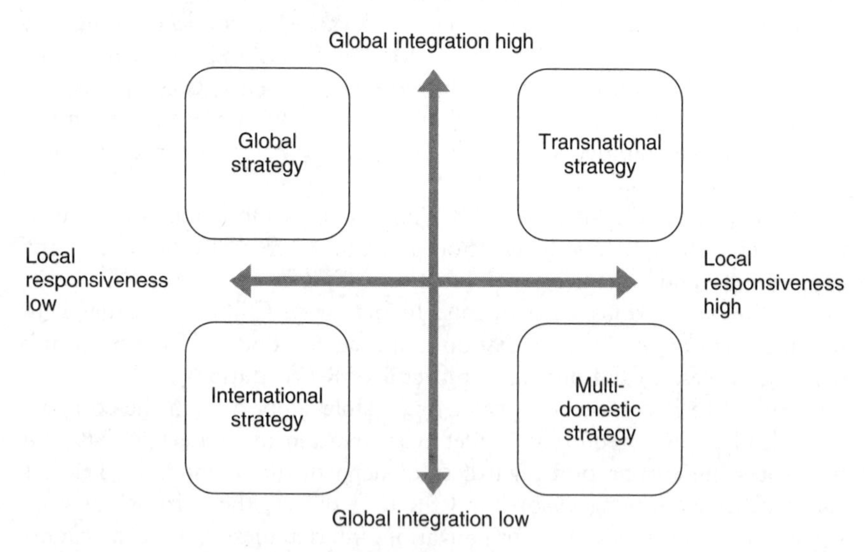

Figure 1.1 Integration-responsiveness grid

egy. The international strategy is when a corporation takes what it does successfully in the domestic market and tries to repeat it internationally. Practices in the home country are replicated in the host countries. When global integration is low and local responsiveness is high, managers can employ the multidomestic strategy. The multidomestic strategy involves locally adapting products (through marketing and production) to the host market and targeting country-specific consumer needs.

When global integration is high and local responsiveness is low, managers can utilize a global strategy. The global strategy involves viewing the world as a single market and using one standardized approach. When both global integration and local responsiveness are high, managers can choose the transnational strategy. The transnational strategy involves combining global scale and local responsiveness. A fusion is created that attempts to avoid making trade-offs between the two (Bartlett & Ghohsal, 1989). Generally, the transnational strategy is considered to be the most effective strategy for MNCs. Although there is some empirical evidence to support the claim, the evidence is not overwhelmingly favorable (Wasilewski, n.d.). The strength of the transnational strategy rests in its ability to derive the benefits associated with both globalization and localization. A corporation creates consistency (globalization) while maintaining flexibility (localization). However, we should resist anointing one, perfect strategy. The point of the I-R grid is that proper strategy depends upon the nature of the pressures faced by the MNC.

Another lens for exploring the CSR globalization-localization discussion is the area of ethics in international public relations. Kruckeberg (1996) has written at length on this subject. The concern is that the internationalization of public relations forces corporations to confront differing ethical perspectives. The public relations ethics in a particular country will naturally reflect the culture's view of morality, or what counts as right and wrong. If public relations ethics is "local," conflicts may erupt as practitioners attempt to engage in public relations across national and cultural borders. One common example is whether it is acceptable to pay for a news story to be published. In some countries this practice is acceptable, but in other countries this is considered an unacceptable form of bribery. Should practitioners adapt to the ethics of a culture or apply their ethical beliefs regardless of the culture? The answer is that the higher ethical standard should apply. Just because a country has a more lenient view of ethics is not justification for engaging in "less ethical" behavior. Kruckeberg (1996) argued that as professions become more international, a shared global professionalism develops. In turn, the emerging profession eventually will develop a shared set of universal ethical standards. The profession will reach agreement on what constitutes professional (acceptable) behavior, and those will evolve into a shared set of ethical standards. There is a belief that certain ethical concerns should be universal and applied wherever public relations is practiced. This deontological perspective suggests we must focus on discharging our duties – following professional codes of conduct or rules and fulfilling obligations – when determining what is ethical (Bowen, 2005a, 2005b). Adhering to global professional standards should eliminate self- interested behavior (Stoker, 2005).

So how can these efforts to grapple with globalization versus localization contribute to our thinking about CSR? From international business strategy, we find value in both globalization and localization. The overall commitment to CSR should be global. Management should try to integrate CSR wherever it operates. CSR initiatives should not be reserved only for highly visible areas or locations with high CSR expectations. Stakeholder expectations and stakeholder ability to pressure for change vary from country to country. However, a country's lack of interest in CSR coupled with stakeholders' inability to pressure for CSR is not an invitation for neglect or abuse. Many critics feel the cultural differences relevant to CSR facilitated the Bhopal tragedy in India. There should be a global commitment to CSR and minimal standards for its application regardless of the location.

However, the emphasis on stakeholder definitions of what constitutes effective and acceptable CSR argues for localization. If CSR efforts do not match stakeholder CSR expectations, the CSR effort will be a failure for all involved. Stakeholders who are dissatisfied because they do not see the organization acting properly may engage in stakeholder churn, a topic explored in detail in chapter 4. Managers may be unhappy because stakeholders reject the CSR and engage in churn. CSR must adapt to local conditions – the demands of the stakeholders. The transnational strategy's ability to effectively fuse globalization and localization is ideal for the CSR function. There always will be pressure for both globalization and localization for CSR. Globally, an organization needs a consistent approach to CSR to avoid accusations of ignoring locations where CSR is not considered to be important. But at the same time, the CSR efforts must be tailored to fit the needs of the local stakeholder expectations. When both pressures are high, the transnational strategy is considered to be the best alternative.

The debate over international public relations ethics echoes the globalization concern of not lowering one's standards for CSR to fit a culture. Just because a country will not apply pressure for CSR does not mean CSR can be ignored there. MNCs have global stakeholders who will expect a certain level of commitment to CSR across locations. Consider how NGOs can pressure organizations that fail to address stakeholder concerns in a particular country even when stakeholders from the country in question cannot. We could argue that there are evolving universal standards for CSR. In some ways, the GRI system and ISO 26000 reflect the emergence of shared standards for CSR. The contents of these two reporting systems are described in more detail in chapter 6. While not overly prescriptive, the GRI does provide guidance on general approaches to CSR. Managers should stay alert to developments and possible changes in the emerging universal standards of CSR.

Conclusion

The concept, philosophy, and practice of CSR are as complex as the world in which corporations are embedded. This chapter described our definition of CSR and explained its relationship to a corporation's mission, stakeholders, and culture. We believe that corporations will be more successful in implementing CSR initiatives, achieving their CSR goals, and contributing to the betterment of society when they are true to their mission and recognize the value of stakeholder engagement. A commitment to CSR requires support from the corporation's leadership as well as coordination among different functional units that can contribute to CSR goals. Internal and external communication plays a significant role in the CSR process described in this book.

We anticipate that the tension between making a profit and making a difference in the world will continue. Many financially successful corporations have been criticized for creating and perpetuating the social and environmental problems their CSR programs are designed to address (e.g., Waddock, 2007). CSR initiatives should not be designed to misdirect public perceptions or conceal wrongdoings. CSR is not a cure for misdeeds or unethical conduct. Rather, the decision to embrace CSR is necessarily complex and should be predicated on knowledge that it will help develop and implement a sound underlying process. This book's process-oriented framework is grounded in a communication perspective that acknowledges a corporation's interdependence with stakeholders, culture, political systems, and economic systems.

The chapters that follow elaborate on our communication approach to the CSR process. Chapter 2 develops a rationale for strategic CSR by exploring issues that affect a corporation's approach to CSR, including its own characteristics, stakeholders, reputational concerns, and motivations for pursuing CSR. Chapter 2 concludes with a brief synopsis of the five phases in our CSR Process Model. The CSR process is designed to help corporations systematically research, design, implement, communicate, and evaluate CSR initiatives that reflect the reality of the corporation's environment. Chapters 3 through 7 detail the CSR Process Model. Chapter 8 offers concluding thoughts on the CSR process. Together, these chapters try to present a balanced view of the potential dialogues and dilemmas that confront corporations seeking to develop and implement successful CSR programs.

Greenpeace's thank-you card to Kimberly-Clark for its response to the Kleercut campaign. Greenpeace protests over Kimberly-Clark's use of wood fiber from the Boreal Forest motivated Kimberly-Clark to change its sourcing practices. © Greenpeace/Andrew Founier

2

Strategic CSR

In essence, CSR becomes strategic when it is integrated into the larger corporate plans and goals. We use the term *strategic* to emphasize that effective CSR initiatives – CSR that benefits social concern(s) and the corporation – must be deliberate, planned, and evaluated. CSR doesn't just "happen." It reflects careful information gathering, prioritizing, and decision making to determine where resources should be invested to accrue the greatest benefit for the business, the social concern, and stakeholders. Why engage in CSR if it does not make a difference to the social concern or to the corporation?

CSR should not be a stand-alone entity designed to pacify critics or to demonstrate the adoption of the latest management fad. CSR should not be an attempt to divert attention from corporate misdeeds or transgressions. Rather, CSR can be integrated into the overall corporate strategy to help it remain successful and competitive. Corporations must be profitable to remain in business. Strategic CSR should contribute to the success of the corporation and not drain resources, the core of Milton Friedman's opposition to CSR (Friedman, 1970). Our definition of CSR – the voluntary actions an organization implements as it pursues its mission and fulfills its perceived obligations to stakeholders, including employees, communities, the environment, and society as a whole – acknowledges the importance of the triple bottom line. Both business goals

Managing Corporate Social Responsibility: A Communication Approach, First Edition.
W. Timothy Coombs, Sherry J. Holladay.

and CSR goals are included in this definition such that CSR is linked with financial success.

In chapter 1, we introduced the idea that a CSR philosophy can encourage companies to use their expertise and other resources to improve society. Viewing societal interests and business interests as complementary rather than competitive or mutually exclusive opens the door for a win-win orientation to strategic CSR initiatives. This definition of CSR privileges both business concerns and stakeholder concerns. Recall that *stakeholders* are defined as *any group that can affect or be affected by the behavior of an organization* (Freeman, 1984). CSR philosophy is grounded in social responsiveness and responsibility and acknowledges the importance of stakeholders and *stakeholder engagement – anticipating and addressing stakeholder expectations in the development of organizational strategy* (Sethi, 1975). Attending to stakeholders helps the corporation understand the larger environment in which it operates and address stakeholder concerns. Doing so makes good business sense. The importance of stakeholders and the stakeholder engagement process is woven throughout this book. We also demonstrate how effective communication processes are fundamental to engagement and the CSR process.

Corporations can utilize CSR to differentiate themselves from competitors, thereby creating a commercial advantage. However, CSR must honor the social component by making meaningful contributions to society or risk being exposed as participating in CSR washing. *CSR washing* refers to cases where organizations claim to be more socially responsible than they really are. CSR washing obviously can have negative ramifications for the corporation and may even call into question the validity of the social concerns the CSR initiatives purported to address.

Businesses can become more competitive by investing in society. For instance, CSR initiatives can work to lower costs, reduce waste, or better serve customer needs in some way. As Porter and Kramer (2006) observed, Whole Foods developed a strategic advantage by selling organic and natural foods. The business successfully targeted a market and supplied stakeholders with products and services in a way that satisfied their social concerns. Business and social interests are not mutually exclusive and can be integrated via strategic CSR (McWilliams, Siegel, & Wright, 2006). The business case for CSR argues that "the right thing to do" can also be cost-effective.

The remainder of the chapter explores factors to consider in strategic CSR initiatives. This chapter continues to set the stage for the CSR Process Model that is the focus of this book. It provides a foundation for the model by discussing corporate characteristics, stakeholders, reputational concerns, and perceptions of motivations for engaging in CSR.

Characteristics of the Corporation

Numerous factors should guide a corporation's CSR efforts, and these factors can be difficult to prioritize. However, the most obvious factor to consider is the corporation itself. We believe that the most appropriate starting point for strategic CSR is the corporation's mission and resources. This is a logical place to begin thinking about CSR because the choice of particular CSR initiatives should be consonant with the corporation's mission, values, business goals, and capabilities (Bhattacharya & Sen, 2004; Kotler & Lee, 2005; Werther & Chandler, 2006, 2011).

In her book *Body and Soul* (1991), Anita Roddick, founder of The Body Shop, explained her orientation to business:

> Social and environmental dimensions are woven into the fabric of the company itself. They are neither first nor last among our objectives, but an ongoing part of everything we do . . . not a single decision is ever taken in The Body Shop without first considering environmental and social issues. (p. 23)

Anita Roddick's values and her belief that The Body Shop could be a force for social change were evident from the inception of her business in 1976 in Brighton, England. The Body Shop's CSR initiatives were a natural outgrowth of its founder's vision of business as more than profit making. (In 2006, The Body Shop was taken over by L'Oreal, the large cosmetics company. Loyal stakeholders seemed shocked by Roddick's decision to sell because they felt she was abandoning the social responsibility mission that was so central to The Body Shop's and Roddick's identity. However, Roddick argued she could invest the proceeds from the sale in social causes, and Roddick continued her activism until her death in 2007.)

Not all corporations were far-sighted enough to integrate CSR concerns into their mission statements or fortunate enough to be founded by an individual strongly committed to a particular set of values. Not all senior management passionately embrace particular social concerns and incorporate those into their CSR visions. But that does not mean they will be ineffective at pursuing CSR.

When a corporation lacks an obvious starting point for exploring CSR, the corporation's leaders can begin by assessing their current business resources, capabilities, and values. They can consider questions like the following: What values guide the way the company does business? How are these values related to larger social and/or environmental concerns? What services or products are provided to customers? How could groups in need benefit from the corporation's outputs, including their expertise? What does this corporation do well, and how could these competencies relate to societal concerns? How could the corporation be a better environmental steward by modifying its operations to consume fewer natural resources?

Another factor affecting strategic CSR is the *size* of the corporation. Many of our examples represent the CSR activities of large multinational corporations (MNCs) that can draw upon a wide range of resources and personnel. Stakeholders might expect large MNCs to have better-developed CSR programs because their size translates into access to more resources. Moreover, large corporations may operate in numerous countries and may try to be responsive to more diverse stakeholders. Stakeholders cannot realistically expect the same types of CSR initiatives from small businesses that they expect from large MNCs. Smaller corporations can engage in CSR but on a reduced scale and with reduced scope. The same strategic processes still apply. But small local businesses may benefit from being particularly sensitive to their unique circumstances, including their values, capabilities, employees, specific communities in which they operate, and more localized social concerns such as particular educational needs, recreational opportunities, local charities, and so forth (Kotler & Lee, 2005; Thompson & Smith, 1991).

Stakeholder Expectations and the Importance of Organizational Identification

In addition to being driven by the corporation's mission and values, strategic CSR should be driven by stakeholder expectations. The stakeholders should be an inspiration for CSR and help identify the social issues that underpin an organization's CSR efforts. Consider how CSR has evolved from a fringe concern in business to "an inescapable priority for business leaders in every country" (Porter & Kramer, 2006). CSR now matters because an increasing percentage of stakeholders decided social concerns were important enough to influence their relationships with corporations. Investors began to place their money in socially responsible corporations while consumers began to seek products and services from companies operating in a socially responsible manner. Making money was no longer the only benchmark for evaluating a business' contribution to society. Various stakeholders supported the belief that businesses must consider the social interest. If stakeholders never showed an interest in CSR, we would not be writing this book and you would not be reading it.

Experts agree that CSR activities must reflect stakeholder values and desires. The social issues that comprise CSR need to be meaningful to the stakeholders (Bhattacharya & Sen, 2004; Maignan & Ferrell, 2004; Porter & Kramer, 2006). The need to consider stakeholder interests places a premium on management understanding of stakeholders, how they view CSR, and what social issues they value. Communication is essential to developing relationships with stakeholders. It is no coincidence that the concept of stakeholder engagement has emerged as interest in CSR has escalated. Stakeholder engagement is a formal conceptualization of listening to stakeholders and conducting formative research about CSR.

The salience of stakeholder expectations for CSR becomes clearer when we consider the value of identification for CSR. Stakeholders *identify* with an organization when they see some element of themselves in the organization. In turn, stakeholders are more likely to support a corporation when they identify with that corporation. More precisely, Bhattacharya and Sen (2004) define *identification* as "the sense of attachment or connection consumers feel with companies engaging in CSR activities they care about" (p. 15). Through the identification process, stakeholders realize part of their own identity is reflected in the corporation's identity. Identification can be a valued component of CSR initiatives when there is alignment between the certain social interests of the stakeholders and the corporation. If corporations pursue social interests that their stakeholders do not value, CSR will not promote identification. Hence, communication with stakeholders generates awareness of shared social concerns and facilitates identification with the corporation.

However, the danger is that many social issues will become "orphans" if they do not catch the eye of stakeholders. At what point does a corporation consider social concerns outside those of keen interest to their stakeholders? How might a corporation champion a neglected social concern in order to build stakeholder support for the concern? A business takes a risk, from an identification perspective, when it tries to build support for an orphan social issue. But that does not mean a corporation should not try to promote an orphan issue or that identification is the only route to CSR benefits. We return to the potential business value of a social issue to provide some insight to these questions.

While creating identification with stakeholders is important, it is not the only potential business benefit that CSR initiatives can yield. Social issues can have a more direct effect on aspects of a corporation's competitiveness such as improving the labor pool by addressing local health problems (Porter & Kramer, 2006). Still, the need for a business benefit can cause some social issues to be marginalized and remain unaddressed. Unfortunately, there is no simple answer to this risk, with the burden of change often falling to those who wish to redress the social concern.

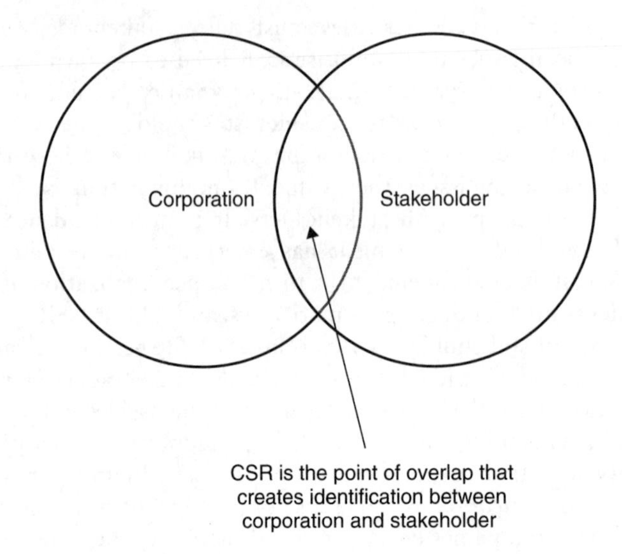

Figure 2.1 CSR as identification

We believe in extending the application beyond consumers to all stakeholders. Figure 2.1 offers a visual representation of CSR as identification. The social issues that comprise CSR become the point of identification. Awareness of the social issues (CSR) permits identification. There are times when management needs to educate stakeholders about their corporation's CSR initiatives. Communication is a central component in linking CSR to identification. Educating stakeholders about how a corporation actually embodies the social values relevant to their stakeholders is a critical task. Theory and research indicate that CSR as identification results in increased stakeholder support for the corporation such as stronger purchase intention (Maignan & Ferrell, 2004; Sen, Bhattacharya, & Korschun, 2006). When there are expectation gaps, differences between how stakeholders expect a corporation to behave and how they perceive the corporation actually behaves, stakeholders may withdraw their support for the company by engaging in negative word of mouth or organized boycotts. These informal and formal methods of communication ultimately are designed to persuade the corporation that it is out of step with stakeholder expectations and changes are needed to bring values into alignment.

The importance of internal stakeholders (employees) should not be overlooked in discussions of stakeholder concerns and the benefits of identification. Hopefully, employees already experience some degree of identification with the corporation that may facilitate their identification with CSR initiatives. But the fact that employees already have ongoing relationships with the company should not lead their concerns and expectations to be marginalized. In addition, it is especially important to inform them of specific CSR initiatives so they will understand how those relate to their jobs and the company overall. However, a major difference may relate to their perceptions of potential threats stemming from CSR initiatives. Employees naturally are concerned about their jobs. If employees believe the corporation's focus on CSR could be detrimental to their jobs, they may experience uncertainty and fail to support the CSR efforts. For example, jobs are contingent upon profits. Activities that detract from profits may threaten job security. Similarly, CSR activities that lead to the elimination of positions will not be welcomed by most employees. If you pit saving the planet against saving jobs, it seems likely that employees will resist the CSR program. Hence, corporations should be sensitive to how CSR initiatives may be perceived by employees and work to address their concerns.

Reputational Benefits of CSR

When we address the strategic aspect of CSR, we must discuss the increasing role of reputation in the corporate world. Though a business concern since the 1950s, interest in reputation exploded in the first decade of the twenty-first century (Meijer, 2004). This intense interest is driven by the business value of reputation. In general, a reputation is how stakeholders perceive an organization. A more precise definition of *reputation* is the *aggregate evaluation that stakeholders make about how well an organization is meeting stakeholder expectations based on past behaviors* (Fombrun & van Riel, 2004; Reinchart, 2003; Wartick, 1992). A strong, favorable reputation has been linked to such tangible assets as attracting customers, motivating employees, retaining employees, generating investment interest, increasing job satisfaction, generating positive comments from financial analysts, generating positive news media coverage, attracting top employee talent, and improving financial performance (Carmeli, 2004; Dowling, 2002; Fombrun & van Riel, 2004).

A key shift in the corporate realm is the integration of CSR into the conceptualization of reputations. Historically, financial factors dominated the assessment of corporate reputations. The financial factors became the proxy for stakeholder expectations used to evaluate corporations. *Fortune* magazine's "Most Admired Companies" list and The Reputation Institutes' RepTrak™ (originally the Reputation Quotient, or RQ) remain among the most widely accepted measures of reputation, and each focuses on financial concerns as the drivers of reputation. Although social responsibility is a component within these measures of reputation, it plays a more minor background role.

The RepTrak™ includes seven dimensions: leadership, performance, products and services, innovation, citizenship, workplace, and governance. CSR is found in the citizenship (e.g., contributes to society), workplace (cares about employee well-being), and governance (e.g., uses power responsibly) dimensions. Interestingly, *Fortune*'s 2007 "Most Admired Companies" edition mentioned the importance of social responsibility, but their evaluative criteria remained unchanged and skewed toward financial factors (Fisher, 2007). More recently, in *Fortune*'s 2010 rankings of "Most Admired Companies," only one of the nine dimensions speaks directly to CSR. In addition to social responsibility, the dimensions are as follows: wise use of corporate assets, retaining talent, quality of product, innovation, long-term investment value, quality of management, financial soundness, and global effectiveness.

CSR has been moving from the background to the foreground of reputation discussions. An illustration of this shift is how Fombrun (2005), a leader in the measurement and discussion of organizational reputation and one of the creators of the RepTrak™, is now referring to CSR as an integral aspect of corporate reputation. An argument can be made that CSR is rapidly developing as *the* driver of reputation. As the earlier definition of *reputation* noted, reputations are evaluations and can range from favorable to unfavorable. We should consider the people making those evaluations – stakeholders. When stakeholders increasingly value CSR, those values will be reflected in reputation evaluations. Moreover, we see the overlapping concern for stakeholder expectations with reputation and CSR. The circle of relevant stakeholders for a corporation's reputation has widened with the inclusion of CSR. Reputation is no longer simply the provenance of investors and customers. Greater numbers of people consider themselves to be organizational stakeholders, and greater numbers of stakeholders are concerned about CSR.

The link between CSR and reputation reinforces the business aspect of CSR and the value of identification. A focus on social responsibility accentuates the differentiation benefits of reputation. A corporation with a strong positive reputation for CSR initiatives can distinguish itself from the crowd of competitors. CSR represents the widening definition of what counts as a stakeholder. Many different types of stakeholders are concerned about a variety of business practices and their impact on the environment and society as a whole. Managers can no longer focus exclusively on investors and their financial interests in order to maintain a positive reputation. CSR is quickly becoming a prominent evaluation criterion for reputations.

One way to understand the value of CSR to reputation is to consider ways to build reputations. Let's discuss two options for crafting a distinct corporate reputation: (1) being first to do something of value and (2) being perceived as an industry leader (Dowling, 2002). Being the first is purely a matter of timing, and only one corporation in each industry can be the first. For CSR, being first can translate into being the first in the industry to embrace CSR in general or being the first to address a specific social concern. McDonald's pioneered integrating environmental concerns into fast food in 1989 when it entered into a joint partnership with the Environmental Defense Fund (Svoboda, 1995).

Early adopters of social concerns are often viewed as industry leaders as well but only if stakeholders are aware of their actions. CSR initiatives do not accrue benefits if people do not know about them. However, a corporation need not be the first to establish itself as the market leader for a specific social concern in order to separate itself from the competition and build a competitive advantage. To become the market leader on a social concern, a corporation must demonstrate it is doing more than anyone else in the industry to address the social concern. Marks and Spencer is pushing its "Plan A" (originally "Look behind the Label") campaign to highlight its social concern by featuring a variety of FairTrade items, including cotton and coffee, and emphasizing health issues by offering healthier prepackaged foods (2010). McDonald's and Marks and Spencer have adopted social concerns that provided, at least temporarily, a way to separate themselves from their competitors. Ben & Jerry's, Patagonia, and Green Mountain Roasters, in contrast, have built strong reputations around social concerns since their inceptions. The Body Shop developed an identity around social concerns and its founder's commitment to social responsibility. Anita Roddick, the aforementioned founder of The Body Shop, promoted the idea of social activism by providing recycling and informing people about ways to participate in other social concerns such as reducing domestic abuse, trading with poor communities, protecting the rights of indigenous people, and promoting human rights around the world. Her concerns resonated with many of her customers and led them to identify with the "beyond-business" mission of The Body Shop.

The reputations not only create differentiation but also can create alignment of stakeholder and corporate interests and facilitate stakeholder identification with the corporation. Businesses can focus on CSR initiatives that will appeal to stakeholders by reflecting their values. Figure 2.1 depicts the shared CSR concerns of corporations and stakeholders. The business defines its corporate identity in part as the social issue. If stakeholders accept that the business does indeed reflect the desired social issue, the stakeholders also are inclined to view the business's reputation as being socially

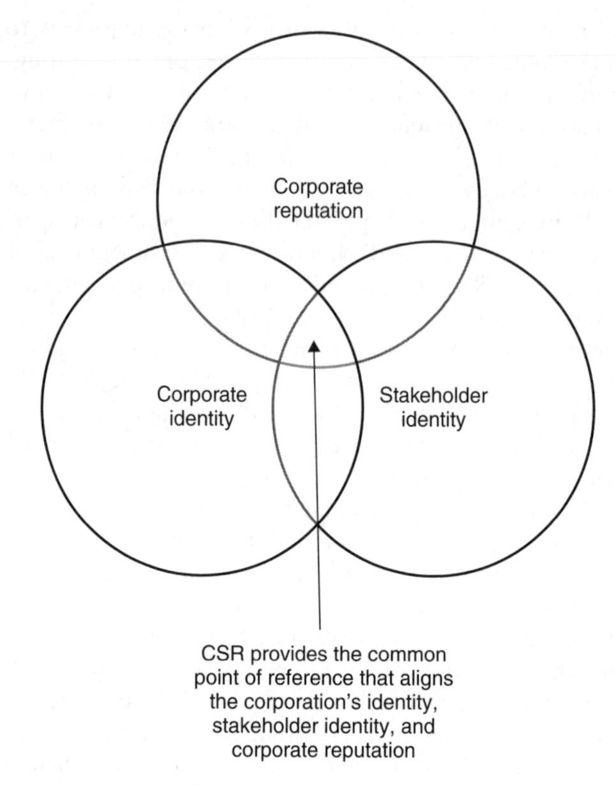

Figure 2.2 Alignment process for CSR and reputation

responsible. In essence, there is an alignment between the corporation's identity, the stakeholders' identity, and corporate reputation. Figure 2.2 illustrates this alignment process. Note the similarity between Figures 2.1 and 2.2. Alignment is a form of identification because it builds on the overlap between corporate identity and stakeholder identity. Alignment adds a third circle representing stakeholder perceptions of the corporation – its reputation. CSR is becoming a vital element within reputation management: "The level of corporate investment in social concerns makes it clear CSR is viewed as key for many firms to build reputation and to create differential advantage" (Ellen, Webb, & Mohr, 2006, p. 155).

Perceived Motives for CSR Initiatives

Stakeholder perceptions assume a critical role throughout the discussion of strategic CSR. Those perceptions often include the corporation's motives for engaging in CSR. Motives are attributions that stakeholders make about CSR activities, not simple objective statements about CSR intentions. Stakeholders may question motivations for engaging in CSR, and perhaps deservedly so given the negative attention attracted by greenwashing. It would be unrealistic to claim a corporation's motivations cannot include an economic component in order for it to be socially responsible. In fact, we assume multiple motivations guide CSR initiatives. Clearly, making a profit to ensure the survival of the corporation – and the CSR initiative – is a central motivation. But motivations may also stem from the founder's values and vision about how businesses can contribute to society. The point is that the profit motive does not preclude more altruistic motivations. They can coexist.

Yvon Chouinard founded Patagonia in 1973 to provide outdoor and adventure sport clothing. What began as a business making climbing pitons is now a global leader in the manufacturing and sales of outdoor clothing and gear. From the start, Chouinard has had a respect for the environment that guided his business. A 1974 catalogue included an article about clean climbing. Here is a line from that environmental statement: "No longer can we assume the Earth's resources are limitless; that there are ranges of unclimbed peaks extending endlessly beyond the horizon. Mountains are finite, and despite their massive appearance, they are fragile" (Patagonia, 2009a).

To get a better sense of Patagonia's commitment to CSR, here is a statement from their CSR web page:

> Patagonia is a $316 million a year, privately owned company based in Ventura, California. We design, develop and market clothing and gear for a wide range of outdoor sports, travel and everyday wear, and are best known for our innovative designs, quality products and strong environmental conscience. Our Mission Statement goes like this: "Build the best product, cause no unnecessary harm, and use business to inspire and implement solutions to the environmental crisis." To that end, we use environmentally sensitive materials (organic cotton, recycled and recyclable polyester, and hemp among them) and both sponsor and participate in a host of environmental initiatives that range from promoting wildlife corridors to combating genetic engineering. To date, we have given some $35 million in grants to grassroots environmental organizations. (Patagonia, 2010)

CSR initiatives, through environmental concerns, have been a core part of Patagonia since its inception. Since 1985, Patagonia has donated 1% of sales to the restoration and protection of the natural environment. In 2001, Yvon Chouinard joined with Craig Mathews of Blue Ribbon Flies to found 1% for the Planet. The organization encourages businesses to donate 1% of sales to environmental groups. The mission is simply to build an alliance of "businesses financially committed to creating a healthy planet" (Patagonia, 2009b). Since 1993, the Patagonia Employee Internship program has allowed employees to leave their jobs for up to two months to work for the environmental group of their choice. Patagonia pays the employee's benefits and salary during that time. Patagonia is on the forefront of recycling equipment and clothing. This includes recycling the thermal underwear worn by their customers. There is concern for social issues as well. As a part of the apparel industry, Patagonia has had to contend with "sweatshop" issues. In 2002 Patagonia hired a social responsibility manager to monitor compliance with its Workplace Code of Conduct throughout its supply chain. Moreover, Patagonia has third-party supplier audits, communicates its social responsibility program to all its factories, and has reduced the total number of factories it uses from 100 to 65, thereby making monitoring more effective (Patagonia, n.d.).

Corporations like Patagonia and The Body Shop have a long legacy of CSR involvement that stems from their founders' visions. Because their CSR initiatives seem to be a natural outgrowth of their founders' passions, stakeholders may be unlikely to question their motivations for CSR. However, some might ask if motivations matter when the CSR initiatives have a positive impact on the environment or society. After all, who can determine what is the "right" reason, or constellation of reasons, for pursuing CSR initiatives? If the focus is on the "good" produced through CSR, second guessing motivations and dismissing the positive effects of economic motivations seem futile. Stakeholders seem to recognize that businesses have a profit motive and that more profitable businesses can devote more resources to CSR. We explore this idea in more detail later in this chapter, when we discuss stakeholder perceptions and four CSR motives.

In sum, CSR can be a win-win for the corporation and society. This stance reflects an ethical perspective termed *rule utilitarianism*. The values underpinning rule utilitarianism focus on the consequences of an action for the collective good. What rules of conduct will produce the greatest good for society? Ethical behaviors are those that produce a desired outcome that benefits the public good. The challenge lies in accurately forecasting both short-term and long-term consequences of an action or a CSR initiative. Unfortunately, a short-term "good" does not preclude a long-term nightmare. This emphasizes the need for strategic CSR based on corporate objectives, careful planning, implementation, and evaluation. This process is cyclical, and communication must play a vital role. We contend that communication is central to successful CSR initiatives.

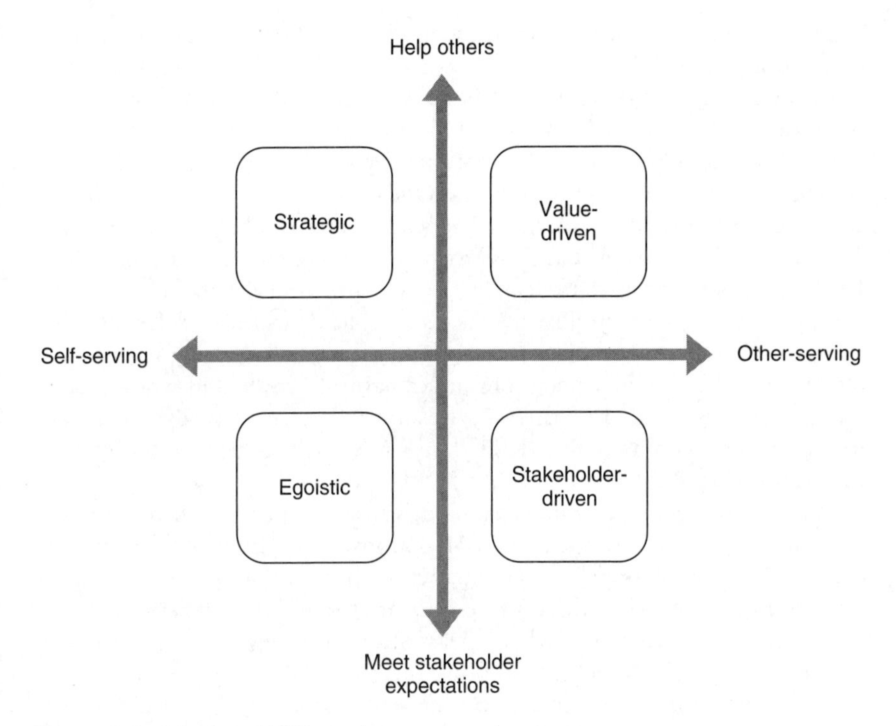

Figure 2.3 Matrix of CSR motives

Communication is the glue that binds together the different departments responsible for CSR.

To further investigate people's perceptions of corporations' motivations for engaging in CSR, Ellen et al. (2006) created a 2 × 2 matrix for evaluating CSR motives. Figure 2.3 offers a visual presentation of the matrix. The matrix includes a duty-alignment dimension that addresses the reason for initiating CSR activities, and is composed of the negative (CSR is enacted to meet stakeholder expectations) and the positive (CSR is performed to help others). The economic dimension involves how CSR relates to performance objectives and ranges from self-serving to other serving. Four motives appear when the two dimensions are crossed: (1) value driven, or caring about the cause; (2) stakeholder driven, or responding to expectations; (3) egoistic, or being obviously self-centered; and (4) strategic, or helping with traditional business objectives.

The four CSR motives are an oversimplification because any CSR effort can be a mix of multiple motives. Research supports this belief because respondents indicate they see multiple motives for CSR efforts. There is an interaction between perceptions of a corporation's CSR motives and the fit of CSR efforts. In general, *fit* is when the CSR effort is consistent with what the business does (Bhattacharya & Sen, 2004). Some examples of CSR fit are useful here. Cargill is a multinational producer and marketer of food and agricultural products and services. One of their CSR initiatives involves working with Feeding America. The CSR initiative helps to feed over 1,600,000 Americans during the Christmas holiday season (Cargill, 2009). Feeding the hungry is a perfect fit for an agricultural company such as Cargill. IKEA is known globally for its flat-pack furniture. IKEA actively seeks to source its wood from forests that are certified as being responsibly managed and to avoid wood from intact natural forests and wood that is illegally harvested (IKEA, 2010a). Responsible forest management is a logical fit for a company like IKEA that is so closely associated with wood furniture.

People perceive CSR as more value driven and strategic when there is a fit between the corporation and its CSR actions. Perceptions of CSR motives can influence how stakeholders interact with an organization. Purchase intention increases when the CSR motives are perceived as value driven and strategic, and it decreases when the motives are viewed as stakeholder driven and egoistic (Ellen et al., 2006).

The views of the CSR motives can be very instructive. Stakeholders can accept a strategic focus to CSR when they believe a corporation cares about the cause. On the other hand, stakeholders reject the CSR efforts when they perceive the corporation was forced into the change as a response to stakeholder pressure and is acting in its own self-interests. In the end, stakeholders recognize the business side of CSR. Stakeholders realize that CSR includes an element of helping to achieve business interests. The challenge is that the strategic element cannot dominate the CSR process. Stakeholders must also believe the corporation has an other-serving element as well. People must perceive that the organization does care about the issue and the interests of those helped by the issue. As we shall discuss in later chapters, balancing strategic and value-driven perceptions of CSR poses a difficult communication challenge.

So how do we reconcile a stakeholder-driven view of CSR with these findings? Part of the answer lies in when stakeholder expectations were used to create the CSR efforts. It is appropriate to distinguish between *proactive* and *reactive* utilization of stakeholder expectations. When management works to anticipate stakeholder social concerns, the CSR will not appear to be a reaction to stakeholder expectations. We can call this *proactive stakeholder expectation utilization*. It includes situations where CSR is part of a founder's vision. In contrast, CSR appears to be a reaction to stakeholder expectations when the CSR efforts are adopted after stakeholders publicly challenge the corporation to change. We can call this *reactive stakeholder expectation utilization.*

As noted in chapter 1, timing is important for CSR implementation. Voluntary, early adopters realize greater benefits from CSR. Managers are quick to identify the social concerns as they emerge from stakeholder engagement and traditional and online media coverage. When those same CSR efforts are adopted later and seem to be "forced" on a corporation, such as through stakeholder pressure including unfavorable media attention, no benefits are realized (Husted & Salazar, 2006).

Kimberly-Clark makes paper products, including Kleenex and Scott, and provides an illustration of forced change. Paper production utilizes wood fiber from some source. From 2004 to 2009, Greenpeace took issue with the source for some of Kimberly-Clark's wood fiber. The effort was named "Kleercut: Wiping away Ancient Forests." The focus of the campaign was protecting the Boreal Forest, an ancient forest located in Canada. Greenpeace wanted Kimberly-Clark to stop sourcing wood fiber from this ancient forest. Kleercut relied on a combination of protests and stakeholder pressure (especially from consumers) to pressure Kimberly-Clark into changing its wood fiber policies. Over 50 protests were launched during the campaign. Under the final agreement, which was announced on August 5, 2009, Kimberly-Clark agreed it would not purchase wood fiber from mills using trees from the Boreal Forest unless strict ecological criteria were used for their harvesting (Kleercut, 2009).

Kleercut is a case of forced changed related to CSR. As the Greenpeace announcement stated,

> It is finally time to celebrate a major victory for the Boreal Forest! Kimberly-Clark has, as a result of public pressure, released a new environmental fibre policy that governs how it will help conserve forests and support sustainable forestry and use more recycled fibre. (Greenpeace, 2009b)

The announcement did go on to report that Greenpeace and Kimberly-Clark were now moving from conflict to a collaborative relationship that they hope will foster forest conservation. Even though Kimberly-Clark is praised, the statement clearly indicates that the change was a result of pressure from stakeholders. Kleercut stands as an example of how businesses can be pressured into adopting CSR initiatives.

Strategic CSR must be anticipatory. Through stakeholder engagement, management anticipates what social concerns are emerging as important and shapes the CSR efforts to match those emerging demands. As a result, the corporation does not appear to be reacting to stakeholder expectations. Instead, the organization appears to be a proactive leader in the area of the social concern, resulting in business benefits from the social issue as well as the betterment of society. Failure to be anticipatory creates gaps between stakeholder CSR expectations and corporate performance. The CSR expectation gaps can prompt stakeholders to take action against a corporation and to generate pressure for change. The idea that CSR expectation gaps and stakeholder pressures can prompt corporate changes is detailed in chapter 4 on formative research.

General Strategic Guidance: Approaching the CSR Process as Change Management

Our final area of discussion frames the strategic CSR process as a form of change management. No single, best method exists for creating a CSR initiative. However, the general framework offered by change management provides useful insights into CSR development and management. The CSR Process Model described in this book is grounded in general principles of change management. We focus on how a corporation's involvement in CSR poses challenges and opportunities that can be managed through rational analysis, development, implementation, and evaluation. We emphasize that stakeholder engagement must be integrated throughout this process.

One type of organizational change is administrative. *Administrative change* involves altering an organization's "structure, strategy, policies, reward systems, labor relations, coordination, and control systems" (Smeltzer, 1991). New CSR initiatives qualify as administrative change. Change is conceptualized as a progressing through four phases: (1) exploration, (2) planning, (3) action, and (4) integration. Exploration involves the identification of the need for change and the decision to pursue a change effort. Planning assigns resources and constructs a roadmap for implementing the change. Action involves the implementation of the plan; the change is disseminated to others. Integration is when the change becomes a part of day-to-day activities (Bullock & Batten, 1985; Timmerman, 2003). There is a clear parallel between the change management process and the CSR process when we consider the central importance of *acceptance of the proposed change*. Both internal and external stakeholders need to perceive the new CSR initiative as legitimate for the CSR initiatives to have positive effects. What benefits are accrued if a new CSR initiative is ignored or ridiculed?

The change management literature often notes the need to create buy-in to the change. *Buy-in* is a common phrase referring to people accepting and supporting a change. An effective way to create acceptance is to have people participate in the development of the change. Through the stakeholder engagement process, management can involve internal and external stakeholders in the creation of a CSR initiative. Because stakeholders play a role in formulating the CSR initiative, they are more likely to support it once the CSR initiative is implemented. Stakeholders will see a part of themselves in the CSR initiative and feel a sense of ownership (Heath & Coombs, 2006).

Communication plays a critical role in change acceptance. It is through communication that stakeholders become a part of the change process (Timmerman, 2003). The engagement for CSR requires communication as stakeholders make their ideas and opinions known to management. For instance, focus groups can be used to generate ideas for possible CSR efforts or to gauge reaction to a proposed CSR initiative. Communication is vital to identification, a specific form of support for a change. Through identification, stakeholders see themselves reflected in the change. For our purposes, stakeholders realize that the CSR initiative reflects their self-identity. Stakeholders build support for the CSR initiative and the corporation through identification (Sen et al., 2006).

Everyone Loves a Good Story

Narratives (stories) offer one way for managers to build acceptance of and cooperation with CSR initiatives. Change management can be viewed as a narrative process; change is a story told to – and told by – those involved in the process. Change managers are successful when people accept their change story. But we also believe that stakeholders must participate in this narrative process such that they become co-creators of these narratives. This view is consistent with the stakeholder engagement process that permeates this book.

Narratives can be viewed as "a chronological account of an event sequence indicating causality through actions explained in terms of intentions, deed, and consequences" (Buchanan & Dawson, 2007, p. 672). In change management, it is helpful to create narratives that go beyond description and capture the causality inherent in change. People need to understand *why* events are unfolding as they are. When CSR initiatives are considered a change, managers need to consider how these narratives can be structured to include the shared vision, values, and social concerns that promulgated the change. Some stakeholders will readily identify the "why" connection between the corporation's mission and values and a focus on CSR. Others may be more skeptical or apprehensive. Narratives will help them see the reasons behind the change and increase their likelihood of participating in the change.

Walter Fisher (1987) claims that people are natural storytellers and that they are persuaded by narratives. A good story will convince people to accept claims such as the legitimacy and value of a CSR initiative. People evaluate narratives by evaluating narrative probability and fidelity. *Narrative probability* deals with the internal consistency of the story. Does the narrative "hang together" and seem logical based on the audience's experiences? Listeners determine whether or not the story has all the right elements and characters, and makes sense to them. *Narrative fidelity* reflects whether the story seems "truthful" and is consistent with their beliefs, experiences, and values. Values play an important role in narrative fidelity because audiences look for how their values are implicated in the story (Fisher, 1987). If the values embedded in the narrative resonate with their own values, the story will be perceived as more believable and desirable. Naturally, narrative probability and fidelity will be enhanced when stakeholders have participated in the creation of the narrative through the engagement process. The narrative should ring true with their experiences, and they should be able to see themselves and their values within the narrative.

The CSR initiative narrative is the story of how the new initiative will be created (a chronological sequence of events). Critical elements for narrative probability are the characters, the intentions, the process, and the consequences. The characters include the corporation, various stakeholders, and society as a whole. All three "characters" have concerns about the consequences of the CSR initiative. The CSR initiative narrative must capture the needs and values of key characters. The narrators also should be sensitive to the emotional needs of listeners. Discussions of corporate social responsibility often evoke strong passions, and those emotional elements should not be neglected.

The CSR initiative narrative should explain why the change is occurring (intentions) and how the decision will be reached. These elements help to construct a narrative that has the right elements to resonate with listeners. Managers must make sure they use those elements to create internal consistency – a good storyline – as well.

Narrative fidelity concerns whether or not the CSR initiative narrative appears to be consistent with the corporation's strategic plans, the corporation's culture and values, and stakeholder needs. If the CSR initiative is inconsistent with the corporation's strategic plans, other managers are unlikely to support the effort. If the CSR initiative is inconsistent with the corporate culture or incompatible with stakeholder concerns, both internal and external stakeholders will question its validity. The CSR initiative narrative should be easy to develop because the CSR process provides the raw materials necessary to construct effective narratives. Throughout the CSR process, managers will have been addressing concerns about narrative probability and fidelity. The collaborative process (stakeholder engagement) will permit co-creation of the story. The resulting narrative content and form should be satisfying to those involved and easy to repeat to others. Telling and retelling the CSR narrative will not only provide information about the CSR process but also reinforce important values, feelings of ownership, and identification with the CSR initiative.

The CSR Process Model: A Brief Preview

The remaining chapters in this book are built around the CSR Process Model shown in Figure 2.4. We believe that strategic CSR requires a commitment to both process and outcomes. Strategic CSR should enable the corporation to pursue business objectives while participating in the process of stakeholder engagement to enact meaningful CSR initiatives. The model depicts a continuous process composed of stages that should inform a strategic CSR effort:

1. Scanning and monitoring
2. Conducting formative research
3. Creating the CSR initiative

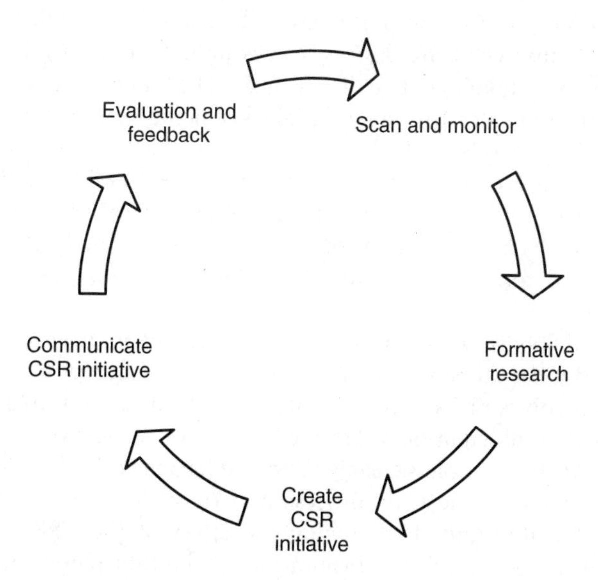

Figure 2.4 CSR Process Model

4. Communicating the CSR initiative
5. Conducting an evaluation and providing feedback

The first process, scanning and monitoring, requires the corporation to search its surrounding environment to identify emerging social and environmental CSR concerns that could affect stakeholder perceptions of their operations. This process also involves identifying stakeholders interested in those CSR concerns. Because these concerns and stakeholder expectations change over time, the scanning and monitoring process is continuous.

The second process, formative research, focuses attention on the concerns or problems to assess opportunities to benefit society and the corporation as well as to identify problems that may create negative effects. Formative research involves the collection and evaluation of information necessary for selecting CSR concerns to convert into CSR initiatives. Intensive research is conducted to study the issues and to begin the process of stakeholder engagement that carries through all steps in the model. This step is important for understanding stakeholder expectations, identifying gaps between what the company is currently doing and what stakeholders believe the company should be doing, and cultivating meaningful dialogue with stakeholders.

The third phase, creating the CSR initiative, translates the CSR concern into practice. The information gleaned from previous stages is used to plan concrete actions involving the corporation and stakeholders. However, the corporation should anticipate possible opposition to the corporation's actions – and inactions – on particular CSR issues. Because different stakeholders have different CSR priorities, it is unlikely that any CSR strategy will satisfy all stakeholder expectations. The stakeholder engagement process that permeates this stage involves stakeholders in the discussions of proposed initiatives and objectives. Ideally the involvement will contribute to a sense of ownership as well as understanding of the selected CSR initiatives. When stakeholders are disappointed with CSR-related decisions, involvement in the process should at least help them feel like their ideas and concerns received a fair hearing prior to the final decision making.

The fourth phase, communicating the CSR initiative, involves helping internal and external stakeholders learn about and accept the CSR initiatives. This involves tasks such as content formulation and media selection that ensure that information about the CSR effort is conveyed to those who are interested. The last phase, evaluation and feedback, enables the corporation to determine if the CSR process and outcome objectives were met. Assessment is important for gauging the effect of the CSR initiative on society, stakeholders, and the corporation. To be transparent, the corporation must provide evaluation data and solicit feedback from stakeholders concerning the process and outcomes of the CSR initiatives. The model depicts an ongoing process such that the evaluation and feedback phase provides the foundation for the scanning and monitoring phase. The cycle continues; it should not stop with the completion of an initiative. The CSR process requires a continuous commitment to research, planning, implementation, and evaluation.

Attendees voice their opinions at a town hall meeting on behalf of the Agency for Toxic Substances and Disease Registry (ATSDR). The purpose of these meetings is to collect community concerns and share health messages about local environmental issues. Courtesy of Centers for Disease Control and Prevention/Dawn Arlotta

3

CSR Scanning and Monitoring

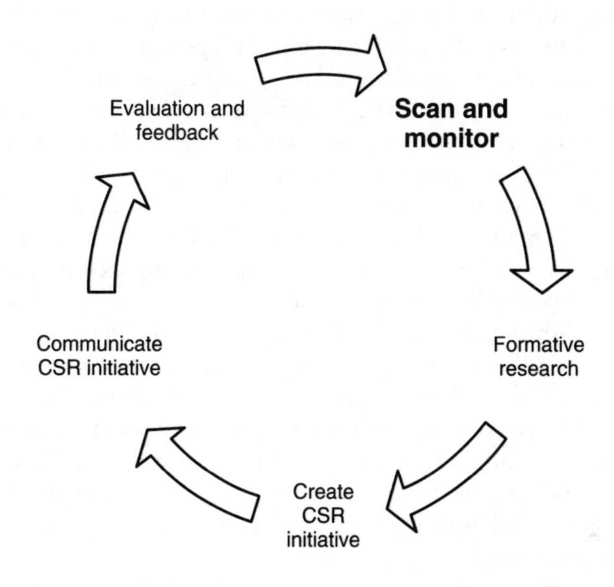

Management strategy should be constructed from a solid base of knowledge. Information must be collected and analyzed to provide the foundation required for strategy formulation. Strategic management plots the direction of the corporation, develops a plan for achieving the desired objectives, and allocates resources for the endeavor. Since the late 1960s, *environmental scanning* has been a core element of strategic decision making. *Scanning* gathers information from the environment that serves as a basis for creating

Managing Corporate Social Responsibility: A Communication Approach, First Edition.
W. Timothy Coombs, Sherry J. Holladay.

knowledge of emerging threats and opportunities. Strategy is predicated on assumptions about the environment, and environmental scanning attempts to determine the "correctness" of those assumptions (Muralidharan, 2004). In other words, scanning helps us assess if the situation we *think* the corporation is facing is really the situation the corporation *is* facing. Scanning moves us from reliance on "gut instinct" or intuition to evidence-based decision making.

From the corporate perspective, effective CSR needs to be integrated into the larger corporate strategy. Hence, CSR is part of the overall strategic management process. CSR is linked to the environment through stakeholder expectations, values, and conceptualizations of what constitutes CSR. As with any element of the environment, stakeholder expectations change over time and require regular assessment. For example, consider how prominent current events such as the BP Deepwater Horizon explosion in the Gulf of Mexico, food and toy safety concerns over Chinese imports, and revelations of worker exploitation in garment factories influence stakeholder perceptions of corporations and expectations for responsible corporate behavior. In 2007, over 2 million toys manufactured by RC2 and Mattel in China were recalled for lead paint. These were prominent, well-known brands, and it raised stakeholder awareness and concern over toys and lead paint. The public health threat created a CSR concern and expectations that corporations would take more effective actions to prevent toys with lead paint from reaching children. CSR strategy must change to reflect the new environment within which the corporation operates. Both the content of the CSR strategy (the objectives and how to reach them) and the strategic controls used to implement the strategy are subject to revision. That is why we begin our discussion of the CSR process with scanning and the related concept of monitoring.

The CSR process begins by identifying potential CSR concerns that may be translated into CSR actions for corporations. Managers "find" potential CSR concerns by using scanning and monitoring to understand their external and internal stakeholders and the corporation's environment. We must recognize that although scanning and monitoring attempt to be objective, they do involve subjective elements as well. Different managers might identify different CSR concerns from the same set of stakeholder data. The important point is that managers must consider stakeholders to be an integral part of the CSR process. Effective strategic CSR is premised on meeting stakeholder expectations for corporate CSR behaviors. Scanning and monitoring provide ways for managers to determine which CSR concerns are relevant to stakeholders and how well the corporation is meeting those expectations. Managers may find opportunities for future CSR initiatives or discover flaws in their current CSR practices. Either insight provides initial guidance for refining CSR activities.

Issues Management

Issues management, the identification of and actions taken to affect issues, has long preached the value of environmental scanning to identify potential problems early (Heath, 1990). Issues are problems ready for some resolution (Jones & Chase, 1979). For example, issues may range from childhood obesity to greener packaging to food safety. Early identification of issues should promote early intervention to reduce the impact of the potential problem on the corporation. In some cases, the potential problem can be converted into an opportunity. Early intervention will result in a greater likelihood of success and be less expensive than if a corporation waits to take action on the problem (Crable & Vibbert, 1985; Jones & Chase, 1979). Issues are frequently closely tied with social concerns. Actions designed to manage an issue may be managing a social concern as well. It follows that the principles of issues management can be applied effectively to CSR and managing social concerns.

In 2009, Nike announced steps to help address the issue of Amazon deforestation. Nike does not operate in the Amazon area but does purchase leather sourced from the Amazon. One source of leather is from cattle raised on land in the Amazon that is illegally cleared by ranchers. Greenpeace had been documenting how leather and meat production were contributing to the Amazon deforestation issue. Nike created stronger guidelines for leather sourcing called the "Nike Inc. Amazon Leather Policy" and only uses suppliers that join the Leather Working Group. Amazon deforestation is not a new issue, but applying the issue to the athletic shoe industry through leather sourcing was innovative (Nike, 2009). Nike was positioning itself to be a leader in the ethical sourcing of leather and received supportive statements from Greenpeace for its efforts.

For CSR, scanning searches inside and outside the corporation for potential issues rather than simply focusing on the corporation's external environment. Managers should cast a wide net to capture as much information as possible. Moreover, the boundary of what separates a corporation from its environment is ill defined at best (Brownlie, 1994). Scanning is similar to a radar system looking for "blips" that could be meaningful. The blips attract attention and then are scrutinized more closely. When a promising issue is found, managers examine it in more detail. In contrast to scanning, *monitoring* evaluates *current efforts* to address a social concern. Monitoring is a form of evaluation because it assesses how stakeholders respond to existing CSR efforts. Scanning helps managers identify new issues that require action and monitoring, and determines if existing social concerns need further action. In this chapter, we explore how scanning and monitoring can be applied in the strategic CSR process. The concepts of scanning and monitoring are translated from strategic management and issues management to the CSR process, and the role of stakeholder engagement in both is discussed.

Scanning and CSR

Scanning is essentially a search of the corporation's environment. The search focuses on emerging social and environmental concerns that could impact CSR-related perceptions of the corporation. The CSR concerns in the environment can shape stakeholders' CSR expectations. Because expectations are evolving, expectations are moving targets. However, some concerns predictably are associated with some industries. For example, the restaurant industry is linked to obesity, food safety, and other health issues; the diamond industry is associated with human rights; the garment industry is connected to child labor and sweat shops; and the petrochemical industry is tied to environmental degradation and health concerns.

CSR scanning is a specific type of scanning that analyzes a myriad of information sources including activist discussions, potential government actions, reputation evaluations, and polling data results. CSR scanning should include internal sources by examining the CSR concerns of employees. Corporations cannot meet stakeholder expectations if they are not aware of them. A mosaic of the social concerns prominent among stakeholders emerges as relevant information is collected and analyzed.

As with issues management, CSR managers must decide which of the emerging CSR concerns warrants further attention. The challenge is to identify those social concerns or issues that will arise as focal points for the corporation's stakeholders. This is challenging because managers must anticipate which social concerns are gaining traction and likely to reach prominence. While such projects may seem like an educated guess, the guess should be informed by research, including the process of stakeholder engagement. Once identified, management must decide if a CSR concern warrants further consideration. The focus then turns to prioritizing social concerns.

Prioritizing CSR Concerns

Managers must interpret these initial data to determine which CSR concerns hold the most promise for the CSR efforts. Though based on data, interpretations are tinged with subjectivity grounded in managers' personal beliefs, values, and experiences. Nevertheless, managers should strive to be objective at this prioritizing stage.

Managers can draw upon the issues management literature for guidance and use the evaluative dimensions of likelihood and impact to assess CSR concerns. *Likelihood* is the potential of the CSR concern to attract interest from a wide array of stakeholders, especially powerful stakeholders. If a large number of stakeholders and powerful stakeholders may be drawn to the CSR concern, it has high likelihood. In this way, likelihood is an assessment of the CSR concern's ability to attract adherents and advocates – and to develop into CSR expectations. *Impact*, the second evaluative dimension, is the effect the CSR concern can have on society and the corporation. Stakeholders want corporations to address CSR concerns that have a major impact on society. To maximize resources, managers want to address CSR concerns that can significantly impact the corporation. This can include CSR concerns that have the potential to significantly harm or benefit the corporation.

The likelihood and impact ratings can be used to create an initial prioritization system. There will be more potential CSR concerns than a corporation has time or resources to consider. As a result, the CSR concerns with the highest likelihood and impact scores should be examined in more detail. We can call these *emerging CSR concerns*. Management then assesses how well or poorly the corporation is positioned to address these emerging CSR concerns. If the corporation is already taking actions that address the social concern, no further action is required. An exception might be if the corporation is not effectively communicating its efforts to stakeholders. In this situation, the corporation would need to develop a more effective communication plan to convey its actions to stakeholders. If the corporation currently is taking action to address the social concern, it will appear concerned about the emerging CSR concern as it develops and be perceived as a leader in addressing the issue. An example will help to illustrate the idea of leadership through early action on stakeholder CSR concerns.

Mobile phones are a ubiquitous global product. The odds are that you have a mobile phone and will own many throughout your lifetime. Do you know the sustainability of your phone? Stakeholder research found that 44% of UK mobile users would. People may not be demanding sustainability information about phones but think it is a good idea. It seems that people generally like to have sustainability information about the products they use. Mobile phone sustainability is a latent CSR concern as stakeholders have not been publicly clamoring for such information but do see it as a benefit. So where do you find information about your mobile's sustainability? Enter telecommunication corporation O2 in August 2010. In collaboration with Forum for the Future, a UK-based sustainability organization that partners with businesses and universities, O2 created the Eco rating, the first UK rating system of mobile phone sustainability (Miner, 2010).

Here is a section of text from O2's announcement of the rating system:

> The Sony Ericsson Elm tops the list of 65 mobile phones from six manufacturers, rated 4.3 out of 5. The scores reflect the environmental impact of a

> mobile phone, how it helps people lead more sustainable lives and the ethical performance of the manufacturer. They will be published online and in O2 stores from this week.
>
> Eco rating has been developed in partnership with independent sustainability experts Forum for the Future, in close collaboration with handset manufacturers. It's a key initiative within O2's Think Big sustainability programme and part of its commitment to bringing sustainable products and services to its customers.
>
> There are 4.1 billion mobile phones in circulation worldwide with a combined carbon footprint over their lifetime of more than 100 million tones. That's the equivalent of taking every car and HGV in the UK off the road and grounding domestic flights for a year. With 1712 mobile phones being replaced every minute in the UK it's easy to see how small improvements can make a huge difference, and Eco rating looks at much more than just CO2. (O2, 2010)

O2 is using the Eco rating to establish CSR leadership because they are the first to offer the mobile phone sustainability rating. The Eco rating system is part of their larger sustainability effort. Scanning through surveys of mobile phone customers enabled O2 to discover the potential CSR concern that became a CSR initiative for O2.

If the corporation fails to act on the emerging CSR concern, a potential problem exists. If nothing changes, eventually stakeholders will perceive the corporation is operating counter to their social concern or constellation of social concerns. The corporation loses its alignment with its stakeholders. Conflict (churn) can erupt if stakeholders feel the need to "make" the corporation address the emerging social concern. Once conflict emerges, the CSR efforts are no longer strategic or beneficial but something that must be done to prevent further damage to the corporation. In this case, the corporation is being reactive and is unlikely to benefit from involvement with the social concern. It will be seen as lagging behind the expectation curve and as merely taking action in order to catch up to industry leaders.

The prior discussion of scanning highlights the importance of early detection of the CSR concern. Early detection means the corporation learns of the CSR concern before a wide number of stakeholders accept the social concern and definitely before any public challenges to the corporation on the CSR concern occur. Again, we should be mindful that detection has a subjective element, and potential CSR concerns can be missed because managers view the information as irrelevant. When managers miss the harbingers of a CSR concern, the social concern will appear in later scanning once stakeholders act upon it. In those cases, scanning reveals the existing problems, as stakeholder anger about a lack of action on the CSR concern is already manifest. When scanning uncovers stakeholder anger, the CSR process becomes reactive rather than proactive. Still, the CSR-related problems are likely to intensify if they are ignored or remain unnoticed.

Monitoring and CSR

In contrast to scanning, which focuses on identifying emerging issues, monitoring involves assessing reactions to *current* CSR initiatives. How are stakeholders perceiving and reacting to a corporation's current CSR efforts? Monitoring is much narrower than scanning because it is limited to current CSR efforts. Managers can focus on existing CSR efforts and determine whether or not the efforts are meeting stakeholder expectations. Just because stakeholders were satisfied with your CSR efforts last year does not mean they will have the same level of satisfaction this year. The factors that drive CSR expectations today may be very different in one, three, or five years. In addition, unexpected events or crises can turn the spotlight on a concern or issue. Consider how concerns with offshore drilling became prominent after BP's Deep Horizon disaster in the Gulf of Mexico. Failure to adapt to changing CSR expectations will result in corporations being perceived as socially irresponsible because expectation gaps develop – the corporation fails to meet the CSR expectations of its stakeholders. We elaborate on the development and management of expectation gaps in Chapter 4. Again, corporations cannot adapt to changing stakeholder expectations if they are not aware that expectations are changing.

If a CSR effort is no longer meeting stakeholder expectations, management must consider corrective action. The initial question is whether or not the CSR concern embodied in the program is still relevant. If the CSR concern is dated and no longer of interest to stakeholders, managers must consider a new direction for the CSR efforts. If the CSR concern is still valued but the CSR actions are considered inadequate or outdated, the CSR program requires modification rather than a new direction. Marks and Spencer, a UK-based retailer, illustrates the evolutionary nature of CSR initiatives. In 2006, Marks and Spencer introduced a CSR initiative called "Look behind the Label." The Look campaign centered on FairTrade goods and healthier foods. The two highlighted CSR concerns were FairTrade cotton and reduced salt in the food Marks and Spencer sold (Marks and Spencer, 2006). In 2007, Look was replaced by "Plan A." Plan A included a list of 100 different CSR-related commitments from Marks and Spencer. Each year, Marks and Spencer reports progress on those commitments and adds new commitments as well. Plan A is built on five pillars: (1) climate change, (2) waste, (3) sustainable raw materials, (4) fair partners, and (5) health. The overarching goal is for Marks and Spencer to become the world's most sustainable major retailer by 2015 (Marks and Spencer, 2010). The point is that Marks and Spencer realizes the fluidity of CSR concerns and incorporates new concerns as they begin to emerge.

Monitoring also can refer to efforts designed to keep an eye on a CSR concern. Scanning may detect a CSR concern and rate it fairly high as a concern. However, its potential to spread among stakeholders may be low. Managers may monitor the CSR concern for any signal that its potential to spread among stakeholders is developing. This might be called placing the CSR concern on a "watch list." If the CSR concern shows increased signs of likelihood, the managers can then act upon it.

Scanning and Monitoring in Concert

Scanning and monitoring should be conducted continuously to benefit a corporation. Irregular scanning and monitoring will not provide the timely data required for a strategic, proactive approach to CSR. Scanning and monitoring are complementary. Scanning can identify new CSR concerns while monitoring can assess known CSR concerns. Both scanning and monitoring provide the starting point for further action. An opportunity or problem is identified, and the process of addressing the CSR situation is initiated. Scanning and monitoring provide information about a specific CSR concern that warrants further attention.

Effective CSR scanning and monitoring are premised on proper information searches. Managers must know where to look for relevant CSR information, how to collect the information, and how to evaluate the information. Sources will include traditional news media, online news media, social media, and key stakeholders. Collection techniques include searching databases, polling data, surveys, focus groups, and interviews. The proper sources and research techniques can vary according to the CSR demands of the corporation's industry. Managers will need to develop their own definitions for *likelihood* and *impact* when evaluating the information they have collected.

Scanning and monitoring provide two foundational elements for the CSR process: (1) the identification of potential CSR concerns and (2) the identification of stakeholders associated with those CSR concerns. It is really a matter of the "chicken-and-egg" dilemma when discussing which comes first. Managers may find a CSR concern emerging in traditional and online media. The managers could then specify the stakeholders that might be involved with the CSR concern. Conversely, managers might discuss CSR in general with stakeholders and discover specific CSR concerns through those conversations. The managers would then conduct additional research to explore the potential of the CSR concern. Ultimately, managers must extract both the CSR concern and stakeholders relevant to that concern for scanning and monitoring to have value.

Stakeholder Engagement's Role in Scanning and Monitoring

Stakeholder engagement for scanning and monitoring begins with identifying the various stakeholders to be engaged. The stakeholders that are engaged can vary by the specific CSR concern being discussed. Still, corporations must carefully consider whom to involve in the process. The Global Reporting Initiative (GRI) specifies that organizations discuss how they define and select stakeholders for engagement. Stakeholder engagement is an element of the GRI, so it appears in numerous CSR and sustainability reports. As a review, GRI reporting covers economic, social, and environmental reports by corporations. The GRI includes these specific statements about stakeholder engagement (the numbers reflect the GRI numbering system):

> 4.14 List of stakeholder groups engaged by the organization.
> *Examples of stakeholder groups are:*
> - *Communities;*
> - *Civil society;*
> - *Customers;*
> - *Shareholders and providers of capital;*
> - *Suppliers; and*
> - *Employees, other workers, and their trade unions.*
>
> 4.15 Basis for identification and selection of stakeholders with whom to engage.
> *This includes the organization's process for defining its stakeholder groups, and for determining the groups with which to engage and not to engage.*
>
> 4.16 Approaches to stakeholder engagement, including frequency of engagement by type and by stakeholder group.
> *This could include surveys, focus groups, community panels, corporate advisory panels, written communication, management/union structures, and other vehicles. The organization should indicate whether any of the engagement was undertaken specifically as part of the report preparation process.*
>
> 4.17 Key topics and concerns that have been raised through stakeholder engagement, and how the organization has responded to those key topics and concerns, including through its reporting. (Global Reporting Initiative, 2006, p. 24)

Identifying stakeholders actually is part of scanning and monitoring. The organization scans the environment for CSR concerns and relevant stakeholders. Those CSR concerns and stakeholders are then monitored for initial information on the topic. The engagement begins as the corporation reaches out to the stakeholders and asks for their input on CSR issues.

One example of engagement is the use of stakeholder panels. The *stakeholder panel* is composed of representatives from the various stakeholder groups that might be interested in a particular CSR concern or in CSR in general. The panel meets regularly and can be used to examine corporate policies and actions for comment and recommendations. The panel offers advice on future CSR actions and critiques of current CSR practices. Panels can address general CSR concerns or be structured around specific CSR concerns such as biodiversity. A corporation can even have multiple stakeholder panels. The specific structure all depends on what the corporation is trying to accomplish.

Thus far, our discussion seems to focus on engagement with stakeholders who are external to the corporation. However, the role of internal stakeholders, a corporation's own employees, should not be neglected. Their role in scanning and monitoring mirrors that of external stakeholders. As is the case with external stakeholders, corporations should reach out to internal stakeholders and solicit their input on CSR issues. There is no reason to expect that the CSR concerns of internal stakeholders will differ drastically from those of external stakeholders. However, employees are uniquely positioned to have both knowledge of the corporation and understanding of potential CSR issues. As company members, they probably already identify with the corporation. Moreover, their roles in the corporation mean they will be either directly or indirectly involved in selected CSR initiatives. Failure to consult internal stakeholders when the corporation's initiatives will affect them certainly could lead to alienation and lack of support for CSR initiatives. Corporations benefit when stakeholders identify with the corporation, the CSR concern, and the values underpinning the social concern. This would hold true for a corporation's own employees. Employees are generally aware of the corporation's capabilities and resources, and may be well situated to contribute ideas about how the corporation can pursue CSR initiatives. Corporations would be wise to include their internal stakeholders in the scanning and monitoring process.

Conclusion and Critical Questions

The conclusions of chapters 3 through 7 include tables of critical questions to consider within each phase of the CSR Process Model. The tables use the following format. First, the question is presented. Second, the relevant parties who have an interest in the question are identified.

Scanning and monitoring seek to identify emerging CSR concerns that could be integrated into future CSR initiatives – and develop the knowledge that makes CSR strategic. CSR is driven by stakeholder expectations, and those expectations change over time. This means that scanning and monitoring must be ongoing processes. To be proactive, managers should address new CSR concerns before they generate widespread interest. In this way, the corporation becomes a leader in CSR. Changing expectations also can mean that an existing CSR initiative becomes obsolete as it no longer speaks to salient stakeholder concerns. Monitoring functions as a "checkup" and determines if existing CSR initiatives are still relevant and viable for stakeholders.

Critical Questions for Scanning and Monitoring	*Relevant Parties*	
	Corporation	*Stakeholders*
What sources should be scanned for possible CSR concerns?	X	
What sources should be monitored for possible CSR concerns?	X	
Which stakeholders should be engaged in the scanning process?	X	X
Which stakeholders should be engaged in the monitoring process?	X	X
How will the engagement process for scanning be structured?	X	X
How will the engagement process for monitoring be structured?	X	X
Do stakeholders still consider the existing CSR initiatives to be relevant?	X	X
How are stakeholders reacting to current CSR initiatives?	X	X
Have any events occurred that suggest the need to modify expectations or efforts?	X	X
What criteria should be used for the preliminary identification and assessment of CSR concerns?	X	X

Effective scanning and monitoring require careful consideration of the sources to examine for possible CSR concerns. The base materials for scanning should include messages created by activists, online discussions of CSR issues, and news media coverage. Managers must also consider the range of salient stakeholders, which ones to include in the engagement process, and the nature of that engagement process. Engagement can provide managers with insights into what concerns are salient for stakeholders (scanning) and how stakeholders are reacting to existing CSR initiatives (monitoring). The goal of scanning is to produce a tentative list of CSR issues that could be translated into CSR initiatives. Because the tentative list requires an initial prioritization, managers should determine the criteria to be used in the preliminary assessment of the CSR concerns. Likelihood and impact evaluations are commonly used to prioritize concerns. During the stakeholder engagement process, stakeholders would be interested in who is included in the scanning and monitoring process and the criteria for assessing CSR concerns to determine whether or not their interests would be taken into account. Monitoring helps managers keep up-to-date on the CSR initiatives that have been implemented. The results from monitoring may signal the need to reinvigorate the stakeholder engagement process on a particular issue where the corporation has fallen behind expectations.

Indian commuters pass by a billboard of British telecommunications giant, Vodafone, in New Dehli. Vodafone operates globally and emphasizes stakeholder engagement in its corporate social responsibility process. © Prakash Singh/Getty Images

4

Formative Research

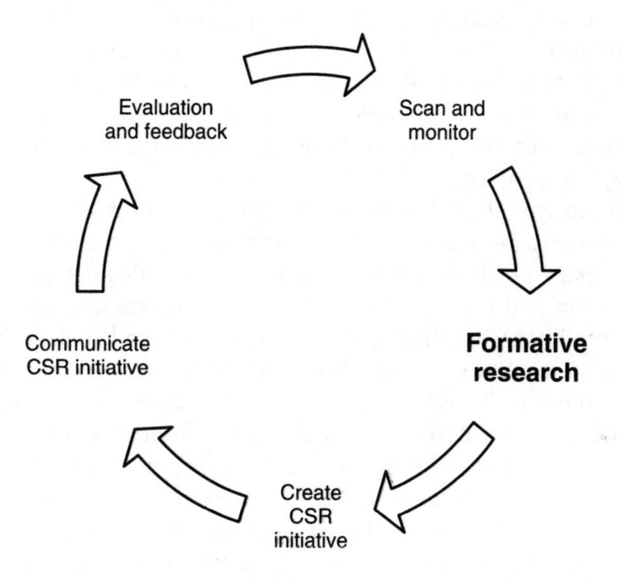

Scanning and monitoring and formative research share an emphasis on narrowing the CSR concerns for a corporation. Scanning and monitoring provide a surface analysis of preliminary CSR concerns that could be translated into CSR initiatives and the stakeholders connected to those CSR

Managing Corporate Social Responsibility: A Communication Approach, First Edition.
W. Timothy Coombs, Sherry J. Holladay.

concerns. The end result is a working inventory of potential CSR concerns that alerts managers to the vast array of potential CSR actions they can pursue. The working list can be a daunting display of potential CSR concerns. By examining the potential CSR concerns in greater depth, formative research helps managers develop a tractable list of options to transform into their CSR initiatives. The working list of CSR concerns is refined to a shorter list of viable CSR concerns. The end result of formative research is an inventory of the CSR concerns the corporation plans to incorporate into its CSR initiatives.

Scanning and monitoring provide insight into CSR concerns that can be viewed as problems and/or opportunities. We suggest a CSR concern can be both because a problem for stakeholders can be an opportunity for the corporation – solving the problem can enhance the corporation's CSR reputation. Formative research examines the opportunity or problem in detail in order to provide the information necessary for selecting which CSR concerns to convert into CSR initiatives. No corporation has the time and resources to address all possible CSR concerns. Managers must make informed decisions, and formative research provides the requisite database for making these choices.

Information is collected about each CSR concern. As a starting point, each CSR concern is examined for its problem and opportunity potential. The *opportunity* portion examines the CSR concern's potential to benefit the corporation and society. The *problem* portion examines the CSR concern's potential negative effects on the corporation and society. Formative research seeks to clarify the situation with additional details and projections about the possible effects (positive and negative) created by the CSR concern and potential costs to both the corporation and society. A thorough list of relevant stakeholders is created. Managers work from the list to identify each group's stake in the CSR concern. A stakeholder map is created for each CSR concern. The stakeholder map should specify which stakeholders benefit from and which might be harmed by addressing the CSR concern. The maps can utilize visual or tabular formats. Figure 4.1 presents a stakeholder map visual, and Table 4.1 offers a sample stakeholder analysis based on a social concern. A wide variety of research methods can be used, including archival research, interviews, real-time media analysis, surveys, panels, and focus groups. The formative research should end in a decision as to whether or not to pursue action on the CSR concern.

Stakeholder engagement is ideal for formative research. Through communication (the application of various research strategies) with stakeholders, the corporation learns more about the stakeholders' CSR interests and views on the focal CSR concern under discussion. Stakeholder panels are one option, but a wider array of data can be collected from surveys of

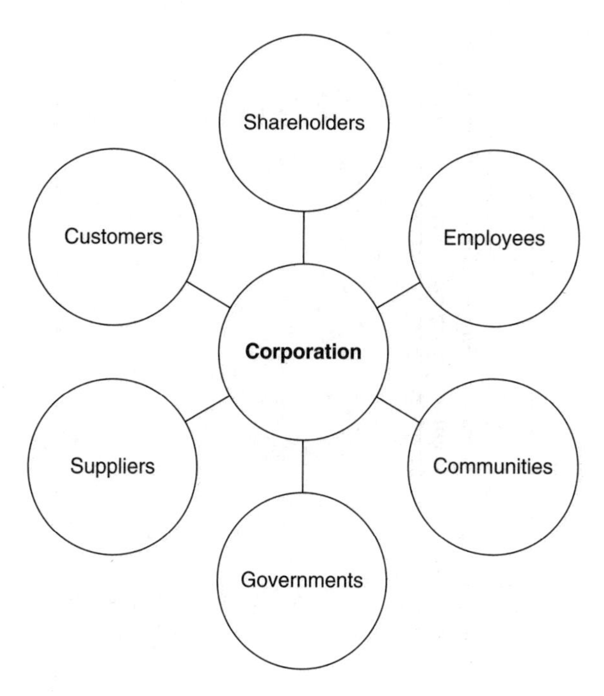

Figure 4.1 Sample stakeholder map

stakeholder and/or focus groups. For example, Heinz surveyed its stakeholders to determine which issues were most important for the corporation to address in its corporate social responsibility report. For social topics, stakeholders chose (1) health and nutrition and (2) malnutrition and poverty work. For sustainability topics, stakeholders wanted more information about goal progress and project case studies (Heinz, 2009). While not the only source of CSR information, talking to stakeholders provides the best insights into their CSR expectations and helps shape CSR practices. Communication with stakeholders also conveys genuine interest in their ideas. This two-way communication is mutually beneficial and influential. Understanding stakeholder CSR expectations is superior to guessing what the stakeholder CSR expectations are. An extended example of how stakeholder engagement benefits scanning, monitoring, and formative research is informative at this point.

Engagementdb is an effort by wetpaint and Altimeter to assess the level of corporate interactivity with stakeholders through social media. Engagementdb rates the top 100 global brands for their social media

Table 4.1 Sample stakeholder analysis

Stakeholder	*Issues*					
	Climate Change and Environment	*Customer Service*	*Health, Safety, and Security*	*Human Rights*	*Supply Chain Responsibility*	*Diversity and Inclusion*
Charities and NGOs	√	√	√	√	√	√
Consumer organizations	√	√	√			
Customers	√	√	√	√		√
Employees	√	√	√	√	√	√
Government and Parliament	√	√	√	√		√
Investors	√	√	√	√		
Communities	√	√	√			√
Regulators	√	√	√			
Suppliers	√		√	√	√	√
Trade unions			√	√		√

engagement. In 2009, Starbucks was the top brand. Their ranking system is based on the interactivity assessment of a corporation's use of the following social media: blogs, branded social network or community, content distribution sites, discussion forums, external social network presence (e.g., Facebook), Flickr or Photobucket, innovation hubs, wikis, ratings and reviews, Twitter, and YouTube. Part of the assessment includes whether or not executives are involved with the various social media.

Starbucks created the http://mystarbucksidea.force.com site where stakeholders submit, comment, and vote on ideas. Each department in Starbucks has a representative assigned as a liaison to the site. The liaison responds to ideas related to their area (Starbucks, 2010b). Box 4.1 contains examples of CSR ideas offered to Starbucks. As of the middle of 2010, there were about 6,000 social responsibility ideas posted to this site. Social media engagement relates directly to scanning and formative research. Social media interaction provides feedback on corporate behaviors and can identify new stakeholder concerns as they emerge. This is a form of scanning and monitoring. Starbucks can review the suggestions on MyStarbucksIdea for reactions to current practices and insights into stakeholder values. Such data are naturally occurring and offer insights into stakeholder attitudes and values. Interacting through social media is a viable way to solicit information about specific CSR concerns from select stakeholders (formative research). Stakeholders even could be asked their views on a specific CSR concern or queried about potential reactions to a hypothetical CSR initiative. Mystarbucksidea.force.com provides ideas for possible CSR initiatives, while people's votes reflect their views on the potential CSR initiatives. This type of interactive site is ideal for collecting information that can be used in the formative research process.

Researching Stakeholder Expectations for CSR

A key theme in this book is the role of stakeholder expectations in creating effective CSR initiatives. It follows that formative research must examine these expectations. Two different approaches for understanding stakeholder CSR expectations can be used in formative CSR research: expectations gaps and alignment. *Expectation gaps* represent a reactive strategy that is used when stakeholders confront corporations about being out of touch with CSR concerns. Managers can miss or overlook CSR concerns, and this can produce expectation gaps and stakeholder churn (conflict between the corporation and stakeholders). In contrast, *alignment* is more proactive. Management tries to anticipate future CSR concerns. By acting on the future CSR concerns, the corporation avoids an expectation gap. While it

Box 4.1 MyStarbucksIdea CSR suggestions

Place recycle bins in every Starbucks

Posted on 3/9/2010 8:05 PM by **merrymorse**
I have been in one Starbucks that has their own recycle bin. How about all the others? People throw away cardboard cups, plastic straws, cardboard cup holders, and papers from straws. These are all recyclable.

I read on one of the posts that your plastic cups are NOT recyclable. If that is true, I can't believe you call yourselves socially responsible. Go to Whole Foods and see what they do to recycle–EVERYTHING in their newer stores is recycled and reused. Starbucks should be at least on a par with Whole Foods.

http://mystarbucksidea.force.com/ideaview?id=
08750000000GoCnAAK (accessed December 15, 2010)

reusable cup sleeves

Posted on 7/31/2010 5:09 AM by **holen1** *Catlettsburg, KY Venti soy chai latte, sugarfree vanilla, no water, double protein,stirred well, EXTRA hot*
I believe that all the throw away cup sleeves are very wasteful. My idea is to make reusable sleeves for sale at the register just as the cups are for sale. I have purchased many cups but would love to see reuasble sleeves with designs like those on cups. People would buy these!!

http://mystarbucksidea.force.com/ideaview?id=
08750000000Gyw7AAC (accessed December 15, 2010)

Locally sourced (organic) baked goods

Posted on 3/19/2008 12:24 PM by **cpresso**
Offer locally sourced (organic or not) high quality baked goods similar to some of the baked goods Whole Foods offers, instead of the nationally consistent scones, cookies, pastries, cakes, and breads offered now. This sacrifices some of the national consistency now in place (though there is some variance already) but brings better quality, better tasting food to Starbucks, supports the local community, and elevates Starbucks above other coffee outlets (national outlets now also serving coffee) by cranking up the quality level and local

community/local business tie ins. As a result, Starbucks will feel more like a local coffee store again rather than some big national chain.

http://mystarbucksidea.force.com/ideaview?id=087500000004D3TAAU (accessed December 15, 2010)

Sources: Starbucks (2010a) and Li (2008).

is better to be proactive than reactive, a CSR manager must be familiar with both approaches.

The Expectation Gap Approach

Stakeholder churn is rooted in a disconnection between what stakeholders want and what corporations provide – there is a failure of the corporation to meet stakeholder expectations. Sethi (1979) referred to this disconnect as a legitimacy gap. We prefer the more direct label of *expectation gap* to avoid the debate over what constitutes legitimacy. CSR is premised on corporations addressing social concerns or issues.

Expectation gaps develop when stakeholders perceive that a corporation has failed to meet their expectations. Corporate responses to expectation gaps are reactive. A corporation is forced into changing its behavior by redressing the CSR concern. As noted earlier, forced CSR change results in little benefit to the corporation but does remove the damage associated with stakeholder churn. Stakeholders benefit from the change, but the problem persists during the time it takes to convince the corporation to address the CSR concern. Scanning and monitoring research works to locate expectation gaps. Once an expectation gap is identified, formative research is used to explore the depth and breadth of the problem. Through formative research, the company develops a more complex appreciation of the nature of the gap. Questions to ask include the following: What did the corporation do – or fail to do – that created the expectation gap? Which stakeholders are most concerned with this expectation gap? What are the extent and severity of the gap? Might stakeholders mobilize against the corporation?

There are two types of expectation gaps: (1) perception gaps and (2) reality gaps (Coombs & Holladay, 2010). *Perception gaps* occur when corporate policies and behaviors actually *do* meet stakeholder expectations but stakeholders fail to recognize the match. At first blush, this may seem puzzling. But consider this fact. Globally, research shows a lack of stakeholder knowledge about corporate CSR activities. Even when stakeholders claim their CSR concerns shape their decision making, their knowledge of actual CSR practices often is limited (Dawkins, 2004; Pomering & Dolnicar, 2008). This CSR ignorance provides the foundation for a perception gap for CSR. Proper CSR communication, discussed in chapter 6, is one way to resolve the perception gap.

Reality gaps occur when corporate policies and behaviors are out of step with stakeholder expectations. The corporation fails to meet expectations. Corporations must find some way to address the reality gap, or stakeholder churn could ensue. In formative research, the reality gap is the most important type of expectation.

IKEA, a Swedish company, is an extremely popular global brand. The IKEA website provides an extensive discussion of child labor. The CSR concern is explained, and IKEA's work in the area is described in detail. For instance, IKEA has "The IKEA Way of Preventing Child Labour." Here is the summary statement by IKEA:

> IKEA has a special code of conduct called The IKEA Way on Preventing Child Labour, which is part of The IKEA Way on Purchasing Home Furnishing Products. Monitoring of compliance with The IKEA Way on Preventing Child Labour is done by IKEA trading service offices and with unannounced visits by KPMG to suppliers and sub-contractors in South Asia. (IKEA, 2010b)

A more detailed presentation of IKEA's code is presented in Box 4.2.

IKEA has a 10-year partnership with UNICEF to address global concerns for children that include child labor. Here is how UNICEF describes IKEA:

> But what makes IKEA Social Initiative a true partner, is the company's deep commitment to social responsibility and their direct engagement with issues affecting children. They have truly joined with UNICEF to tackle issues like child labor at their root causes. (UNICEF, n.d.)

IKEA's commitment to child labor as a CSR concern was born through the pain of a reality expectation gap. From 1994 to 1997, three separate documentaries linking IKEA to child labor were aired on German and Swedish television. The abuses focused on facilities in Pakistan, Vietnam, the Philippines, and India. One way for suppliers to hold down costs is to exploit child labor (Bailly, Caudron, & Lambert, 2006). The media attention resulted in stakeholder churn. Stakeholders expected IKEA not to use child labor and reacted negatively to the revelation that IKEA suppliers

Box 4.2 IKEA Child Labour Code of Conduct

1. General Principles

IKEA does not accept Child Labour.

IKEA supports the United Nations (UN) Convention on the Rights of the Child (1989). The IKEA Child Labour Code of Conduct is based on this Convention, stipulated in:

> Article 3; 'All actions concerning the Child shall take full account of his or her best interests.'
>
> Article 32.1 'the right of the child to be protected from economic exploitation and from performing any work that is likely to be hazardous or to interfere with the child's education, or to be harmful to the child's health or physical, mental, spiritual, moral or social development.'

In addition, this Code of Conduct is based on the International Labour Organisation (ILO) Minimum Age Convention no. 138 (1978).

According to this convention, the word "Child" is defined as any person below fifteen (15) years of age, unless local minimum age law stipulates a higher age for work or mandatory schooling, in which case the higher age would apply. If, however, the local minimum working age is set at fourteen (14) years of age in accordance with exceptions for developing countries, the lower age will apply.

This Code of Conduct also incorporates the ILO Convention on the Worst Forms of Child Labour no. 182 (1999).

2. Implementation

All actions to avoid Child Labour shall be implemented taking the Child's best interests into account.

IKEA requires that all suppliers shall recognize the U.N. Convention on the Rights of the Child, and that the suppliers comply with all relevant national and international laws, regulations and provisions applicable in the country of production.

Suppliers are obligated to take the appropriate measures to ensure that no Child Labour occurs at suppliers' and their sub-contractors' places of production.

If Child Labour is found in any place of production, IKEA will require the suppler to implement a corrective action plan. If corrective

(*Continued*)

action is not implemented within the agreed time-frame, or if repeated violations occur, IKEA will terminate all business with the supplier concerned.

A corrective action plan shall take the Child's best interests into consideration, i.e., family and social situation and level of education. Care shall be taken not merely to move Child Labour from one supplier's workplace to another, but to enable more viable and sustainable alternatives for the children.

The supplier shall effectively communicate to all its sub-contractors, as well as to its own co-workers, the content of the IKEA Way of Preventing Child Labour, and ensure that all measures required are implemented accordingly.

3. Young workers

Young workers of legal working age have, until the age of 18, the right to be protected from any type of employment or work which, by its nature or the circumstances in which it is carried out, is likely to jeopardise their health, safety or morals.

IKEA therefore requires all its suppliers to ensure that young workers are treated accordingly, this includes measures to avoid employment during school hours. Limits for working hours and overtime should be set with special consideration to the workers' low age.

4. Labour force register

The supplier shall maintain documentation for every worker verifying the worker's data of birth. In countries where such official documents are not available, the supplier must use appropriate assessment methods as per local practice and law.

5. Monitoring

All suppliers are obliged to keep IKEA informed at all times about all places of production (including their sub-contractors). Through the General Purchasing Conditions for the supply of products to the IKEA Group of Companies, IKEA has reserved the rights to make unannounced visits at any time to all places of production (including their cub-contractors) for goods intended for supply to IKEA. The IKEA Group furthermore reserves the right to, at its sole discretion, assign an independent third party to conduct unannounced inspections in order to ensure compliance with the IKEA Way of Preventing Child Labour."

Source: IKEA (2010b).

were using child labor. IKEA responded positively to the stakeholder churn by seeking to eradicate child labor from its supply chain and working with groups such as UNICEF to improve the life of children around the world. IKEA admitted its mistakes and continues to take steps to address the CSR concern. Child labor is a CSR concern that demands continued attention as IKEA must monitor suppliers for compliance with their codes, including assessing the validity of birth certificates. IKEA's handling of the child labor issue is not perfect, but it has committed serious resources to preventing its appearance in the IKEA supply chain.

Origins of Expectation Gaps

The expectation gaps between how corporations behave and how stakeholders want them to behave can develop for different reasons. Understanding the origins of expectation gaps provides insights into how best to manage the gaps. Expectations require strategic action because stakeholders can contest a corporation's CSR efforts and commitment when its behavior and policies fail to meet their expectations. CSR is contested when stakeholders challenge the corporation's current behaviors and/or policies. The effects of the contests are in part dependent on the nature of the challenges. CSR challenges can be (1) organic, (2) exposé, and (3) villain.

Organic CSR challenges arise from changes in stakeholders' CSR expectations coupled with the corporation's failure to recognize those expectation shifts. Consider how quickly climate change and sustainability became central to CSR discussions. Corporations may simply fail to keep pace with societal shifts, and the organic challenge provides a chance to regain alignment with stakeholder expectations. The organic challenge brings the gap to the attention of management, thereby offering management a chance to learn and to correct their CSR activities. This would be an illustration of what we term *instructive churn* – management has an opportunity to learn from the conflict (Coombs & Holladay, 2010). There is a slight disruption in the corporation-stakeholder relationship, but it can be "fixed" by altering the CSR efforts to align with the current stakeholder expectations.

In *exposé* CSR challenges, stakeholders reveal how a company's CSR claims are exaggerations or outright lies. Exposés are the most damaging challenges because they erode trust by raising doubt about a corporation's honesty. Moreover, exposé challenges directly threaten reputations. As noted in chapter 2, CSR can be used to build corporate reputations. If a foundational element of a reputation is shown to be false, the company's reputation is severely damaged. Trust is one of the pillars in most conceptualizations of organizational reputation (Berens & van Riel, 2004). Exposé challenges reveal how companies use false or deceptive claims about their CSR activities to promote a favorable reputation. The false use of CSR for reputational gain is referred to as various types of *washing*, including greenwashing, pinkwashing, and bluewashing.

Greenwashing is probably the best-known form of washing. Corporations claim to be environmentally friendly through practices and products when they really are not. Or an organization has a public "green" front while it continues to harm the environment with its other actions and products. Essentially corporations attempt to create the impression that they care about the environment without demonstrating the underlying commitment to the environment. Greenpeace maintains a website dedicated to exposing greenwashing and educating people about its practices (http://www.stopgreenwash.org). Greenpeace offers four criteria for identifying greenwashing: (1) dirty business, (2) ad bluster, (3) political spin, and (4) "it's the law stupid." *Dirty business* promotes green actions while ignoring the fact that core business practices are polluting and unsustainable. *Ad bluster* uses advertising and public relations messages to exaggerate environmental claims and distract people away from environmental problems. *Political spin* occurs when corporations claim to be green while lobbying against environmental laws and regulations designed to protect the environment. *It's the law stupid* occurs when a company praises its environmental actions when it is simply complying with existing laws and regulations (Greenpeace, n.d.). It is not doing anything more than the minimum it is supposed to be doing to meet legal requirements.

Consider the case of Sephora and their "Naturally Gorgeous" claims. Sephora is a major cosmetic retailer. To be part of the green movement, the "Naturally Sephora" seal was created. Green, Naturally Sephora seals appear on products that meet the company's internal standards. As the Sephora website states, "[W]e created an internal logo to help you spot the products carried at Sephora that have been formulated with and without certain ingredients" (Sephora, n.d.). However, not everyone agrees with how Sephora defines *natural*. The Environmental Working Group (EWG) maintains a cosmetic database that rates cosmetics in terms of hazards. A rating of 0 to 2 is a low hazard, 3 to 6 is a moderate hazard, and 7 to 10 is a high hazard (Reuben, 2009). This is part of the EWG's Campaign for Safe Cosmetics. A handful of the Naturally Sephora products are rated as high hazards according to the EWG criteria. This is not the most egregious example of greenwashing, but it does reveal the often subtle misrepresentation of green to build a reputation (Tennery, 2009). Corporations can claim to be green to build false reputations through misrepresentation and misdirection. In reality, the corporations are not significantly reducing their environmental impact.

Another type of "washing," *pinkwashing*, involves connecting the sale of products with support for breast cancer research while the corporation actually sells products that may contribute to breast cancer risks. Breast

Box 4.3 Pinkwashing Detection

Breast Cancer Action's Pinkwashing Questions

- How much money from my purchase will actually go to the cause?
- What is the maximum amount that will be donated?
- How much money was spent marketing the product I want to buy?
- What organization will get my donation, and what types of programs do they support?
- What is the product manufacturer doing to assure that its products are not contributing to causing breast cancer?

Source: Think before You Pink (n.d.).

cancer is a highly emotional and visible disease globally. Companies try to build positive reputations by associating their products with helping those with breast cancer. Products have included soup, cosmetics, automobiles, tools, kitchen utensils, yogurt, soft drinks, and fast food. However, automobile exhaust, chemicals in some cosmetics, and bovine growth hormones in yogurt have all been linked to breast cancer. Consumers like the idea of "buying pink" because they can be socially conscious simply by shopping (Landman, 2008). Box 4.3 provides guides to pinkwashing detection by explaining how to separate legitimate ways to support breast cancer research and treatment from the hype of pinkwashing.

Bluewashing refers to a corporation's attempts to build visible ties to the United Nations (UN) in order to create a positive reputation based on humanitarianism with little commitment to the effort. Bluewashing occurs because the partnerships with the UN often provide no mechanism for monitoring behavior. For example, a corporation can sign an agreement to support the UN Global Compact but never take any action to support the agreement. The agreement is public, but the corporation's actions remain shrouded in mystery. Bruno and Karliner (2000) talk about companies wrapping themselves in the UN flag without taking any substantive humanitarian actions. Corporations that sign the UN Global Compact often are accused of bluewashing. The UN Global Compact proposes 10 guiding principles but provides no screening or enforcement mechanisms to guarantee that corporations follow the principles. It is considered bluewashing when the signing of the UN Global Compact is the only real action taken in an effort intended to improve a corporation's reputation.

Companies that claim to help the environment, support breast cancer, or follow the UN Global Compact open themselves to exposé challenges if they fail to honor their commitments to these social concerns. Exposés that prove a corporation's deceptive practices can have a devastating effect on the reputation the corporation is trying to craft around these social concerns. An exposé can call all other CSR claims into question and a corporation's reputation into disrepute.

Villain CSR challenges occur when activist stakeholders, typically a non-governmental organization (NGO), have targeted a corporation for a series of attacks. There is an ongoing cycle of conflict between the corporation and the activist stakeholders, with the CSR challenge being one act in a larger play. Consider how the People for the Ethical Treatment of Animals (PETA) regularly challenges KFC on a variety of issues, including the humane treatment and slaughter of chickens. The two sides regularly exchange negative messages. For instance, KFC wanted to pay for repairs to potholes in Warren, Ohio. All they asked in return was for "refreshed by KFC" to be sprayed on the filled-in potholes. PETA offered twice as much money for the repairs – provided signs would be placed near each filled pothole that depicted an evil Colonel Sanders (WKBN.com, 2009). It is easy for other stakeholders to ignore villain CSR challenges because they just become background noise in continuing feuds (Coombs, 2010).

CSR exposé challenges are increasing in their importance as ways to contest CSR. Two factors account for this growth. First, the value of CSR for reputation development continues to increase. CSR claims can become a point of vulnerability. If the CSR claims can be discredited, the corporation's valuable reputational assets will diminish. Second, the Internet makes it easier to engage in CSR exposé challenges. The Internet can be an information source about corporations that engage in "washing" by failing to honor their social commitments. In addition, the Internet has the potential to quickly spread the information about "washing" to a wider range and number of stakeholders. As with CSR, if stakeholders do not know about an exposé, it has no effect on the company. Through websites, blogs, tweets, discussion boards, and email, the Internet provides the potential to reach other stakeholders with the exposé (Coombs & Holladay, 2007a).

The organic and exposé CSR challenges can be treated as challenge crises. In a *challenge crisis*, someone or some group contests the appropriateness or morality of a corporation's behaviors and/or policies (Coombs, 2007; Lerbinger, 1997). Managers need to evaluate the likelihood and impact of the challenge when determining a course of action. Recall that we discussed likelihood and impact as two important evaluation tools in chapter 3's coverage of the scanning and monitoring stage. In the context of a challenge crisis, *likelihood* is the possibility that the CSR challenge will reach other stakeholders and that they will agree with that challenge. *Impact* is the effect that the CSR challenge can have on the corporation. Although the primary effect is on the corporation's reputation, the crisis can create a cascading effect onto financial assets.

Not all stakeholder expectation gaps are the same. One key difference is in how the stakeholder churn to the corporation's CSR actions or inaction developed. The nature of the CSR challenge affects how managers must address the expectation gap. Organic CSR challenges are easier to address and more likely to promote instructive churn where the company can learn from the conflict between stakeholder expectations and organizational actions. Exposé CSR challenges are more damaging to reputations and more difficult to address because trust in the corporation is eroded. Villain CSR challenges are simply one battle in an ongoing war and are unlikely to create additional problems for a corporation. The lesson is that managers must consider the nature of the CSR challenge when contending with expectation gaps. Part of formative research must include exploring the nature of any expectation gaps.

Relevance of Operant Conditioning Theory to Stakeholder Challenges

One critique of stakeholder churn and CSR is the focus on punishment. Often stakeholders seek to punish the organization through reputational damage, boycotts, and negative word of mouth. It has been suggested that stakeholders should rely more on rewards and less on punishment to shape corporate CSR. To fully appreciate that point, we need to explore the roots of this discussion, operant conditioning. *Operant conditioning* is a motivation theory that explains that behavior is a function of its consequences. Behavior modification can occur through the application of contingent consequences. Consequences can be used to either increase a desirable behavior or decrease an undesirable behavior. To be effective, the consequences must be consistent and contingent upon the behavior rather than random responses to behavior. The subject we hope to motivate (the corporation) must associate the consequence with the behavior. In addition, operant conditioning is more than just rewarding desirable behaviors and punishing undesirable behaviors.

To increase the likelihood of a behavior, reinforcers are utilized. Reinforcers can be positive or negative and are administered after the desired behavior. *Positive reinforcers* (reinforcement) are stimuli or outcomes that the subject views as favorable. For example, a dog may be given a treat for sitting properly. *Negative reinforcers* (escape) are adverse stimuli or outcomes that the subject views as unfavorable. A rat performs the desired behavior, and a loud noise is removed from its cage. To decrease the likelihood of a behavior, punishments are used. Punishments can be positive or negative. A *positive punishment* (punishment) is when an adverse stimuli or outcome is introduced after an undesired behavior. A cat is sprayed with water for climbing on the kitchen counter. *Negative punishment* (penalty) is when a desired stimuli or outcome is removed when an undesirable event occurs. A child cannot use the computer after he or she has done something wrong. It can be difficult to distinguish between negative reinforcers and positive punishment. A negative stimulus must be present (positive punishment) before it can be removed (negative reinforcer).

Reinforcers must be considered desirable by the subject. If the subject does not really care about a reinforcer, its introduction or removal will have no effect on the subject's behavior. Similarly, subjects must view an adverse stimuli or outcome as unfavorable. If subjects do not consider the stimuli or outcome to be negative, its introduction or removal will have no effect on the subject's behavior (Huitt & Hummel, 1997; Learning Technology Center, n.d.). Corporations are not animals – so how does operant conditioning relate to stakeholder challenges to a corporation's CSR?

Corporations are stakeseekers; they desire the stake held by various people populating their environment (Heath & Coombs, 2006). For instance, companies want customers to buy a service and investors to purchase stock. Money is the stake and takes the form of the purchase of either a service or stock. Corporations as stakeseekers want some type of support (a stake granted) from stakeholders. The stake is the source of the stakeholder's power in the organization-stakeholder relationship. Power can be defined as the ability to influence the behavior of others. A has power over B if A can cause B to do something B would not otherwise do (Coombs & Holladay, 2007b; Motion & Leitch, 2009). Stakes and reputation provide the foundation for connecting operant conditioning with CSR. Having the stake and maintaining a favorable reputation are desirable for a corporation. Losing the stake and damaging a reputation are undesirable for a corporation. Stakeholders draw upon this knowledge when seeking to alter corporate behaviors and policies.

Stakeholders favor using punishment to change CSR-related behaviors. The approach is logical when stakeholders want to change what they view as negative behaviors (lack of social responsibility) enacted by a corporation. To promote change, stakeholders can (1) generate negative publicity to damage a corporation's reputation (positive punishment), (2) withhold

Table 4.2 Translating operant conditioning in contesting CSR

Operant Terms	*Application to Stakeholder Churn*
Reinforcement (positive reinforcers)	• Praise a corporation for their CSR efforts. • Buy-cott.
Escape (negative reinforcers)	• Remove boycott or protest when new CSR behaviors are enacted.
Penalty (negative punishment)	• Boycott when corporation is irresponsible.
Punishment (positive punishment)	• Protests and other pressure applied when an corporation is irresponsible.

their stakes (negative punishment), and (3) utilize a combination of the two. Let's use a boycott as an example. Boycotts withhold a stake, typically the purchase of a product. However, it is rare for a boycott to have a serious financial effect on a corporation. In other words, the negative punishment does not really harm the corporation. Most boycotts succeed because they threaten the corporation's reputation. Boycotts generate negative publicity (stakeholder churn). By highlighting negative aspects of a corporation, a boycott damages its reputation.

We can use the boycott example to illustrate reinforcers used to promote positive behaviors. When a corporation engages in the desired CSR behaviors, a boycott ends and restores the stake (negative reinforcer). Or stakeholders may say they will start buying from a corporation (called *buy-cotts*) if the desired CSR behaviors are adopted. This provides new customers, so the change is a positive reinforcer because the corporation gains new stakes. However, given that boycotts rarely are a punishment, it is unlikely that a buy-cott will be enough of a reward. Positive reinforcers can be verbal. Stakeholders can pledge to publicly praise a corporation if it adopts the desired CSR behaviors. But just how rewarding would such praise be to a corporation? It would be wrong to discount positive reinforcers completely. Inherent in the business argument for CSR is that responsible businesses are rewarded with supportive behavior from stakeholders, including purchasing, investing, and favorable reputations. Refer to Table 4.2 for a summary of the relationship between operant conditioning principles and stakeholder churn generated by CSR.

If stakeholders are seeking to end an undesirable behavior, punishment is the logical choice. Punishment is the way to remove a behavior. If a corporation is harming indigenous people, stakeholder churn can create the pressure to end the behavior. Punishment does work in tandem with positive reinforcers in many efforts to shape CSR. When the desired behavior is enacted, a punishment is removed, the critics can then praise the corporation, and the socially responsible behavior should attract other stakeholders to the organization. It is unrealistic for managers to expect stakeholders to switch to positive reinforcers and to abandon punishment. Managers must anticipate that stakeholders will contest CSR (enact churn) by applying punishment and penalty coupled with a small dose of reinforcement. Managers should plan to maximize the value of any praise (positive reinforcement) in their CSR communication. Operant conditioning helps to shed light on the dynamics of stakeholder churn. In turn, these insights can help managers better prepare for the stakeholder churn emerging from CSR concerns.

The Alignment Approach

Being more proactive with shifting stakeholder CSR concerns can provide greater benefits to the corporation and society. The corporation becomes a leader in the CSR concern, and society is improved by the actions taken on the CSR concern. The alignment approach is proactive because it treats CSR as issues management. Issues management places a priority on environmental scanning for the early detection of threats (issues). Early detection leads to early intervention, thereby increasing the likelihood of success in managing the issue (Jones & Chase, 1979). The CSR Process Model we propose in this book is grounded in the issues management approach. The corporation selects the most promising of the emerging CSR concerns. The selected CSR concerns are embodied in the company's values, policies, and actions. To prevent a perception gap, the company must effectively communicate its CSR to stakeholders. The stakeholders must perceive the shared social concern with the company. Stakeholders accept the evidence that the company embodies the shared social concern. In short, the social concerns and values align between stakeholders and the corporation.

This CSR alignment approach is based on alignment principles derived from reputation management as well as issues management. Reputation management involves, in part, selecting a corporate identity that will resonate with stakeholders. Corporate identity and corporation reputation align when stakeholders perceive a similarity between their values and the values espoused in the corporate identity (Hatch & Schultz, 2000). In this way, CSR alignment is the opposite of an expectation gap. By anticipating where a CSR expectation gap may develop, a corporation can proactively change behaviors and policies to prevent an expectation gap. By the time the social concern becomes salient to stakeholders, the corporation is already reflecting the social concern. This is similar to anticipating consumer taste shifts in products such as music or automobiles.

Stakeholders are a logical starting point for identifying their own future social concerns. NGOs, as professional activists, are eager to share their views on social concerns. The NGOs are often a bellwether for social concerns that may spread to other stakeholders. Engaging NGOs and other activists helps organizations identify a developing social concern and prevent an expectation gap. A case study will help to illustrate the value of engagement and expectation gap prevention posited by the alignment approach.

As a global brand, Coca-Cola faces many social concerns, including water use and marketing to children in schools. As a large corporation, Coca-Cola must contend with its contribution to global warming and climate change. Part of Coca-Cola's operation is the use of vending machines around the world for the storage and sales of its products. Vending machines keep the Coca-Cola products cold. The vending machines rely on hydrofluorocarbons (HFCs) for their cooling systems. HFCs are over 11,000 times more harmful than carbon dioxide (Pasternack, 2008). Although most stakeholders are currently unaware of the problems of vending machines and climate change, this issue has the potential to develop into a larger social concern. Greenpeace is one of the NGOs interested in vending machines and their greenhouse gas emissions. Their effort to promote the social concern is known as Greenfreeze. With Greenpeace's promotion, the social concern has the potential to grow and attract the attention of additional stakeholders.

Coca-Cola had been experimenting with vending machines cooled by carbon dioxide (CO_2) at the Athens Olympics in 2004 and on a larger scale at the Beijing Olympics in 2008. In Beijing, all of Coca-Cola's 5,600 vending machines were CO_2 cooled. Coca-Cola was the soft drink sponsor of the Olympics, and the Olympics have added a green mission. The end result was Coca-Cola using their sponsorship of the games to test the new technologies (Pasternack, 2008).

In December 2009, just before the Copenhagen climate summit, Coca-Cola announced that by 2015, all of its vending machines would be HFC free. The declaration was made jointly with Greenpeace. The announcement noted that Coca-Cola had been working with Greenpeace since 2000 on developing a viable solution for the HFC in vending machines. The announcement from Coca-Cola included this statement from Amy Larkin, director of Greenpeace Solutions: "Greenpeace increasingly works with businesses to make fundamental manufacturing and sourcing changes by connecting regulation, economies of scale and supply chain security. Coca-Cola's commitment today runs ahead of regulation and takes some fear out of rapid change" (2Sustain, 2009). Various social media messages related to sustainability, such as the blog 2Sustain, and online news concerned about the environment, such as http://www.greenbiz.com, reported favorably on Coca-Cola's HFC-free vending machine strategy (GreenBiz.com, 2009; 2Sustain, 2009). Coca-Cola successfully leveraged the reach and utility of online media for its CSR promotional communication. Third parties like Greenpeace and stakeholders concerned with the social issue can create awareness of the CSR initiative and help Coca-Cola avoid the stigma of appearing overly interested in self-promotion. Because Coca-Cola is ahead of the HFC vending machine social issue, it has prevented a potential expectation gap and may be viewed as an industry leader for this CSR initiative. As we discussed, "being there first" to address a social concern in an industry provides greater reputational benefits than being forced to comply with new regulations.

Vodafone's website clearly demonstrates an alignment approach in that it provides numerous opportunities for the corporation to solicit information and ideas from stakeholders as well as share information with stakeholders. This innovative website is designed to stimulate discussion and debate about issues related to both the corporate and stakeholder interests. Within the "Corporate Responsibility" section of its website, Vodafone provides a "CR Dialogues" option (http://www.vodafone.com/start/responsibility/cr_dialogues.html; Vodafone, n.d.-f). The general purpose of its CR Dialogues is described as follows:

> The Vodafone CR Dialogues explore key issues we face in our relationship with society. They cover topics that are specific to the telecommunications industry (such as privacy and accessibility) and also those that reflect approaches to corporate responsibility (such as stakeholder engagement and assurance).
>
> **Learning from many experiences**
>
> There is more than one point of view to any issue and sometimes achieving consensus can be difficult. We want to explore these issues fully and the opinions of others are therefore of great value. Our aim is to consider new ideas and stimulate debate. Through Dialogue we hope to make our CR investment more effective and to help other organisations do the same by bringing together a wide range of informed views and experiences.
>
> **Convergence of CR Reporting and Stakeholder Engagement**
>
> The Vodafone CR Dialogues are at the interface of our reporting and engagement programmes. Our CR report identifies our most material issues and our engagement probes the views of experts and other stakeholders. Through the Dialogues we have an opportunity to explore subjects in depth from different perspectives.
>
> We will only succeed if we stimulate responses. We want to debate what works and what doesn't and to be prepared to challenge accepted wisdom.

> We plan to test new proposals through Vodafone's own CR programme. (Vodafone, n.d.-f)

This Vodafone site then provides clickable links to CR dialogue topics that include e-waste, privacy and mobile, stakeholder engagement, assurance of reporting, and economic empowerment.

When readers click for "more information" at the stakeholder engagement listing, they are taken to a lengthier presentation of the topic of stakeholder engagement. The "Dialogue: Stakeholder Engagement" information (Vodafone, n.d.-c) includes the following:

> Engagement is extremely valuable for Vodafone and we think that it is also valuable to our stakeholders. We have learned a lot from our engagement experience globally and we think that sharing this knowledge could be useful for other companies and stakeholders.
>
> We have also found challenges and opportunities for improvement that we would like to discuss. This is the first of the Vodafone CR Dialogues and we want to stimulate debate to take stakeholder engagement a step forward. Please send us your comments, opinions or ideas.
>
> Initially we would like to propose five discussion themes:
>
> - Should multinationals engage locally or globally?
> - Is it legitimate to engage with 'opinion formers' such as pressure groups who claim to represent views of a wider public?
> - Or is it important to engage a mass stakeholder group through large surveys?
> - What is the company's side of the engagement bargain? Must there be a promise to take the messages to senior executives?
> - Does too much engagement create "Stakeholder fatigue"? (Vodafone, n.d.-c)

The site also provides a clickable link to a downloadable PDF on stakeholder engagement. It explains, "This pdf summarises what Vodafone has learned from experience about Stakeholder Engagement" (Vodafone, n.d.-c).

The "Please send us your comments, opinions or ideas" link takes readers to an email form where they can record their comments with the promise that comments will be sent to the Corporate Responsibility team.

Another topic listed at the "CR Dialogues" site is "Privacy and mobiles" (Vodafone, n.d.-b). When readers click on "for more information," they are taken to a site that reads,

> Welcome to this Dialogue on privacy.
>
> About the subject issue: Privacy and mobiles
>
> Technology is transforming the nature of communications and the way we communicate. This can be both liberating and exciting – no longer are we tethered to the desk phone or desktop; information can be created and shared

instantly anywhere and anytime. At the same time, the greater political focus on tackling terrorism and other serious crime has led to greater efforts at harnessing technology for surveillance purposes, including communications technology. These twin trends throw up a range of inter-related complexities around privacy which this Dialogue seeks to explore.

Four different perspectives on the subject to stimulate discussion –We have collected four expert views on Privacy and Mobiles to inform and stimulate discussion. Click below to access each essay and then join the Dialogue by adding your comments. (Vodafone, n.d.-b)

This section is followed by four essays written by four individuals with different affiliations and perspectives, not just those of Vodafone. Following the essays is an invitation to participate in the debate:

Stimulating the debate

We want to know how you think companies, governments and others should be responding. Here are some specific questions we would like your views on:

- How far should companies be able to go to use information about you for commercial purposes such as targeting advertising?
- Some commentators take the view that users do not really care about their privacy – look at how many people are prepared to publish intimate personal details on their Facebook page. Do you care if companies allow your personal information to be used to target advertising to your personal tastes and interests? How much control would you want to exercise, e.g. to consent, to opt out, to limit the types and amount of data, etc?
- Should we co-operate with government authorities which make urgent requests for user data without proper procedures if the purpose is urgent enough, eg a terrorist threat? If so, what safeguards would you expect companies to adopt?
- Should we accede to information requests from private firms such as copyright holders without requiring a court order, if we believe the request is legitimate, for example because we believe a user is engaged in piracy?. Or should we go in the other direction and fight such court orders in the interests of our users' privacy?
- What do we need to do to educate customers about privacy risks? (Vodafone, n.d.-b)

As with the other "Dialogue" site, Vodafone provides a link where readers can submit their ideas.

Overall, the Vodafone website is innovative and informative, and it clearly communicates a desire to create a dialogue with stakeholders. Listening carefully to stakeholders is the foundation for an effective application of the alignment approach. Only by understanding and being responsive to stakeholders can a corporation anticipate imminent CSR concerns and position itself as the industry leader on those concerns.

The Counterbalance: Corporate Concerns

As noted in the discussion of CSR as strategic, CSR initiatives must reflect corporate needs, not just those of stakeholders. While we might feel that CSR should be executed to make the world a better place, a "business case" must be made for CSR initiatives. In simple terms, the CSR initiative must fit the corporation. *Fit* means a consistency with the corporation's strategic plan, the nature of the industry, and a favorable cost-benefit ratio from the corporation's perspective. CSR selection is a balancing act. The right CSR initiative effectively merges stakeholder and corporate interests. Managers, working with stakeholders, use the information collected during the first two phases to create a final list of potential CSR concerns.

Creating the list requires narrowing down the preliminary list created during scanning and monitoring. The additional information collected during formative research provides the basic materials for assembling the list. But information itself is raw and must be processed into usable knowledge. Managers must develop criteria for evaluating the potential CSR concerns. By consistently applying the criteria, the managers can systematically narrow the options to a viable final list. What are the perfect criteria? The answer is "It depends." Again, we return to the notion of balance. The criteria must find the proper balance between stakeholder and corporate interests. Unfortunately, that balance varies according to the social concern, the nature of the stakeholders, and the nature of the corporation. That means there is no magical set of criteria we can offer to managers. Instead, we provide the key questions that managers should be asking themselves when working to assemble a viable list of CSR concerns. We review the key questions associated with formative research in the next section.

Conclusion and Critical Questions

Scanning and monitoring identify the preliminary list of social and environmental concerns that could be translated into CSR initiatives. The purpose of formative research is to examine each of the potential concerns in detail to determine which CSR concerns will actually be addressed in CSR initiatives. Formative research helps to narrow the field of CSR concerns that will become part of CSR initiatives. The end result of formative research is a list and explanation of the CSR concerns the corporation could incorporate into its CSR initiatives.

Critical Questions for Formative Research	*Relevant Parties*	
	Corporation	*Stakeholders*
What sources of information should be utilized in the formative research?	X	X
Which stakeholders should be engaged in the formative research?	X	X
How will the engagement process for formative research be structured?	X	X
Do the stakeholders perceive the engagement process as just?	X	X
Which stakeholders could be positively affected by the CSR concern(s)?	X	X
Which stakeholders could be negatively affected by the CSR concern(s)?	X	X
How salient is the CSR concern to stakeholders?	X	X
Are there expectation gaps?	X	X
Are the expectation gaps perception or reality gaps?	X	
How should each gap be addressed?	X	X
Is there a possibility to use the alignment approach – is a social concern emerging?	X	X
Is there chance for the corporation to become an industry leader on an emerging CSR concern?	X	
How might the corporation utilize an alignment approach beyond being an industry leader?	X	X

Formative research relies on solid information sources to be effective. Managers need to know where to go to find the necessary information about the CSR concerns. Understanding how stakeholders view CSR concerns is critical. The expectation gap and alignment approaches provide guidance on how to uncover stakeholder CSR expectations. Managers must decide the best way to engage stakeholders to collect the information necessary to find expectation gaps or to determine alignment. Alignment may be more beneficial because it is proactive. However, corporations cannot afford to miss or ignore expectation gaps because that can evoke the wrath of stakeholders.

Realistically, not all stakeholders will benefit from any given CSR initiative. Identify which stakeholders are most likely to benefit from the CSR concern. Conversely, some stakeholders may find their concerns ignored or may suffer in some other way as a result of pursuing a particular CSR concern. For instance, switching to suppliers that respect Forest Stewardship Council (FSC) guidelines for timber harvesting can result in harming current suppliers that do not comply with the FSC guidelines. Seriously consider the varying effects of the CSR concern on the stakeholders.

In addition to considering stakeholder expectations, managers need to determine the fit of the CSR concern within their corporation. Fit includes assessing the CSR concern's consistency with the corporation's strategic plan, the nature of the industry, and the costs and benefits the CSR concern can accrue to the corporation. Managers must also consider which CSR concern allows the corporation to have the greatest positive impact on stakeholders and society. Finally, managers must produce final recommendations about what CSR concern or concerns a corporation will pursue through its CSR initiatives. That requires a clear set of evaluative criteria for selecting the final CSR concern(s). It is important to establish those criteria from the start, to share the criteria with the engaged stakeholders, or even to create the criteria through collaboration with the stakeholders.

Greenpeace's "No Fish Farms" campaign protests fish farms that produce sea lice that endanger wild salmon populations. © Greenpeace/Daniel Beltrá

5

Create the CSR Initiative

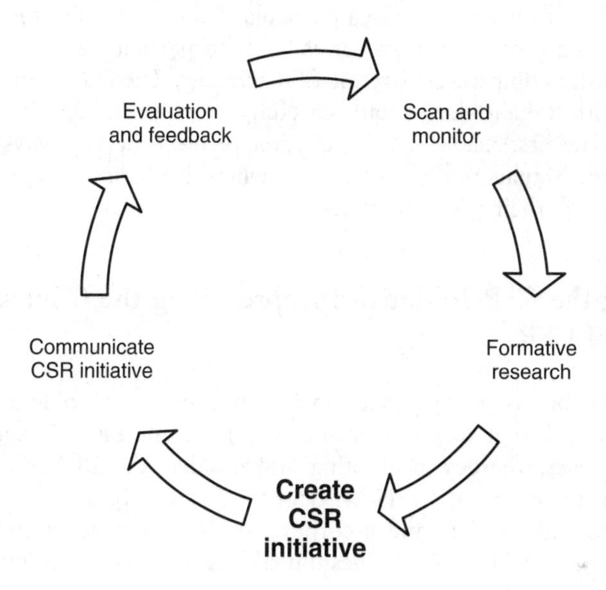

Formative research concludes with a short list of promising potential CSR concerns a corporation might translate into CSR initiatives. In the next stage, creating the CSR initiative, managers make the final decisions about which CSR concerns the corporation will pursue at this time and which it will not. Because all CSR concerns on the short list will have merit, the choice is not easy or purely objective. CSR concerns are likely to be contested by the various parties involved. Conflicting interests and perspectives

Managing Corporate Social Responsibility: A Communication Approach, First Edition.
W. Timothy Coombs, Sherry J. Holladay.

on CSR are a natural part of the final decision-making process. This means everyone will not be satisfied with the final decision about CSR initiatives. In spite of a shared interest in corporate social responsibility in general, all interested parties would rarely agree on the perfect CSR initiative. Corporations and stakeholders must work to produce a set of CSR initiatives that are acceptable for most parties. Choosing to focus on one CSR concern means ignoring another, and parties may disagree as to how to convert the CSR concern into a specific initiative. The implementation of the selected CSR strategy is likely to be challenged as well. We use the phrase *CSR initiative* to refer to a particular CSR effort. But it is important to keep in mind that a corporation is likely to participate in multiple CSR initiatives that comprise its overall CSR strategy. The corporation, in conjunction with stakeholders, should carefully consider and develop each CSR initiative. The first section of this chapter reviews the key ways that CSR is contested. Managers must anticipate where problems will arise as they seek to finalize their CSR initiatives.

Selecting the CSR Initiatives: Appreciating the Contestable Nature of CSR

Ideally, CSR builds stronger relationships between stakeholders and a corporation. Recall that stakeholder and corporate interests can align around CSR initiatives, thereby promoting stakeholder identification with and support for the corporation. However, CSR also can be a source of conflict that divides stakeholders and a corporation. Division occurs when stakeholders contest CSR – they question a corporation's CSR efforts. This chapter explores the key concerns associated with stakeholder challenges of CSR.

Stakeholders can challenge CSR initiatives for any number of reasons. Whatever the reason, contesting CSR affects a corporation's CSR efforts. This chapter examines key factors involved in stakeholder resistance to CSR: (1) differing stakeholder expectations, (2) disputes over what constitutes CSR, (3) determining the "right amount" of CSR, and (4) internal stakeholders (employees) contesting CSR. Taken together, these four factors help managers understand and anticipate the most common challenges they will confront when implementing CSR efforts.

Differing CSR Expectations among Stakeholders

Unfortunately, meeting stakeholder expectations for corporate behavior is not simple or straightforward. As previous chapters have noted, neither stakeholders nor their CSR expectations are monolithic. In light of potential dilemmas, how should a corporation proceed with the CSR process? We can begin with the premise that not all stakeholders carry equal weight in the decision-making process. More precisely, not all stakeholders are equally important to the corporation. Management has limited time and resources. For this reason, some stakeholders garner more attention than others, and some stakeholders can become marginalized.

Stakeholder Salience

Management prioritizes stakeholders based on salience, and these prioritizations also apply to CSR. Mitchell, Agle, and Wood (1997) conceptualized prioritization of *stakeholder salience* as "the degree to which managers give priority to competing stakeholder claims" (p. 854). Stakeholder salience is a composite of three factors: (1) stakeholder power (the ability to affect the organization) (2) legitimacy (the public acceptability of stakeholder demands), and (3) the urgency of the stakeholder claim (pressure to act). Managers assess stakeholders across these three factors. The more of these factors a stakeholder possesses, the more salient that stakeholder becomes. Salient stakeholders figure more prominently in decision making. Box 5.1, "Stakeholder Salience," summarizes the prioritization process based on Mitchell et al.'s (1997) work.

A complicating factor is that stakeholder salience is fluid, not static, because stakeholder salience can change over time. More importantly for our discussion, stakeholder salience depends on the issues being considered (e.g., Buysse & Verbeke, 2003). Stakeholder salience need not be the same for CSR issues as for competitiveness issues. Moreover, the same stakeholders may not be salient for the different CSR issues a corporation addresses. For instance, different stakeholders may be salient for human rights issues versus environmental issues. Greenpeace would be more salient for environmental issues but less relevant to human rights issues. Global Alliance would be salient to both issues. Our discussion of stakeholder salience informs the CSR challenge of identifying and managing differing expectations.

If all stakeholders valued the same social and environmental concerns, CSR would be much easier! The stakeholder engagement process would reveal the core issues of concern that could then be translated into CSR initiatives. But the reality is much more complex. A series of differing expectation problems confront CSR initiatives at this stage in the process and can be organized around the following questions:

1. Which CSR issues should be addressed, and how are these prioritized?

Box 5.1 Stakeholder Salience

Mitchell et al. (1997) use their three attributes of stakeholders to help managers understand the salience of stakeholders. Stakeholders that have only one attribute are considered latent stakeholders. *Latent stakeholders* are passive because they lack the attributes necessary to pressure a corporation. *Expectant stakeholders* possess two attributes and therefore have greater salience. Expectant stakeholders are more active because they are beginning to expect a response or reaction from the corporation. *Definitive stakeholders* have the greatest salience because they demonstrate all three attributes. Expectant stakeholders should be monitored carefully because they need to attain just one more attribute to become definitive. For instance, dependent stakeholders can join with a stakeholder who has power to become definitive. Stakeholder salience is a dynamic process as stakeholders can both attain and lose attributes over time (Mitchell et al., 1997).

Latent stakeholders have only one attribute.
Dormant: have power but lack legitimacy and urgency
Discretionary: have legitimacy but lack power and urgency
Demanding: have urgency but lack power and legitimacy
Expectant stakeholders have only two attributes.
Dominant: have power and legitimacy but lack urgency
Dangerous: have power and urgency but lack legitimacy
Dependent: have legitimacy and urgency but lack power
Definitive stakeholders have all three attributes.

2. How should the CSR issues be addressed? What should the CSR initiatives "look like"?
3. What is the "right amount" of CSR? How much can be done, and for whom? Should the CSR concern focus on the local community, region, country, or world?

What Constitutes CSR?

The greatest strength and weakness of CSR is that it can cover so many different issues and be enacted in so many different ways. CSR can cover concerns as diverse as child labor, HIV prevention and treatment, worker rights, environmental preservation, clean energy, water rights, disaster relief, and the treatment of indigenous people, to name but a few. How is management to select and prioritize CSR issues when stakeholders advocate for different issues? Given that CSR initiatives can take many forms, how should management select the form(s) of the initiatives? Previous chapters have described the myriad forms that CSR can take ranging from philanthropy to social marketing to ethical sourcing to sustainability. There are no easy answers to "what constitutes CSR," but a return to the strategic use of CSR is instructive at this point.

Through stakeholder engagement, managers learn what CSR issues are most important to their stakeholders. This information can be translated into a *stakeholder rating system* of CSR issues. We can create a table that lists the stakeholders, their salience to the corporation, and the relative importance of various CSR issues to those stakeholders. The table can be extended to include additional cells such as how the stakeholders think the organization could address the CSR issue or the extent to which stakeholders seem willing to be active partners in the CSR process. We could even develop a weighting method for the scores to reflect the salience of the stakeholders for CSR in general and for specific CSR concerns. One option for narrowing a list of CSR concerns is to identify what issue or set of issues appears most frequently among the stakeholders. If the corporation were to pursue CSR initiatives addressing the issues identified by these stakeholders, this would reflect a utilitarian approach. The organization would seek to address concerns representing the greatest number of stakeholders. However, there are limits to a utilitarianism approach to stakeholder engagement. For example, a salient stakeholder lobbying for a less popular issue or a worthy CSR issue can become marginalized. Additionally, the "top" issue or issues and how they should be addressed may not fit well with the corporation's strategic plans and operations.

Thus far, we have focused heavily on the importance of stakeholder concerns in driving the CSR process and decision making. But any prioritization and selection of CSR issues must necessarily consider the corporation as well. In fact, the corporation must be the starting point when considering CSR initiatives. What are the corporation's core values? What CSR issues have a natural fit with its capabilities and business functions? How can the CSR issues be integrated in its strategic plan? These issues were raised during our earlier discussion of how strategic corporate social responsibility must mesh with characteristics of the corporation. CSR issues should be consistent with a company's competencies (e.g., pharmaceutical companies are well suited for addressing health-related CSR issues, food production companies are positioned to use ethical sourcing for their ingredients, and manufacturing companies are in the position to modify their energy use) and other objective characteristics we discussed earlier such as size, location, and mission. CSR initiatives can drain resources, become a distraction, and be generally ineffective when they are inconsistent with competencies, characteristics, or strategic plans. A clear lack of synergy with a corporation's values, mission, and operations could invite criticism from industry experts and shareholders (Heath, 1994; Heath & Coombs, 2006; Kotler & Lee, 2005). Although stakeholder concerns are important to selecting CSR issues, the characteristics of the corporation must take precedence over stakeholder concerns.

There is no perfect system for selecting the CSR issues and determining how to address them. Using a systematic approach, such as the CSR Process Model we are advocating, increases the likelihood of an effective CSR effort. Scanning and monitoring followed by formative research help to identify and to rank CSR issues. Identifying what to address is a significant starting point. Management must examine the most promising issues and possible actions to determine which fits best with the corporation and its strategic plans. As noted earlier, stakeholder engagement should continue throughout the CSR process. Management needs to communicate with stakeholders about how decisions are being made and provide rationales for the final decisions on CSR issues. Managers will not satisfy all of the stakeholders all of the time, but they can supply a well-reasoned explanation of the decision.

Stakeholder Participation in Decision Making

Translating a CSR concern into a corporation's CSR initiative is dominated by three major factors: (1) strategic planning, (2) balancing costs, and (3) stakeholder concerns. Part of weighing these concerns is deciding what role stakeholders will play in the decision-making process as part of engagement. Creating the CSR initiative through engagement is perhaps the most challenging task in the CSR process. Engagement requires some amount of collaborative decision making to be effective. With collaborative decision making comes some degree of power sharing with stakeholders. Engaging stakeholders in the CSR decision requires allowing them some say over the nature and shape of the CSR initiative – a sharing of power. Serious engagement involves stakeholder participation in the CSR decision-making process. Of course, the role of the stakeholders in the decision-making process can vary, but it does involve the corporation relinquishing some power.

Stakeholder participation can range from involvement to collaboration to empowerment. *Involvement* occurs when the corporation seeks to understand the stakeholders' concerns and desires and to incorporate them into the decision-making process. Stakeholders do not have a direct voice in the decision, but their input shapes the options being considered for CSR initiatives, an extension of formative research. *Collaboration* requires giving the stakeholders a say in both the development of the CSR initiatives and the selection of the CSR initiatives. *Empowerment* is when the corporation allows the stakeholders to develop and select the CSR initiatives, thereby relinquishing almost all control over the CSR process.

Involvement limits the power sharing to shaping the CSR options. Corporations must communicate their decisions, both the process and the outcomes, thoroughly to stakeholders. A dominant reason why stakeholder engagement fails is that stakeholders feel removed from and uninformed about the final decision about the CSR initiative. If stakeholders have committed their time and effort, they want to know what decision was made and why that decision was made. Stakeholders want to feel their input was treated with respect and understand the criteria used to justify the final decision. Knowing the decision criteria helps stakeholders to determine whether or not the process was just. Effective stakeholder engagement establishes the decision criteria and the nature of the decision-making process early in order to foster the perception of a just decision. Involvement can be used when there is strong consensus about a particular CSR initiative and stakeholders will be receptive to it.

Collaboration increases stakeholder power and the transparency of the process by giving them a vote in the decision. Stakeholders will understand the various options that were considered and how the vote resulted in the final selection of a CSR initiative and/or choice not to pursue a particular option. Again, the criteria for the decision need to be clarified during the engagement process along with the details for how the decision-making process is to occur. Collaboration is useful when the CSR concern is contentious and the corporation needs the stakeholders to accept the CSR initiative. As we have discussed, one motivation for CSR is a desire to prevent stakeholder churn (Porter & Kramer, 2006). Therefore, corporations are wise to facilitate acceptance of their CSR initiatives. Collaboration helps to build buy-in to CSR initiatives, thereby decreasing the likelihood of opposition to the actions. One possible reason for opposition to the CSR initiative is that it needed to be modified to fit the corporation's strategic goals. The ideas of the stakeholders have to mesh with the needs and capabilities of the corporation when a CSR initiative is crafted. Stakeholders could oppose the modification of their ideas. However, the possibility of churn is reduced if stakeholders understand how and why the modifications occurred. Being part of the decision-making process clarifies why the final CSR initiative decision was selected.

Empowerment allows the stakeholders to determine the CSR initiative. While this is rare, there are instances when corporations rely on the stakeholders in this way. When stakeholders are angry and oppose current policies, the corporation can involve stakeholders by asking them to plot a viable CSR course. Corporations will retain some veto power if the proposed CSR initiative lacks viability from a business perspective. When McDonald's was frustrated in its efforts to cope with its pollution problem associated with styrofoam, it turned to the Environmental Defense Fund (EDF) to solve the CSR problem for them. The EDF plotted the CSR initiative that helped transform McDonald's into an environmental leader in the fast food industry (EDF, 1991).

Another formula is to have stakeholders vote on the CSR options. The Co-operative Group in the United Kingdom illustrates the stakeholder voting approach to CSR initiatives. The customers decide in what areas the bank will not invest their money. If customers decide a specific industry should not be supported, the bank does not invest money in that industry. Here are two examples of CSR-related investment guidelines developed by the customers:

1. "We will not finance the manufacture or transfer of indiscriminate weapons, eg cluster bombs and depleted uranium munitions."
2. "We will not finance any business whose core activity contributes to the development of nanotechnology in circumstances that risk damaging the environment or compromising human health." (Co-operative Financial Services, n.d.)

The Co-operative Bank's philosophy states,

> The views and concerns of The Co-operative Bank customers have shaped the Ethical Policy for over 16 years, and their views have shaped our Ethical Policy – ultimately deciding how we invest their money. We understand that people's views can change, so we will continue to ask our customers their opinions, in order to ensure that our policy remains an up-to-date reflection of their concerns. (Co-operative Financial Services, 2006)

The customers, through the bank's ethical engagement process, determine CSR investment initiatives for the corporation.

Organizational Justice in the Engagement Process

The concept of organizational justice provides valuable insights into the engagement process surrounding a company's CSR-related decision making. Generally, *organizational justice* examines perceptions of fairness about events involving an organization (Folger & Cropanzano, 1998; Greenberg, 1990; Greenberg & Colquitt, 2005). Although the organizational justice literature typically focuses on employees, the ideas can be expanded to include stakeholders in general (e.g., Fediuk, Coombs, & Botero, 2010).

People are more accepting of outcomes, such as decisions about CSR activities, when the decision embodies justice. Hence, engagement should seek to establish a decision as being a just one. In addition, the corporation should encourage and manage stakeholder involvement in a way that demonstrates the engagement process itself is just.

Justice in corporations is a multifaceted concept. There are actually three primary types of justice: (1) distributive justice, (2) procedural justice, and (3) interactional justice. *Distributive justice* involves perceptions of fairness in the allocation of resources. For CSR, distributive justice can include what CSR issue(s) are selected and the actions that are taken on those issue(s). Stakeholders might feel their issues were not addressed or were not addressed in sufficient depth. *Procedural justice* involves perceptions of the fairness of the decision-making procedures themselves. For CSR, stakeholders can view the company as having a just or unjust process for making CSR decisions. Ideally, engagement is used to explain the CSR decision-making process and to establish that it is just. Distributive and procedural justice do interact. People can dislike the allocation of resources but accept the decision because the process was just. The stakeholders may not be happy with the specific decision option but are unlikely to take action against the corporation because the decision was fair. However, they can still lobby for change.

Interactional justice concerns perceptions of how people were treated interpersonally and is composed of interpersonal and informational justice. The first aspect, *interpersonal justice*, involves whether or not people felt they were treated with respect and dignity. Effective engagement procedures should seek to build interpersonal justice. For example, the concept of dialogue and its emphasis on perspective taking and power sharing should contribute to perceptions of interpersonal justice. The second aspect of interactional justice, *informational justice*, concerns perceptions of fairness about the explanations that people receive about the decision-making process and outcomes (Colquitt, 2001; Colquitt, Greenberg, & Zapata-Phelan, 2005). It is critical that engagement includes thorough information on and explanations of the decision, and answers to any stakeholder questions about the decisions.

Perceptions of interactional justice increase the acceptance of decisions, while perceived violations increase the likelihood of people taking action against the corporation. For CSR, this could mean the difference between stakeholders publicly stating they disagree with the corporation's choices but acknowledging the validity of the decision based on the information or publicly attacking the corporation for its unjust decision. Perceptions of justice do not satisfy all parties but do reduce the conflict generated from decisions by making them more palatable.

The "Right Amount" of CSR

Critics of the idea that stakeholder expectations should drive CSR initiatives maintain that stakeholders will never be satisfied and will always want more. In this sense, stakeholders are likened to extortionists. Once their original demands are met, they will demand more. We would argue this is plausible and even desirable. CSR is fluid and should change as societal values evolve. What is acceptable CSR today may not be so in one, two, or three years. As noted earlier, instructive churn is based on the dynamic nature of CSR. Recall that instructive churn enables a corporation to learn from conflict with stakeholders. The activist stakeholders keep a corporation alert to potential expectation gaps and ways to refine their CSR initiatives. Hence, the "right amount" of CSR is always a point of negotiation. The scanning and monitoring step and formative research step in the CSR process help a corporation monitor trends and reactions to CSR initiatives.

The idea of negotiation between the corporation and stakeholders returns us to the utility of stakeholder engagement. Part of the discussion of CSR involves explaining and justifying the corporation's current investment in CSR: the focus and breadth of CSR initiatives. There are times when a corporation cannot expand CSR initiatives due to financial, legal, and/or cultural limits. This requires managers to explain CSR-related choices to stakeholders. That does not mean that stakeholders will be satisfied and not agitate for more CSR or for different CSR actions. Even partners need to be free to be critical of CSR initiatives. But it is better for a corporation to enact some of the CSR initiatives expected by stakeholders than no CSR or the "wrong" CSR.

We have pointed to the idea that characteristics of the corporation will help guide the selection and creation of CSR initiatives. Larger corporations, especially multinational corporations, are more likely to be identified by activist groups as companies that could be persuaded to pursue large-scale CSR initiatives that could affect entire countries, regions, or the world. In comparison, smaller corporations may be best suited to addressing more local issues, although their size alone does not preclude them from participating in CSR efforts that address global problems like poverty and insufficient health education. Stakeholders are likely to assume that larger companies have more to give. They also may assume that larger companies are obligated to devote more resources to CSR because of their larger negative impact on the planet (e.g., consumption of resources and carbon footprint). However, it is important to note that large and small corporations alike should be attentive to locally based stakeholders who expect the corporation to contribute to the community in which it is based. Even the large multinational corporation that addresses social justice issues worldwide should be concerned with social justice issues in its own community. The point is that stakeholders will expect a corporation to enact CSR initiatives that are commensurate with its size and reach.

When Employees Challenge CSR: Considering Internal Stakeholders

Employees are a significant internal stakeholder in any CSR effort. As organizational members, they should be well positioned to understand the corporation's mission, values, and capabilities. Like external stakeholders, they also may support particular social issues. Although they have a common employer, employees are not necessarily monolithic in their interests. However, the common denominator for internal stakeholders is that they have a vested interest in the company. In many ways, they resemble shareholders who have an economic interest in the company. In fact, many employees *are* shareholders in their corporation. Their interest in CSR initiatives may be spurred by their commitment to the social concern as well as the anticipated effects of CSR initiatives on their positions and the company as a whole. Employees want and need to be aware of what the corporation is doing. Their role as both receivers and senders of CSR-related opinions and information should not be overlooked.

Although we hope that employees will function as cheerleaders for the corporation's CSR initiatives, this may not be the case. Employees are unlikely to support a CSR initiative if they perceive it may threaten their jobs and/or the overall economic well-being of the corporation. In addition, they may not support a CSR initiative they perceive to be greenwashing. On the one hand, a new sustainability initiative may mean reassignments or layoffs for some employees. On the other hand, it may create the need to hire additional employees. It is natural that stakeholder attitudes and behaviors reflect self-interest. As discussed in the earlier section "What Constitutes CSR?" the concept of organizational justice, coupled with the process of internal stakeholder engagement, may help us understand, manage, and benefit from negative employee reactions to CSR. Internal stakeholders expect to be valued in the same way that external stakeholders are valued when it comes to engagement and decision making. Information sharing is essential to this process. But sometimes employees may not perceive the CSR-related information to be "good news."

As a form of uncontrolled social media, employee blogs and tweets may be regarded as credible information sources that are unfiltered by corporate interests. The next chapter, on communicating the CSR initiative, explores the positive impact of employee blogs and tweets on external stakeholder knowledge of a corporation's CSR initiatives. Our concern here is employee communication of negative information. Employee blogs and tweets can be critical of CSR. Dissatisfied employees may blog about their perceptions of the futility of CSR efforts, the "real" costs to the corporation, the lack of "real" benefits to those groups the CSR initiative was supposed to serve, and so on. The Internet provides a forum for employees to air their concerns and complaints as well as praises. Employees can become stakeholder activists. It would not be in the spirit of engagement to silence or restrict employee communication about CSR.

So how should a company respond to situations where employees communicate negative information or opinions about CSR? Systematic monitoring of what is said about a company, including its CSR initiatives, is a recognized business practice, and both traditional and online media typically are examined (Coombs, 2007). Organizations can conduct their own monitoring or hire another firm to provide the service. Recall that chapters 3 and 4 described scanning and monitoring and formative research as the first and second stages, respectively, in the strategic CSR process. Although such monitoring of employee communication may smack of "Big Brother" to internal stakeholders, companies do want to know what is being said by both internal and external stakeholders. This can function as instructive churn. In addition, companies would be wise to assess if comments are gaining traction – sparking additional comments in the online world – and spreading to more stakeholders (Coombs & Holladay, 2007a).

As would be the case with external stakeholders, the corporation should contact the employees to arrange a meeting about their concerns. Recall that we also recommended meeting with dissatisfied external stakeholders to better understand their concerns. The engagement process should be beneficial in this case, too. It would be unwise and unjust to simply censor negative comments from employees. The engagement process should be used to dialogue with the employees and discover the roots of the critiques. Employees can offer useful insights into perceptions of CSR and the enactment of CSR initiatives. Managers will benefit from seriously considering and responding to employee criticisms.

The point of reviewing the contested characteristics of CSR is to illustrate the difficulties surrounding the final selection of the concerns to pursue as CSR initiatives. The decision is challenging, and managers should not expect to go unscathed with their final selections. The lesson is to recognize the ways that CSR can be contested and to account for them in the CSR decision-making process. Managers do need to decide what CSR concerns to address and how they will address them. We believe that considering the contested aspects of CSR creates a better process and better choices among the CSR initiatives.

Preparing for Negative Stakeholder Reactions: Message Mapping

It is important for managers to anticipate that some stakeholders will react negatively to the selection of a specific CSR initiative. Stakeholders may feel the CSR initiative does not go far enough or does not address their CSR concerns. Hence, stakeholders might have issues with distributive justice. Managers cannot expect to please all of the stakeholders all of the time with their CSR initiatives. Because corporations cannot address every CSR concern, they must prioritize and select concerns based on specified criteria. Engaging stakeholders in the CSR process helps to establish procedural justice for the CSR initiative selection. Managers also can prepare to handle the stakeholder complaints with the CSR initiative selection.

By monitoring stakeholder reactions throughout the CSR process, managers can anticipate challenges to the CSR initiative. Managers will deal with negative stakeholder reactions to CSR initiatives both in this stage and in the CSR communication stage of the CSR process. Risk communication utilizes a concept known as *message mapping*. Message mapping involves anticipating questions and concerns that might arise and preparing detailed responses for those questions (Covello, 2003). Detailed responses provide specific supporting evidence such as facts or testimonials. For CSR communication, the message map would identify the stakeholder group, their likely concerns with the CSR initiative, a detailed response to the concern, and appropriate channels for delivering the message. Box 5.2 provides a template that can be used to develop message maps. The exact questions will vary by CSR initiative, and managers should use engagement and other sources of information to anticipate the questions. Engagement is helpful because stakeholders probably will raise the concerns during the engagement activities. Managers always should anticipate questions about procedural justice and be prepared to defend the fairness of the CSR initiative selection process. As we have discussed, it is important to consider procedural justice because it promotes transparency and helps stakeholders understand the decision-making process and their role within it.

Developing CSR Objectives

Once the choice to pursue a specific CSR initiative is made, managers must then plan how they will bring the initiative to life. Entire books are written on planning, including how to develop project management documents and budgets. In many ways, planning is unique in each corporation. There are basic activities that must be accomplished, but *how* they are enacted varies.

Box 5.2 Message-Mapping Template

CSR Message Map
Stakeholder:
Concern with CSR initiative:
Basic response:
Supporting information (1):
Supporting information (2):
Supporting information (3):
Appropriate channel(s):

We have chosen to reduce the discussion of planning to the central concept of objectives because of its critical role in the CSR process. We return to the use of objectives in chapter 7, which covers evaluation and feedback.

If we believe that CSR initiatives are strategic, the CSR actions should be built around objectives. Objectives provide guidance and a mechanism for evaluation. Goals provide only a general direction for behavior. In contrast, an objective moves from the general direction embodied in a goal to greater specificity. An objective seeks to pin down what is expected from the strategic effort and must be measurable. Keep in mind that the term *objective* can have multiple meanings, and this can create confusion. Therefore, it is important to distinguish between two types of objectives, (1) process and (2) outcome objectives, when discussing objectives. While both are useful, mistaking one for the other creates problems.

Process versus Outcome Objectives

A *process objective* specifies what steps will be taken to create and to execute the CSR effort. As part of the process, managers would identify what tasks need to be completed, when the tasks are to be completed, and who has responsibility for the tasks, and then monitor the cost of the task. A process objective allows the corporation to determine only if they took the actions or steps they were supposed to take. Were tasks A, B, and C performed by their assigned completion dates? The problem is that simply performing tasks is not the same as obtaining desired results from the performance of the tasks. This is why we must consider the value of outcome objectives.

An *outcome objective* seeks to determine whether or not a CSR initiative was successful. Toward that end, an outcome objective specifies what the CSR effort hopes to achieve and within what time frame. An effective outcome objective quantifies what the CSR effort should accomplish. CSR efforts hope to create changes that benefit society. The objective should specify the amount of desired change or target behavior as a percentage or number (Coombs, 2005; Stacks, 2002). An outcome objective must be measurable and specific. You cannot evaluate a CSR effort if you cannot measure it. The outcome objective is used to determine the success of the initiative.

There are three types of outcome objectives: (1) knowledge objectives that focus on stakeholders learning and recalling new information (e.g., 40% of the customers who purchase lumber will report knowing of the corporation's partnership with the Forestry Stewardship Council), (2) attitude objectives that focus on changing how people feel (e.g., at least 60% of customers will approve of XYZ's sale of FairTrade coffee in the café), and (3) behavior objectives that specify that stakeholders will engage in prescribed behaviors (e.g., 75% of employees will recycle beverage containers purchased in the workplace). CSR initiatives often focus on changing behaviors. The corporation wants to persuade employees, suppliers, customers, and other stakeholders to do something – or to not do something – that comprises the CSR initiative (Coombs, 2005).

Process objectives can be converted into outcome objectives. For example, perhaps the CSR initiative involves donating products to a local women's shelter. The process objective might simply state, "To donate clothing to the shelter." That can be converted into an outcome objective by reformulating it to state, "To donate $5,000 in clothing to the Hope House women's shelter by December 10th." Or the process objective may state, "The company will supply additional paper and plastic recycling bins throughout the building to encourage recycling." That can be converted to an outcome objective by rephrasing it to say, "Employees will increase their amount of paper recycling by 40% and their amount of plastic recycling by 30% by the end of fiscal year 2010."

Two common confusions haunt CSR initiatives: (1) confusing a goal for an objective, and (2) confusing a process objective for an outcome objective. *Goals* simply state "general directions." Hence, they are vague and difficult to use when evaluating progress toward a target. In contrast, the details provided by an objective facilitate evaluation. Process is what you are going to do – not the effect of those actions. Corporations and stakeholders need to know the intended effects of a CSR initiative and the actual effects produced by the CSR initiative. Only then can we properly evaluate a CSR initiative, a point developed further in our discussion of evaluation and feedback in chapter 7. Hitachi's 2007 CSR report can be used to illustrate these confusions. The report contained information about Hitachi's CSR objectives. Here are some sample statements:

1. Contributing to society based upon a plan.
2. Publishing CSR report.
3. Developing environmentally friendly products.

The first statement is a goal. Saying the corporation will be "contributing to society based upon a plan" is very general! People will want to know what that really means in terms of effects on society. The second statement is a process objective. Publishing a CSR report is a task. Thus, it is a process objective rather than an outcome objective. The act of publishing the report (the process) does not have an effect on society. The process objective only claims the corporation will complete that task, not that the act of publishing the report will have an effect on society. The third statement is a weak outcome objective. "Developing environmentally friendly products" does move us closer to an outcome objective. Products that are environmentally friendly can have an effect on society and can be measured. However, to qualify as an outcome objective, number 3 requires greater specificity to quantify the effect of product development. For example, Hitachi could identify a target percentage of its product line it hopes to make environmentally friendly or identify the total amount of a dangerous chemical it hopes to remove from the environment through its environmentally friendly products. Providing more specifics would make this statement a stronger outcome objective.

We do not mean to be critical of Hitachi. If you examine most CSR or sustainability reports, you will find more process objectives than outcome objectives. The 2007 "Corporate Responsibility Report" by Adidas, for instance, is dominated by process objectives. Here are two examples: (1) "To identify and engage with appropriate technical, brand and NGO partners to support the reduction of energy, waste and water in our core supply chain"; and (2) "To enhance the internalisation of environmental metrics by core footwear suppliers to drive improvements in their reporting and defining reduction targets" (Adidas, 2007, p. 12). It is logical that as corporations build CSR programs, they detail what is being done. Stakeholders do want to know this information, and it is easy for the corporation to document. However, managers must realize that stakeholders want information about the effects of those actions as well.

Barilla's 2008 "Sustainability Report," for instance, includes the objective of eliminating artificial colorants and hydrogenated fats and oils from all products by 2014 (Barilla, 2008). The effect on society is still implied; people should be healthier if they have healthier products, but the progress is easy to monitor. Barilla can demonstrate progress by annually reporting the percentage of its products that still contain artificial colorants and hydrogenated fats and oils. Managers need to develop outcome objectives that can specify and document the effects of their CSR efforts on society.

Developing objectives, especially outcome objectives that specify measurable results and identify the time frames for accomplishing those results, contribute to perceptions of accountability. Outcome objectives should be publicized to ensure that those people responsible for enacting the CSR initiative are aware of the objectives and that those stakeholders who are interested in the initiative can monitor the results. Fear of being held accountable for results may be one reason why some corporations report only process objectives (what actions were taken) rather than outcome objectives (what results were achieved). It is much easier to hide behind process objectives because they do create the appearance that the corporation is doing something. And some people may argue that doing something is better than doing nothing. However, corporations that are serious about producing positive outcomes for society will see the value of developing and reporting progress on CSR outcome objectives.

Conclusion and Critical Questions

The preceding step, formative research, helps to identity what effects the CSR concern can have on society and the corporation. The formative research sets the stage for the selection of the CSR concerns that will become the corporation's CSR initiatives. Managers must consider the financial costs of the CSR initiatives and the potential return on investment (ROI), and establish clear outcome objectives for what happens as a result of the CSR initiatives. Managers must also consider the consistency of the specific CSR initiatives. The CSR initiatives should be consistent with the corporation's strategic plan, its corporate culture, and the national culture in which the CSR initiative will be implemented.

Stakeholder engagement continues to be a valuable resource when crafting a CSR initiative. Stakeholders become more invested in the CSR initiatives and feel a sense of ownership over the engagement process and initiatives when they have a greater role in creating them.

Once the CSR concerns are selected, they must be translated into action. Action occurs when the CSR concerns are translated into specific CSR initiatives and implemented by the corporation. The CSR initiatives are what the corporation does to address the CSR concern such as enacting new requirements for suppliers, reducing the amount of pollutants released into the environment, or donating employee time to a local non-profit organization. Outcome objectives should be attached to this decision. Each CSR concern should be accompanied with an objective or set of objectives.

Critical Questions for Creating the CSR Initiatives	*Relevant Parties*	
	Corporation	*Stakeholders*
Which stakeholders should be engaged in creating the CSR initiative?	X	X
How does the corporation assess stakeholder power, legitimacy, and urgency?	X	X
Which stakeholders are latent, expectant, or definitive?	X	X
How will the engagement process for creating the CSR initiative be structured?	X	X
What level of collaborative decision making will be utilized in the engagement process?	X	X
What type of decision-making approach will be used?	X	X
How do stakeholders perceive the procedural justice associated with the decision making?	X	X
What are the stated stakeholder objectives for the CSR initiative?	X	X
What are the measurable benefits of the CSR initiative for stakeholders?	X	X
Which stakeholders will benefit from the CSR initiative, and how will they benefit?	X	X
Which stakeholders might be upset by the CSR initiative, and why?	X	X
Is the initiative likely to trigger churn among those stakeholders who are upset?	X	X
How will the process objectives be established?	X	X
How will the outcome objectives be established?	X	X

Critical Questions for Creating the CSR Initiatives	*Relevant Parties*	
	Corporation	*Stakeholders*
What message maps should the corporation prepare in anticipation of negative reactions by some stakeholders?	X	
How consistent is the CSR concern with the corporation's current business strategy?	X	
How well does the CSR concern fit with the corporation's industry?	X	
What are the potential costs of the CSR concern to the corporation?	X	
What are the potential benefits of the CSR concern to the corporation?	X	
Where can the corporation make the most difference?	X	X
What criteria will be used to select the final CSR concern(s) to be implemented?	X	X
What are the financial costs of the CSR initiative to the corporation?	X	
What are the stated objectives for the CSR initiative?	X	
How consistent is the CSR initiative with the corporation's strategic plan?	X	
How consistent is the CSR initiative with corporate culture?	X	
How consistent is the CSR initiative with national culture?	X	

Throughout this process, the degree of decision-making power the corporation shares with stakeholders must be carefully considered. These engagement points have implications for perceptions of procedural justice in the CSR initiative creation process. Stakeholders need to establish criteria for evaluating how well the CSR initiative meets their own objectives in order to prove the CSR initiative actually benefits stakeholders. This raises the issue of which stakeholders actually benefit from the CSR initiative and how they benefit from it. Stakeholders who are not benefiting and/or were not part of the selection process could be upset. Managers must anticipate which stakeholders might become upset, why they would be upset, and the possibility of the CSR initiative triggering stakeholder churn. Stakeholders will share this interest in engagement, decision making, benefits, and objectives because these factors determine the amount of influence they have over the process and how the outcome might affect them and the CSR concern.

Ben & Jerry's three-part mission statement emphasizes practices that benefit people, the environment, and its business. Courtesy of Ben & Jerry's

6

Communicate the CSR Initiative

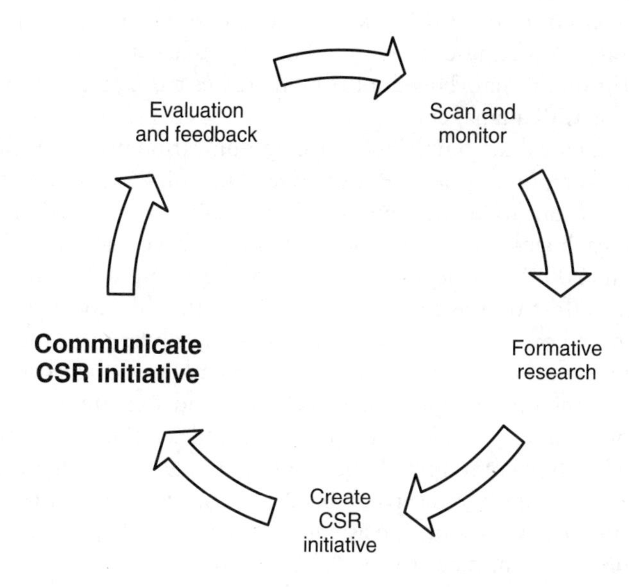

Communication is at the heart of our perspective on the CSR process. Thus, it may seem odd to devote a chapter to "communicating the CSR initiative" when communication is woven into all parts of the process. The purpose of this chapter is to explore how, once the CSR initiative has been created, it can be communicated to stakeholders. The CSR team will need to target both internal and external stakeholders. Employees can be vital communication channels in and of themselves. The external stakeholders will include

Managing Corporate Social Responsibility: A Communication Approach, First Edition.
W. Timothy Coombs, Sherry J. Holladay.

all those affected by the CSR initiative decision and any stakeholders who have a general interest in the corporation's CSR activities. Typical external stakeholders would include local communities, NGOs, traditional and online media, suppliers, customers, investors, and retailers. Effective communication about CSR has been hindered by the assumption that communication is simply the transmission of CSR information from the corporation to its stakeholders. In reality, CSR communication is a challenging process requiring an understanding of stakeholders, their information needs, and communication channels. A central concern is what we term the *CSR promotional communication dilemma*. Stakeholders want CSR information, yet corporate messaging can create a backlash when stakeholders see it as overly self-promotional. This double bind creates a difficult communicative challenge for CSR managers.

Another factor that complicates the communication process is the variety of interests surrounding a CSR initiative. Not all stakeholders want the same information about the initiative. The CSR communication must be tailored to each stakeholder yet maintain an overall consistency (Pomering & Dolnicar, 2008). For instance, investors are interested in the financial effect of the effort on the corporation (e.g., ROI), while local communities want to know how the actions directly affect their lives (e.g., the effects on health and environment). It could be problematic if the corporation is viewed as saying one thing to one stakeholder and something rather different to another simply to please the receivers and tell them what they want to hear. This type of targeted messaging, though well intentioned and designed to meet specific receivers' needs, might backfire and be perceived as disingenuous. A lack of consistency may arouse skepticism about the sincerity of or commitment to the CSR initiative.

The CSR communication stage should develop a plan that outlines the stakeholders to be addressed, channels (media) to be used to reach them, and primary messages to be sent to each stakeholder group. Managers should have a sense of the stakeholders based on the formative research, and the messages must be adapted to their interests as well as the specific CSR initiative. In this chapter, we also discuss how employees and social media are valuable CSR communication channels. Finally, two of the major CSR reporting guideline systems, the Global Reporting Initiative (GRI) and ISO 26000, are reviewed to illustrate how they can provide a framework for organizing communication about CSR.

CSR Promotional Communication Dilemma

Stakeholders report that they would like to know more about the CSR efforts of corporations. However, stakeholders are also skeptical of corporations that are perceived to commit too much time and effort to CSR communication. Without awareness of their CSR initiatives, corporations may draw no reputational benefit from their CSR initiatives. However, too much effort to create awareness can have a boomerang effect as stakeholders become cynical and skeptical when there is excessive self-promotion about CSR initiatives. The challenge is to effectively communicate the CSR initiative without creating a backlash we term the *CSR promotional communication dilemma*.

Globally, stakeholders say CSR actions influence their relationships with organizations (Sen, Bhattacharya, & Korschun, 2006). However, research proves that stakeholders have a very low awareness of corporate CSR activities (Bhattacharya & Sen, 2004; Pomering & Dolnicar, 2009). So even though people report that a corporation's CSR record can be an important decision-making criterion when selecting products and services, stakeholders are underinformed about CSR. This is extremely problematic for corporations. Awareness drives many of the benefits that corporations derive from CSR. The key element is identification through CSR. In chapter 2 on strategic communication, we discussed how CSR initiatives provide common values that allow stakeholders to appreciate how their identities overlap with a corporation's identity. In turn, identification builds support for the corporation and the creation of favorable reputations (Bhattacharya & Sen, 2004). Identification and favorable reputations translate into supportive behaviors for the corporation such as purchase intention (Maignan & Ferrell, 2004; Sen et al., 2006). As Bhattacharya and Sen (2004) noted, "[C]onsumers' awareness of a corporation's CSR activities is a key prerequisite to their positive reactions to such activities" (p. 14).

In light of the importance of CSR to consumer decision making and corporate reputation, it seems obvious that corporations should raise awareness of their CSR activities through communication. Maignan and Ferrell (2004) recommend that CSR be infused throughout corporate communication. They also noted the need for more research into CSR communication because "businesses cannot hope to enjoy concrete benefits from CSR unless they intelligently communicate about their initiative to relevant stakeholders" (p. 17). Their call for more research suggests the challenges to communicating CSR. Sen at al. (2006) refer to communicating CSR as a double-edged sword that challenges corporations to create "optimal communication of their CSR actions" (p. 164). CSR awareness can be increased through the communication tactics of advertising and promotional efforts. However, consumers want CSR facts but dislike a hard sell. Too much "effort" in CSR promotion can cause negative attributions about CSR initiatives and harm an organization's relationship with stakeholders (Bhattacharya & Sen, 2004). For instance, studies in Denmark indicate that people are skeptical about "conspicuous corporate CSR communication" (Morsing, Schultz, & Nielsen, 2008).

We can refine the notion of *too much effort* or *conspicuous communication* to focus on message tone and costs. *Message tone* refers to the idea that the message is appearing too often and too prominently. CSR information can be integrated into various corporate communication tactics but should not always dominate the message and should focus on facts rather than overpromotion and self-congratulation. CSR communication benefits from a tone that is low-key and focuses more on the presentation of facts than on the promotion of the corporation's involvement in CSR.

Armstrong World Industries Inc. provides an example of low-key promotion of CSR. Armstrong linoleum is FloorScore® certified. That means the product can carry the FloorScore® Label. FloorScore is a certification system that "tests and certifies hard surface flooring and flooring adhesive products for compliance with rigorous indoor air quality emissions requirements. Individual volatile organic compounds (VOCs) are evaluated using health-based specifications" (Scientific Certification Systems, 2010). At its corporate website, Armstrong reports and explains the certification under the "Sustainability" link (Armstrong World Industries, 2010). You need to look for this CSR information by opening the "Awards and Certification" link in the "Sustainability" section of the website. The FloorScore is not featured in advertising or other more aggressive forms of promotion.

Stakeholders find it problematic when corporations spend a great deal of money on CSR promotion such as advertising (Alsop, 2004). Thus perceptions of the *cost* of promotion must be considered in addition to message tone. If the corporation is committed to CSR, couldn't they spend the money more wisely on the CSR initiative itself rather than on advertising their involvement in the issue? The goals of CSR communication may benefit from the utilization of low-cost tactics. While constricting, a low-key tone and low-cost tactics do not doom the effectiveness of the CSR-related communication. Instead, it becomes a challenge to overcome the CSR promotional communication dilemma.

The key to managing the CSR promotional communication dilemma is careful analysis of the problem. Managers must address two core issues that emerge from the promotional communication dilemma: (1) source and (2) cost. *Source* refers to who is presenting the message. Corporations lack credibility as sources of CSR information because their communication can appear overly self-serving. Corporations may appear more interested in the benefits they accrue from a positive CSR-oriented reputation than the CSR issue itself. Third-party information sources carry greater weight with stakeholders because they seem more neutral and more interested in the social concern than the corporation supporting the concern.

The second issue is cost. *Cost* refers to the amount of money the corporation spends on the CSR promotional communication tactics. Escalating costs for the CSR promotional communication tactics increase the likelihood of a boomerang effect from the CSR messages. Excessive spending on messages that tout the corporation's involvement in the social concern may create the impression that the corporation is more interested in generating publicity for itself than supporting the CSR concern. It is inappropriate for messages to focus more on the corporation itself rather than the CSR effort, the stakeholders who benefit from the effort, and tangible outcomes. The CSR promotional communication mix must reflect sensitivity to the two core issues of source and cost.

There are limited options for addressing the source issue. A corporation will be the source for various CSR tactics. Time and transparency are keys to building the corporation's credibility as a source. The corporation must establish a track record of disclosing a range of CSR information. This includes providing information about failures (e.g., failure to reach target outcome objectives), not just successes. Interested stakeholders need to be able to access information that reveals when a corporation has failed to reach an outcome objective or has had a lapse in its CSR initiative. For instance, the GAP prides itself on eliminating child labor and is widely recognized as a garment industry leader on this CSR concern. Still, in 2008 there was an incident where a supplier for baby clothes was found to be using child labor. The GAP acted quickly to remedy the problem (Gap Inc., 2007; Global March against Child Labor, 2007). To be perceived as sincere and credible, management must be willing to discuss the good and the bad of their CSR. Trust is enhanced by a transparent process. Transparency allows stakeholders to "see" how a corporation creates and reports its CSR data. The CSR report is a perfect example. Transparency answers key questions such as the following:

- How was stakeholder engagement used in the process?
- What were the objectives of the CSR initiatives?
- How were the data in the report collected?
- Which stakeholders were consulted or engaged in the data-gathering process?
- What were the stakeholder reactions to the CSR data?

As noted earlier, stakeholder engagement aids the transparency process. When stakeholders are a part of the process, they develop a clearer picture of how the corporation is developing and utilizing CSR efforts. Stakeholders must be able to see into the corporation and find the information they are looking for. Building CSR credibility is a long-term investment for a corporation. Only a consistent history of demonstrating transparency and openness about CSR will cultivate the development of credibility.

Third-party endorsements serve to complement and to reinforce CSR messages from corporations. Legitimate third parties transfer their CSR credibility to an organization when communicating their support for that corporation. The third-party endorser must acknowledge the corporation and agree to let its name or logo be used. The value of an endorsement is a function of the relevant expertise and name recognition of the endorser. Publics that are attracted to the third-party organization should then be attracted to the corporation it endorses (Dean & Biswas, 2001). Third-party endorsements can be either direct or indirect. *Direct third-party endorsements* are statements from the third party. Such statements could be communication tactics from the third party, such as a news release, or quotations from the third party in the corporation's communication tactics. Whatever tactic is used, there is some direct statement from the third party supporting the corporation's CSR efforts.

Greenpeace's praise for Apple's elimination of PVC from its PC power cords illustrates third-party support. Greenpeace ranks electronic companies with its "Guide to Greener Electronics" and updates the rankings every few months (Greenpeace, 2010). In its "Green My Apple" campaign, Greenpeace has been critical of Apple for not being very green in the past. However, in October 2009 Apple became the first major computer manufacturer to offer PVC-free PC power cords. The power cords had been the last part of PCs to still contain PVC, a plastic that Greenpeace and others consider toxic. Here is a statement posted by Greenpeace to its website: "This lays down the gauntlet to other major PC makers such as Dell, HP, Lenovo and Acer to catch up with Apple again, and we'll be keeping up our pressure on them to match Apple's lead" (Greenpeace, 2009a). While not wildly ecstatic praise, the comment does offer support for Apple's CSR effort to reduce PVC usage in PCs. Stakeholders concerned about PVC can locate verification of Apple's concern and actions related to the PVC issue.

Indirect third-party endorsements include certification labels and the endorser's name. There are a variety of legitimate certification systems that have direct relationships to CSR efforts. The label verifies the corporation's claims about their CSR activities relative to that certification process. Starbucks using the FairTrade logo and Home Depot selling lumber certified by the Forestry Stewardship Council (FSC) are examples of certification labels in action. The other option is placing the endorser's name on a product and/or in messages from the corporation. The Sierra Club has allowed its name to be used in association with Clorox's "Green Works" line of environmentally friendly cleaners. The Green Works products include the Sierra Club logo on the label and the Sierra Club name on many of its communication tactics such as news releases and the website for Green Works. The Sierra Club name symbolizes approval of this Clorox sustainability effort. Similarly, Ben and Jerry's website describes how, since 2006, it has worked with a paper supplier that uses FSC-certified pulp and has reduced waste by 1,000 tons each year. Pints of Ben and Jerry's carry the FairTrade logo when they contain ingredients that are FairTrade certified. Costa Coffee reports that 100% of the coffee it sells in the United Kingdom is sourced from Rain Forest Alliance-certified farms that demonstrate a commitment to sustainable agriculture.

The certification is a routine process that requires meeting certain standards and allowing inspectors to verify that those standards are being met. Other endorsements can be simple statements of support or complex partnerships between the corporation and the third party. Partnerships are becoming more popular and reflect a strong sense of stakeholder engagement. As noted earlier, partnerships grant the third party some power in the decision making about CSR policies and activities. The communication emphasizes that the corporation worked closely with the third party in creating and perhaps even verifying the CSR efforts. A partnership would seem to be a stronger endorsement than a simple statement of support or approval. The corporation demonstrates a keen commitment to CSR by entering a partnership designed to build its CSR initiative. Partnerships require a significant investment of corporate time, money, and willingness to share power. That is much more involved than simply arranging for a third party to say it likes or supports a corporation's CSR efforts. Refer to the partnership discussion in Box 6.1 for a more detailed discussion of the topic.

As noted earlier, stakeholders dislike corporations spending large amounts of money to promote their CSR efforts. The dislike seems to stem from the perceived costs of promotion more than the act of promoting the CSR. Efforts to heavily promote CSR initiatives, such as advertisements, can be viewed as problematic as well. People are likely to view CSR initiatives as self-serving and self-congratulatory – and question a corporation's motives for engaging in CSR – when there is "overpromotion" of the CSR efforts. Corporations must be effective at disseminating CSR efforts without expending too much on costs. Too much cost is a reflection of effort as well as spending. That is why nonproduct advertising about CSR efforts is often a poor choice.

Public relations has long been an option for the low-cost dissemination of information. Common public relations tactics that can be used for CSR promotion are brochures (still low cost), news releases, sections of a corporate website devoted to CSR, special websites to discuss CSR, employee

Box 6.1 Overview of Corporate-Activist Partnerships

Many experts now recommend corporate-activist partnerships because the results can benefit society and corporations. However, both sides have reservations about partnerships and must be cautious about their creation. Partnerships involve collaborative decision making and raise issues about power (Friedman, 2008). Stakeholders help to shape CSR initiatives with their views of social issues and their conceptualization of CSR. Activists have reservations about partnerships because they fear co-optation (i.e., fear they will begin to think like corporate partners), loss of their own identity, and a loss of power if they are perceived to no longer be challenging the corporation. Corporations have reservations about partnerships because they fear being viewed as weak by capitulating to activist demands and sharing power with activists. Successful partnerships need to (1) allow activists to participate in decision making, (2) allow activists to retain their critical voice, (3) permit corporations to pursue financial concerns along with social concerns, and (4) set clear benchmarks for success with objectives (Coombs & Holladay, 2009a).

blogs, employee tweets, posts to discussion boards, and sending CSR information to CSR social media (bloggers and tweeters). The possible PR tactics for avoiding the CSR promotional communication dilemma provide a transition into a detailed discussion of communication channels.

Communication Channels for CSR Messaging

Starting with the formative research stage, CSR managers should build detailed profiles of the various stakeholders that could be connected with the CSR initiative and their "stake" in it. Messages are adapted to the needs and interests of these stakeholders. Channel selection is critical to ensuring that the stakeholders are exposed to the message. This section overviews the communication channel options for CSR, examines employees and external stakeholders as channels, and details the strategic value of social media for CSR communication.

Overview of Communication Channels for CSR

The public relations tactics list is a mix of controlled and uncontrolled media. *Control* indicates whether or not the corporation has control over if and how the message is used. For instance, a media outlet can ignore a news release (determine *if* the message is used) or write its version of a story based on the news release (determine *how* the message is used). *Uncontrolled tactics* include news releases and sending information to social media sources. Sending information to social media sources mimics a news release and acknowledges the growing power of the social media. Box 6.2 provides an overview of the various social media options available to managers. The upside of uncontrolled tactics is the third-party effect. The news media or social media users become the source of the CSR information because they are the ones reporting it to other stakeholders. The corporation (1) saves on cost, (2) does not appear to be an active promoter, and (3) and gains CSR credibility from the third parties. The downside is that the CSR message may be ignored or be distorted in how it is reported. The media outlet can chose to frame the information as it wishes. For example, a corporation may find that the news media overlooked what the corporation believed to be positive accomplishments and focused instead on how the corporation is "not doing enough" to address a social concern.

The online environment provides some unique opportunities for uncontrolled CSR public relations. There are online outlets that specialize in presenting and discussing CSR information. If a corporation can distribute through these outlets, the reach and CSR credibility of the message are greatly enhanced. Some popular outlets include CSR International, SustainabilityForum.com, and CSRwire.com.

CSR International is one popular online outlet for CSR information. CSR International tries to promote effective CSR practices. It can be followed on Twitter, through an RSS feed, or by subscribing to its email list. SustainabilityForum.com is a clearinghouse for CSR-related information offering news, blogs, and forums for discussion. Their CSR news often features stories about CSR initiatives undertaken by various corporations. You can even become a fan of SustainabilityForum.com on Facebook. The website contains a blog and an archive of CSR research as well as CSR news that is provided by SustainabilityForum.com. Here is how it describes itself:

> The purpose of SustainabilityForum.com is to be a resource for valuable discussion, news, opinion and events all related to the topic of Sustainability. Registration is free and anyone can join our community. SustainabilityForum.

Box 6.2 Social Media Overview

Social media are the collection of online technology tools that facilitate conversations and communication between people. People can share text, audio, video, images, podcasts, and any combination thereof (Safko & Brake, 2009). As recently as a few years ago, social media were more likely to be called *consumer-generated content* because stakeholders, not corporations, were creating the online messages. The tools for social media are too vast to list here, and more will be added between the time we write this text and it is published. In this box, we summarize the primary types of social media and offer a few examples of each. Keep in mind that no categorization system for social media is perfect and that some social media tools can cross between categories.

Blogs and micro-blogs are ways people can post their thoughts. Others can comment on those ideas and share the ideas with others through links and reposting. Micro-blogs such as Twitter are simply shorter messages. In the case of Twitter, the limit is 140 characters. Blogs provide a longer format for the presentation of ideas. Internet forums are original social media. Forums are known by a variety of names including *discussion groups*, *discussion boards*, and *message boards*. An Internet forum is an online location (often called a bulletin board) where people can post messages and replies to messages. A conversation can evolve as people keep responding to the same message – in other words, a thread develops. Internet forums are constructed around specific topic areas. Virtually every topic has an Internet forum somewhere. Corporations need to identify the Internet forums relevant to their operations and their CSR issues. Internet forums provide a place for stakeholders to share and discuss both information and opinions. Starbucks is one of a number of corporations that have begun to operate their own Internet forums as a means of engaging stakeholders with CSR.

Content communities emerge when people converge around some object of interest. YouTube (video) and Flickr (still images) are prominent content communities. People form communities around the video or images, including the ability to leave comments about the content. A corporation may find content communities relevant to their CSR issues. Moreover, videos or images about a company's CSR, posted by either employees or external stakeholders, might create a content community. Most people have heard of social-networking sites such as Facebook, MySpace, LinkedIn, and Bebo (Safko & Brake, 2009).

Social-networking sites can be defined as

> web-based services that allow individuals to (1) construct a public or semi-public profile within a bounded system, (2) articulate a list of other users with whom they share a connection, and (3) view and traverse their list of connections and those made by others within the system. The nature and nomenclature of these connections may vary from site to site. (Boyd & Ellison, 2007)

The unique aspect of social-networking sites is that a person's social network is exposed to others. The ability to "see" the social networks of others provides an opportunity to make additional connections that would not have occurred otherwise. The person's profile is the core of the social-networking sites. People then link others they know to their profiles, and the networking begins. Social-networking sites can offer a variety of applications as well. Many organizations create a Facebook fan page rather than a profile. A fan page looks like a profile and is designed to help connect an organization with stakeholders who are interested in them (followers). Fan pages are public and allow organizations to add a variety of information and to engage directly in discussions with stakeholders (Mucha, 2009). CSR initiatives and issues are a logical topic that would emerge on a fan page.

The final category is social bookmarking or aggregators. Social bookmarks, or aggregators, are used in collections and evaluations of Internet content that are shared with others. Individuals place tags or bookmarks on Internet content. The tags have keywords and evaluations that are then aggregated at a social-bookmarking site such as StumbleUpon or Delicious (formerly Del.icio.us). Other people can then search through the social bookmarks. Here is how StumbleUpon describes itself:

> StumbleUpon helps you discover and share great websites. As you click Stumble!, we deliver high-quality pages matched to your personal preferences. These pages have been explicitly recommended by your friends or one of 8 million+ other websurfers with interests similar to you. Rating these sites you like ( ) automatically shares them with like-minded people – and helps you discover great sites your friends recommend. (StumbleUpon, 2011)

(*Continued*)

Managers can use social-bookmarking or aggregator sites to get a sense of people's awareness of the organization's CSR efforts and their reactions to their efforts.

This is not intended to be an exhaustive list of social media. The point is to highlight key social media tools that could benefit CSR communication. Organizations can use social media to (1) learn what CSR issues are important to stakeholders (find emerging issues), (2) determine if stakeholders are aware of CSR initiatives, (3) assess stakeholder reactions to CSR initiatives, (4) increase awareness of CSR initiatives, and (5) provide an avenue for stakeholder engagement. The number one priority in social media is *listening*. Point 1 through 3 all involve listening. Listening to stakeholders helps managers to understand the stakeholders and their CSR concerns. This CSR knowledge base provides a foundation for engaging stakeholders and eventually promoting awareness of CSR initiatives. Part of listening is learning the proper etiquette for the various social media channels. Violating the rules of etiquette is another way to create a backlash against a corporation and its CSR efforts. Social media are about allowing people to find information they want, not a means of forcing unwanted information onto stakeholders.

com's mission is to be a resource for Sustainability news, opinion and discussion you can trust. We have do not republish any press releases, we do not have sponsored articles. . . . Just interesting news, views, discussions and opinions on how we can make a difference in this world. (SustainabilityForum.com, n.d.)

If a corporation wants to distribute a CSR-related news release, then the best online option is CSRwire.com. CSRwire.com positions itself as "the world's number one resource for corporate social responsibility news as well as the hub for an influential community that has realized the value and necessity of Corporate Social Responsibility and sustainability" (CSRwire, 2010). It offers news release distribution, archives of CSR reports, CSR videos, podcasting, and commentary. You can follow them on Twitter or become a fan on Facebook.

Controlled media do not have to be expensive. Recall that controlled media are controlled by the corporation. The corporation creates the message, selects the medium, and distributes the message. Starbucks, for instance, has long included simple brochures about their CSR initiatives at their cafes. They also provide much more extensive information about their CSR efforts at their website. Websites are low-cost options for providing detailed CSR information. Corporations frequently provide a section on their website about CSR, including any CSR or sustainability reports they produce. For example, Starbucks posts its annual "Global Responsibility Reports" that are available for download as PDF files. Starbucks' website also presents information about its CSR actions in great detail and provides visuals to reinforce the text. A more condensed version of its "Global Responsibility Report" is available online in the form of their "Global Responsibility Scorecard." Most companies provide attractive photographs and links to additional information for those interested in the details of their CSR initiatives. Providing both detailed and abbreviated descriptions of CSR efforts helps to meet the varying needs and interests of the readers.

Vodafone is one of many corporations that devotes a specific section of its corporate website to CSR. Recall that chapter 4 on formative research also presented detailed information about Vodafone's "Dialogues" website. Simply click on the "Corporate Responsibility" link on the Vodafone home page, and you are connected with a wealth of CSR information. The main topics include "Our Approach," "Consumer Issues," "Access to Communication," "Supply Chain," "Our People," "Environment," "Our Network," "Mobiles," "Masts and Health," "Our Socio-Economic Impact," "CR Dialogues," and "Publications & FAQs." Each of the main topics provides detailed information about that area. "Consumer Issues," for example, covers topics that Vodafone feels are important to maintaining consumer trust. Those issues include protection for inappropriate content, spam, responsible marketing, mobile advertising, clear pricing, mobile theft, privacy, safe driving, considerate mobile use, consumer campaigns, and product safety (Vodafone, n.d.-e). We can examine two of these topics further. "Clear Pricing" seeks to increase the clarity and transparency of pricing plans. This includes offering plans that are easy to understand and are written clearly (Vodafone, n.d.-a). "Mobile Theft" offers advice on how to prevent mobile phone theft and what to do if your mobile phone is stolen, and notes the equipment identity registers (EIRs) that Vodafone uses to immobilize and to block stolen mobile phones (Vodafone, n.d.-d).

Some corporations create separate websites focusing on CSR. For example, Intel has a CSR website, "CSR@Intel." The site is primarily a blog for its employees. In November 2009, MillerCoors launched a separate website for CSR under the title "GreatBeerGreatResponsiblity.com." The site provides detailed information to consumers and other stakeholders about MillerCoors CSR initiatives and even invites them to participate in some CSR efforts. The website divides CSR into three broad categories: (1) environmental sustainability, (2) alcohol responsibility, and (3) people and communities. Cornell Boggs, chief responsibility and ethics officer at MillerCoors, noted, "The new Web site gives us a unique opportunity to connect with consumers who enjoy our great beers, and would like to learn more about the responsibility behind those brands" (MillerCoors, 2009). The "Environmental Sustainability" section covers concerns such as water use, packaging sustainability, energy consumption, and waste reduction from the production process. "Alcohol Responsibility" includes discussions of drinking and driving, underage drinking (including responsible marketing), and drinking on college campuses.

The "People and Communities" section discusses the MillerCoors commitment to its employees and the communities in which it operates. Employee volunteerism has been an established practice developed by Coors and carried over into MillerCoors. The website states,

> We take great pride in contributing to our communities and dedicating our time to volunteerism. MillerCoors and its employees have a long tradition of supporting the communities where we live and work. Over the past several years, employee volunteers have collectively posted more than 60,000 hours per year. (MillerCoors, n.d.)

MillerCoors asks the stakeholders to get involved as well with a focus on water conservation and drunk-driving prevention. They provide a section where people can post messages about what they will do to help. People can enter messages up to 140 characters à la Twitter, and those messages are publicly displayed in the "What Will You Do to Help?" section of the "GreatBeerGreatResponsibility.com" website.

Employees as a Communication Channel

Morsing et al. (2008) found that effective CSR communication in Denmark relied upon an "inside-out approach." The *inside* refers to the employees. Effective CSR is grounded in employee support. Corporations must secure employee commitment to CSR concerns, a point we noted earlier in this book. The research reported that CSR communication reflected the CSR concerns that related to employees. The premise is that employees committed to CSR facilitate trustworthy CSR communication. Employees will verify messages that external stakeholders hear from the corporation as well as communicate their own positive messages about the corporation's CSR initiative.

Employees (internal stakeholders) often are overlooked in CSR communication in spite of their importance to the success of a CSR initiative. Employees provide a vital communication channel for a corporation. Friends and family often turn to employees as sources of information about corporations, including CSR efforts. The better informed employees are about CSR , the more effective they are at communicating about the organization's CSR activities. We are not implying that employees should be force-fed the "company line" and instructed to repeat it. Rather, employees should be well informed, and it is up to them to determine when and how they communicate about CSR to those outside the corporation. Research indicates that employees are generally underinformed about their corporation's CSR. As a result, a potentially valuable communication channel to external stakeholders is lost. Moreover, the opportunities for employees to feel a greater sense of involvement and identification with the CSR initiative are overlooked.

Employee blogs, Twitter accounts, and postings to discussion boards are additional low-cost options for extending the reach of CSR messages. Employees with blogs and Twitter accounts can be encouraged to include CSR information in their messages. Again, the corporation provides information and encourages employee discussion of CSR; they do not require the employees to mimic the company line. It is advantageous to have employees who work in CSR to be involved in the social media and to discuss their activities. Employees responsible for CSR initiatives can locate relevant online discussions and contribute their own posts. Such posts should always identify the corporation by name and mention that the employee's job is related to CSR. This disclosure is simply an extension of corporate transparency. Employees can provide a valuable communication channel for CSR if they are well informed on the subject. Their personal involvement and investment in CSR activities often make them highly credible and enthusiastic supporters of the initiatives. That is why employees should be a primary target for CSR communication. Employees want to know about their corporations, and the risk of a boomerang effect is minimized. It also is important to regard employees as receivers of information. Corporations should be interested in employees' formal and informal communication with family members, community members, and online contacts. Employees can be a valuable source of information about how those outside the corporation are reacting to the CSR initiatives.

External Stakeholders as a Communication Channel

External stakeholders can be significant communication assets for addressing the CSR promotional communication dilemma. Engagement can help to coordinate how stakeholders facilitate information dissemination about the CSR initiatives. Stakeholders can issue joint statements to the media, place information about the CSR initiative on their websites, and post information about the CSR initiative to various social media sites. In this way, the CSR promotion appears to be driven and delivered by interested stakeholders rather than the corporation. In addition to avoiding the stigma of self-promotion, the corporation reaps the benefits from the third-party endorsements and word-of-mouth communication.

Although many stakeholders will spontaneously transmit the information, engagement provides a structured approach to help facilitate stakeholder dissemination of CSR-related information. As with employees, the point is to avoid a heavy-handed push for the corporate line. Instead, stakeholders involved in the CSR process have unique insights, and the corporation can suggest ways of sharing that information with other stakeholders. The decision of whether or not to communicate and the nature of that communication still are the provenance of the stakeholders. As with any effective "viral" effort, the corporation plants ideas but does not control if and how they spread. Social media are key components to external word of mouth. The growing importance of social media demands a more thorough analysis of its application to CSR communication.

Strategic Application of Social Media to CSR Communication

Communicating the corporation's CSR messages in social media can be the basis for creating an echo. An *echo* occurs when people pick up the CSR messages and relay them to others – the online version of word-of-mouth communication. The CSR messages become viral. Viral efforts allow other people to transmit a corporation's message just as people transmit real viruses to others. Essentially, your stakeholders do the communication work for you. It is important to recognize that people may also contribute their own interpretations of the messages. However, when others add their own viewpoints, this may increase perceptions of the authenticity of the messages. We also should remember that viral efforts are uncontrolled and may never spread. Some viral efforts never gain traction. Moreover, this does not mean that every effort to communicate about CSR is or should be some type of viral campaign. Rather, the use of social media creates the potential for echoes to emerge.

There are solid theoretical reasons for including social media and hoping for an echo in CSR communication. Early mass communication researchers identified *the two-step flow of communication*. Katz and Lazarsfeld (1955) argued that the mass media's effect on people was through opinion leaders.

The mass media provide the information. Opinion leaders carefully monitor the mass media and collect the information. *Opinion leaders* are an elite group that others turn to for guidance on particular issues, including politics and consumer purchases. Different people can be opinion leaders on different issues. Opinion leaders then share a combination of the information from the mass media and their interpretation of the mass media information with other people. The two steps are (1) mass media to opinion leaders and (2) opinion leaders to others. The personal influence of the opinion leaders is what helps to create the mass media effect (Okada, 1986). The two-step flow requires that the opinion leaders be influential in shaping the attitudes and behaviors of those who turn to them for information and advice.

Although there have been challenges to the value of the two-step flow, it remains viable even today as an explanatory framework. In large measure, the "tipping point" idea popularized by Malcolm Gladwell (2002) is derived from the two-step flow model of information diffusion. Gladwell traces the popularity of some trends, such as Hush Puppy shoes, to opinion leaders who embrace the trend and spread it to others. Gladwell's (2002) work relies on the biological metaphor of epidemics that we find at the root of viral marketing. Burson-Marsteller developed the term *e-fluential* to refer to people who were influential (opinion leaders) online ("E-Fluentials," 2010). The e-fluentials represent about 10% of the US online adult population. Viral campaigns work online because e-fluentials are targeted with the message and then spread it to others. Keller and Berry (2003), authors of *The Influentials*, term these power people *influentials*. The two-step flow concept is at the heart of viral marketing even today.

Duncan Watts, a network researcher for Yahoo and PhD from Columbia University, has a different take on how messages spread through the Internet. Watts has used computer simulations to test the flow of ideas among people. His research concluded that influentials, opinion leaders, and e-fluentials are not the key. His research found that average people, not influentials, are more often responsible for the echoes that create viral effort success (Thompson, 2008). Watts argues that the people who actually create resonating echoes are random and accidental rather than easy to find and purposeful. Moreover, trends will only emerge if people (society) are ready to embrace the trends. The viral effort must have a foundation for success. This means the viral effort serves to amplify an existing need or concern rather than create a new one. The power of influentials is illusionary because researchers work backward from a successful viral effort and thereby impose structure and conclusions about cause and effect that may be unwarranted.

Watts and his colleague Johan Peretti (2007) favor the "big seed" approach. They argue that viral campaigns that target influentials are small seed approaches. A few seeds are planted with influentials with the hope they will take root and spread. This is done in part because people believe only these small seeds can create what they call a *cascade* where the message reaches a wide audience. In contrast, the big seed approach argues that a lot of people (seeds) should be targeted with the initial message. No effort is made to find the influentials; you simply use mass efforts to reach a broad spectrum of the target audience. Watts and Peretti (2007) believe any individual in this mass audience is capable of creating the cascade. You increase your odds of success if you plant a large number of seeds (the big seed approach) rather than gamble on a few seeds that are believed to be important but probably are no more important than any other seed.

The big seed concept retains the essence of the two-step model. The mass media are used to deliver a message (step 1). People who receive that message transmit the message to other people (step 2). The system can continue to multiply as people keep relaying the message to others. The echo rate (the number of new people infected by a person) can be low, but the viral effort can still be successful. Consider the following example. A big seed campaign targets 2,000 people with an average echo rate of 1. A total of 2,000 additional people are reached in the first round of infection. An influential campaign targets 100 people with an average echo rate of 10. A total of 1,000 people are reached in the first round of infection. With the big seed approach, the quantity of new infections relies on the large initial number of those infected rather than a few influentials infecting a large number of additional people (Watts & Peretti, 2007). The argument for using social media is that they facilitate the ability of people to share messages. We should note that Watts's big seed approach does not exclude influentials from the mix of seeds. Rather, he sees folly in relying solely on the influentials (Thompson, 2008).

It may seem that we have drifted far from our initial point of using social media to promote CSR efforts. However, the journey through the two-step flow and viral-marketing process provides a rationale for crafting a CSR social media strategy. With echoes, the CSR communication is carried by the stakeholders. Hence, social media provide an opportunity to reach people while appearing low cost and low effort, and using third parties. Corporations should identify the social media channels to utilize and any specialized online CSR outlets to target. The corporation can post CSR information to the corporation's Facebook and Twitter accounts as well as blogs linked to the corporation. Using the social media is part of the big seed approach. Fans on Facebook, followers on Twitter, and people reading the blogs are exposed to the message and can create echoes through retweets, posts on Facebook, and any other opportunity to share information with others such as social bookmarking using del.icio.us or Digg. The online echoes allow people to add commentary as well. This means there is an opportunity for people to add personal endorsements to the message. Of course, those who disagree can add their criticisms of the CSR efforts as well. Keep in mind that corporations have no control over if or how the CSR message echoes throughout the Internet.

Watts's (in Thompson, 2008) notion that people need to be ready to embrace a trend for one to develop has valuable insights for CSR communication. Management must select CSR concerns that have the potential to be embraced by stakeholders. Engaging stakeholders helps to determine what CSR concerns will resonate with stakeholders. Watts supplies more evidence that selecting the right CSR concern is more important than simply being involved in CSR. Moreover, managers may work to promote a particular CSR concern to reinforce its importance and relevance to stakeholders. Just promoting a CSR concern and not the corporation's CSR efforts in that area should avoid a backlash effect. Promoting a CSR concern in general is more CSR-centric rather than corporation-centric.

The social media posts can be paired with efforts to target important CSR online sources. As we discussed earlier in this chapter, CSR International reports CSR research and organizational actions on its website, through its listserv newsletters, and in its tweets. Also recall that CSRwire is a commonly used source for information about organization CSR efforts. It would be logical for corporations to use CSRwire to announce significant CSR actions. Justmeans.com is a site that, for a price, helps corporations to place their CSR messages on various social networks, track results of the communication, and create advocates for the corporation.

There are any number of CSR blogs that attract a great deal of attention as well. Working with CSR bloggers is a long-term investment. Corporations should resist pitching CSR stories to bloggers. Instead, corporations need to cultivate relationships over time. This involves understanding what type of information the blogger really wants, sharing relevant information with bloggers, and responding to their questions. For instance, do not send a blogger a modified version of a news release detailing a CSR effort. Instead, send a short message describing the CSR effort with links for additional information, an email contact address, and the option to receive future information through RSS. We are simply offering some options here, not making specific recommendations. Refer back to Box 6.2 for a summary of the key ideas for CSR and social media options. The social media offer low cost in terms of both price and effort. People know that online posts cost virtually nothing and do not seem to involve a great deal of effort. This makes it an ideal vehicle for CSR promotional communication.

The Overall CSR Promotional Communication Strategy

Regardless of the communication channels used, the corporation must develop its overall CSR promotional communication strategy for social reporting. Managers must decide if its CSR promotional communication should be annual or more continuous in focus. Some corporations opt for an annual report that ties CSR promotional communication to the corporate responsibility or sustainability report. The corporate responsibility report becomes the focal point of the CSR messaging. Stakeholders should be aware that the annual report has been released, be exposed to its highlights, be encouraged to view the report online, and be asked to provide feedback on the report. Even an annual approach should include engagement through feedback on the report.

While the corporate responsibility report is a natural anchor for CSR promotional communication, it does not alter the fact that corporations are involved with CSR on a continuous basis. Although a corporation may not have CSR-related news to communicate every day, CSR-related activities occur continuously throughout the year. Continuous promotional communication is more robust and should appear as an ongoing conversation with stakeholders about CSR. Being part of a conversation should engender greater trust in CSR messages than the occasional statement on the subject. Corporate websites should be updated frequently to report ongoing activities. Rather than framing CSR as a once-a-year topic, as is the case in the annual report approach, the continuous approach demonstrates it is a topic the corporation contemplates regularly. Again, social media are an excellent resource in this endeavor. Given the nature of social media, periodic CSR messages will not appear to overpromote. Stakeholders expect regular blog entries, tweets, and posts to Facebook. The CSR section of the website or a stand-alone website provides other valuable communication channels. Again, stakeholders expect website content to be updated regularly. Using a combination of social media and websites will not make it appear as though the corporation is devoting too much time and money on promoting its CSR initiatives.

Annual Reports and CSR Communication

Many corporations use annual reports to summarize their CSR efforts. These reports typically are called *CSR reports* or *sustainability reports*. The two names reflect the growing similarity between CSR and sustainability. Some corporations use alternative names. For example, as we discussed earlier, Starbucks calls theirs a "Global Responsibility Report." At present, there are no standardized requirements for CSR reporting in most countries.

Corporations are free to present their CSR information as they wish. They choose what to report about their CSR initiatives as well as how to report it. Of course, corporations with strong CSR performances are probably more motivated to disclose information than those that have not had strong performances.

The concerns surrounding CSR communication have led a growing number of corporations to adopt a more structured reporting method. Here we offer two well-known structured reporting frameworks: the Global Reporting Initiative, which is associated with the UN; and the ISO 26000, which is affiliated with the International Organization for Standards. These comprehensive social-reporting methods offer guidance on balanced reporting.

In 1997, the UN Environmental Program worked with various partners to create guidelines for the voluntary reporting of a company's economic, social, and environmental activities. These guidelines are called the Global Reporting Initiative. GRI is the dominant framework for CSR and sustainability reports globally. It identifies what to report and how to report it. The centerpiece of company reports is the performance indicators for sustainability. The performance indicators report the measured effects of the company in three broad areas: (1) economic, (2) environmental, and (3) social. The social indicator is further divided into labor practices and decent work, human rights, society, and product responsibility. Essentially the performance indicators inventory the key topics that companies must cover in their CSR reporting. Below are the definitions of the three areas and subcategories that can be used to guide the creation of CSR reports based on the GRI.

Economic: "the organization's impacts on the economic conditions of its stakeholders and on economic systems at local, national, and global levels" (Global Reporting Initiative, 2006, p. 26).

Economic performance
Market presence
Indirect economic impacts

Environmental: "an organization's impacts on living and non-living natural systems, including ecosystems, land, air, and water" (Global Reporting Initiative, 2006, p. 27).

Materials
Energy
Emission, effluents, and waste
Water
Biodiversity
Products and services
Compliance

- Transport
- Overall

Social: "the impacts an organization has on the social systems within which it operates" (Global Reporting Initiative, 2006, p. 29).

- Labor practices and decent work
  - Employment
  - Labor-management relations
  - Occupational health and safety
  - Diversity and equal opportunity
  - Training and education
- Human rights
  - Investment and procurement practices
  - Nondiscrimination
  - Freedom of association and collective bargaining
  - Child labor
  - Forced and compulsory labor
  - Security practices
  - Indigenous rights
- Society
  - Community
  - Corruption
  - Public policy
  - Anticompetitive behavior
  - Compliance
- Product responsibility
  - Customer health and safety
  - Product and service labeling
  - Marketing and communications
  - Customer privacy
  - Compliance

The work of well-known organizations such as the United Nations can provide a framework for organizing CSR information. For example, in its "Global Responsibility Report" for 2009, Starbucks (2009b) explains it is a member of the UN Global Compact and that it sees its corporate mission as consistent with the 10 guiding principles of the compact. The website lists the 10 principles of the UN Global Compact, identifies areas of Starbuck's operations it feels are relevant to each of the principles, and identifies areas of its responsibility report that address each operations area. Clickable links provide opportunities to learn more about how Starbucks is addressing the issues. For example, principle number 9 of the UN Global Compact states, "Businesses should encourage the development and diffusion of environmentally friendly technologies." The responsibility report then lists four areas of relevance to Starbucks: (1) environment (including recycling, climate change, energy, water, and green building as subsets of "environment"), (2) climate change, (3) green store design, and (4) cups. Each of these categories also includes clickable links where readers can obtain more information. The report also lists organizations that advise them on their global responsibility initiatives. For example, Conservation International is listed with an explanation noting that the organization advises on issues related to ethical sourcing. The logo for Conservation International also is clickable and provides additional information about the organization and its functions.

ISO is the International Organization for Standards and a familiar name for those in international business. ISO, Greek for "equal," is a name rather than an acronym. ISO is a nongovernmental organization composed of national standards institutes from 129 nations. Its role is to create and publish international standards on a wide array of business concerns. ISO facilitates international business through standardization. In 2001, ISO instituted a committee to investigate the possibility of creating standards for social responsibility. The interest stemmed from the fact that CSR was increasing in importance globally and stakeholders needed some way to assess the social integrity of organizations. Working drafts of CSR documents began circulating in 2005. The 2004 preliminary report noted how social responsibility is complicated because it means different things to different people. As result, ISO focused not on creating the "one" definition of CSR but on identifying the essential characteristics of social responsibility (International Organization for Standardization [ISO], 2004). ISO 26000, the final draft of international CSR standards, was circulated in 2009 with a vote ending in 2010. The ISO 26000 standards were then published in 2010 (ISO, 2010a).

On November 1, 2010, the ISO 26000, providing guidance for social responsibility, was formally released. Here is the announcement describing ISO 26000:

> ISO 26000 is an ISO International Standard giving guidance on SR. It is intended for use by organizations of all types, in both public and private sectors, in developed and developing countries, as well as in economies in transition. It will assist them in their efforts to operate in the socially responsible manner that society increasingly demands. ISO 26000 contains voluntary guidance, not requirements, and therefore is not for use as a certification standard like ISO 9001:2008 and ISO 14001:2004. (ISO, 2010)

The report contains information on scope, terms and definitions, understanding social responsibility, the principles of social responsibility, recognizing social responsibility and engaging stakeholders, guidance on social responsibility core subjects, guidance on integrating social responsibility throughout an organization, and examples of voluntary initiatives and tools for social responsibility.

ISO 26000 provides another set of international guidelines for CSR, but it is a voluntary program, not a certification program, and does not include specific requirements. Instead, ISO 26000 attempts to create a common set of concepts, definitions, and methods of evaluation. It recognizes that CSR is complex and variable from industry to industry and country to country. As ISO stated, "There is a range of many different opinions as to the right approach ranging from strict legislation at one end to complete freedom at the other" (ISO, 2010b). ISO is looking for a golden middle way that promotes respect and responsibility based on known reference documents without stifling creativity and development. ISO 26000 should meet the demands of stakeholders and corporations interested in social responsibility reporting.

As with the GRI, ISO 26000 emphasizes engaging stakeholders in CSR. Section 5 of the ISO 26000 draft is devoted to engaging stakeholders. Section 6 identifies the seven core subjects that should be addressed in CSR efforts: (1) organizational governance, (2) human rights, (3) labor practices, (4) the environment, (5) fair operating practices, (6) consumer issues, and (7) community involvement and development (ISO, 2009). The seven core CSR subjects are defined below.

Organizational governance: "the system by which an organization makes and implements decisions in pursuit of its objectives" (ISO, 2009, p. 21).
Human rights: "the basic rights to which all human beings are entitled because they are human beings" (p. 22).
Labor practices: "encompass all policies and practices relating to work performed within, by or on behalf of the organization" (p. 32).
Environment: considers the impacts of an organization's decisions and behavior on the environment that can include "the organization's use of living and non-living resources, the location of the activities of the organization, the generation of pollution and waste, and the implications of the organization's activities, products and services for natural habitats" (p. 40).
Fair operating practices: these "concern ethical conduct in an organization's dealings with other organizations and individuals" (p. 46).
Consumer issues: these "include providing education and accurate information, using fair, transparent and helpful marketing [of] information and contractual processes and promoting sustainable consumption" (p. 50).
Community involvement and development: seeks to "enhance the public good – helps to strengthen civil society" (p. 58), and "encompasses support for and identification within the community" (p. 59).

Each of the seven CSR subjects is further delineated by identifying key issues within each subject. For instance, the environment issues include prevention and pollution, sustainable resource use, climate change mitigation and adaptation, and protection of the environment and restoration of natural habitats (ISO, 2009).

These two recognized social-reporting frameworks can offer guidance to corporations that want to develop a method of communicating with stakeholders about their CSR initiatives. Both GRI and ISO 26000 provide corporations with ideas of the general content and structure of annual CSR reports. However, such annual reports are just one aspect of CSR communication. Managers must decide how the annual reports fit within their larger CSR communication efforts.

Conclusion and Critical Questions

Communication often is treated as a simple transmission task of sending information to people. Managers develop a CSR initiative and then communicate it to the stakeholders. Although this view oversimplifies the communication process, some communication may seem more one-way than two-way at times. However, no overall communication effort should rely on the simple transmission of information with no concern for feedback from those receiving the messages. The stakeholder engagement process remains valuable for soliciting reactions to CSR-related information provided through controlled and uncontrolled media.

We have identified a series of questions that managers should consider when developing their CSR communication efforts. In the next chapter on evaluation and feedback, we elaborate on how stakeholders should be involved throughout this communication process.

Critical Questions for Communicating the CSR Initiative	*Relevant Parties*	
	Corporation	*Stakeholders*
Which internal and external stakeholders should be targeted?	X	X
How should the CSR message be communicated to internal stakeholders (employees)?	X	
How should the CSR message be communicated to external stakeholders?	X	X
Which communication channels should be used to reach internal stakeholders?	X	
Which communication channels should be used to reach external stakeholders?	X	X

Critical Questions for Communicating the CSR Initiative	*Relevant Parties*	
	Corporation	*Stakeholders*
What steps can be taken to prevent a backlash from overpromotion?	X	
How could early feedback systems be used to help adjust the CSR communication effort, including detection of a backlash?	X	X
Will the communication effort be report driven or more regular in its presentation?	X	X
What is the potential for creating a partnership between the corporation and stakeholders?	X	X
What potential exists for using social media to communicate the CSR concern?	X	
What potential exists for direct third-party endorsements?	X	
What potential exists for indirect third-party endorsements?	X	

The starting point is deciding which internal and external stakeholders should receive the messages. Identifying the targets guides the presentation of the CSR messages and the selection of communication channels. Combined, the targets, messages, and channels provide the raw materials for the CSR communication plan. Internal stakeholders should be an early target because they can then serve as an additional channel for communicating the CSR initiative to external stakeholders. A critical concern is a backlash whereby the communication about the CSR initiative creates harm rather than good. As noted earlier, a variety of actions can be taken to reduce the likelihood of a backlash, including reliance on online channels to reduce the appearance of overpromoting the CSR initiative. It is important to detect any early signs of a backlash and general reactions to the CSR communication effort in order to make necessary corrections to the communication plan. We began the discussion of backlash with the final selection of a CSR initiative because some stakeholders will be aware of the choice at that stage of the CSR process. However, many stakeholders will not learn about the selection of a CSR initiative until it is announced through the CSR communication. Again, managers should prepare messages designed for coping with negative stakeholder reactions to a CSR initiative.

Finally, managers must decide if the CSR initiative communication will be driven by an annual CSR report or a regular exchange of CSR information with stakeholders. Stakeholders have a vested interest in who is targeted, messaging, channel selection, and feedback on the CSR initiative.

Stakeholders want accurate information from the messages, and feedback provides additional influence over the CSR process. At present, there are no standardized requirements for CSR reporting. Companies are free to present their CSR information as they wish. They choose what to report about their CSR initiatives as well as how to report it. Careful attention should be devoted to CSR communication because of its role in the overall strategic process.

Novartis, a major pharmaceutical company headquartered in Switzerland, describes four pillars of citizenship: patients, people and community, environment, and ethical business conduct. Courtesy of Novartis International AG, Basel, Switzerland

The BBC (British Broadcasting Corporation) is the world's largest broadcaster. It provides public service broadcasting all over the world via television, online, and radio. Courtesy of BBC

7

Evaluation and Feedback

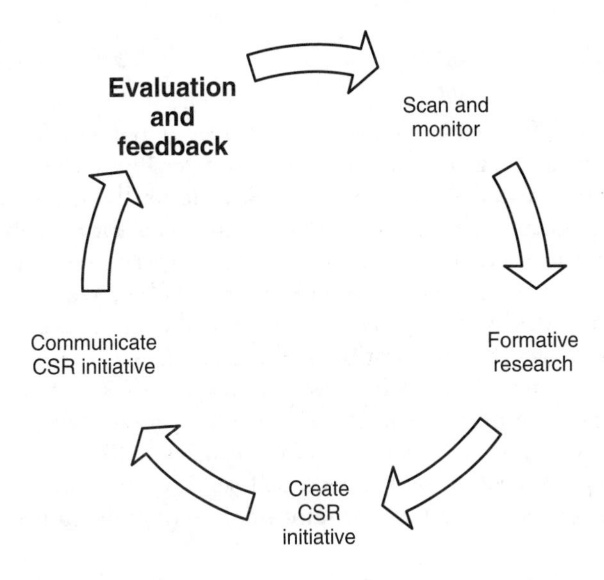

Ultimately, CSR initiatives are about creating change. Effective CSR initiatives should have positive effects on both society and the corporation. CSR is designed to benefit society, and corporate benefits help to justify CSR expenditures. Once the CSR initiative is operational, its effects can be evaluated. Evaluation is predicated on having measurable objectives. Data are

Managing Corporate Social Responsibility: A Communication Approach, First Edition.
W. Timothy Coombs, Sherry J. Holladay.

collected and used to determine whether or not the CSR initiative reached its stated outcome objectives. Feedback from stakeholders is useful as well because it can provide insights into refining the CSR initiative and the overall CSR process. Evaluation is the formal process of assessing the success of the CSR initiative. In contrast, feedback focuses on stakeholders. The corporation collects stakeholder reactions to the CSR initiatives, the CSR process, and the effectiveness of CSR communication. This chapter explores the utility of evaluation and feedback in the CSR process and how this fifth stage naturally segues into the first stage of the CSR process, scanning and monitoring.

Evaluation

Evaluation and feedback comprise the fifth stage of the CSR process. It would be misleading to call evaluation and feedback the "final" step. The evaluation and feedback processes flow naturally into scanning and monitoring processes because feedback really is a form of monitoring. The corporation, working with stakeholders (perhaps including third parties), should assess whether or not the stated objectives were achieved (evaluation). Ideally, the objectives include the desired effects of the CSR initiative on the corporation and the effects on society and stakeholders. Too often, corporations report how the CSR initiative benefits them and provide no information about how it might have affected the stakeholders it was designed to help (Blowfield, 2007; Smith, 2003). This makes the CSR initiative look self-serving, a point we discussed in conjunction with the CSR promotional communication dilemma in chapter 6.

A focal point in evaluation is whether or not the CSR initiative's objectives have been achieved. Managers must avoid the mistake of developing assessments that reflect only corporate concerns such as reputational benefits. Doing so would only confirm stakeholders' fears about exclusion from the full CSR process. The engagement process may appear fraudulent when stakeholder concerns are omitted. Stakeholders may have questions about the veracity of the evaluation data when they are neglected in this process.

As noted in chapter 5 on creating the CSR initiative, process objectives and outcome objectives are commonly confused. For evaluative purposes, processes and outcomes are very different. CSR and sustainability reports lean heavily toward reporting what corporations have done (process) rather than emphasizing the effects or impacts of those actions (outcomes). Recall that *process objectives* track what is done during the communication process, while *outcome objectives* are used to assess the effectiveness (success or failure) of the communication process (Coombs, 2005). Although it is important to document and report process objectives because stakeholders need to know what actions are being taken, true evaluation demands assessment of outcome objectives.

Let's explore further the distinction between process and outcome objectives. Recall that the importance of objectives and the difference between process and outcome objectives were introduced in chapter 5. Process objectives simply describe the CSR activities. Sometimes corporations report only process objectives in an attempt to appear transparent. However, these reports are misleading because actions themselves are not a substitute for measurable effects. Consider these sample objectives from ING's 2009 corporate sustainability report: (1) 15% of the ING management council will be women, (2) 25% of the business units will set targets for electricity and paper use, and (3) ING will develop a program to stimulate sustainable entrepreneurship (ING, 2010). Of these three, only the first objective is a true outcome objective that is measurable. However, even that objective does not develop the societal impact of altering the gender composition of the management council. The effects can be discussed in accompanying text, but that is not the same as providing measured progress on the societal effects. The more significant information about the results of CSR initiatives comes from the evaluation of outcome objectives.

Outcome objectives assess the specific results of the actions that were taken. What happened as a result of these CSR initiatives? Although measurements of effectiveness can be difficult to conduct, they are a necessary component of evaluation. Reporting outcome objectives indicates the extent to which the CSR initiatives were effective and for whom. Did the changes implemented produce the targeted reductions in emissions? How much paper was saved by making all documents electronic? What were the cost savings from installing energy-efficient lighting? How did regular inspections of production facilities reduce the number of labor violations reported in an Indonesian factory? How many children in the target population received free vaccines? Outcome objectives should provide specific data about how the CSR initiative affected society. Reporting outcome objectives also helps the corporation determine its return on CSR investments. This could provide important information for financial stakeholders who are cautious about embracing CSR.

Of course, a potential danger in reporting outcome objectives is that they reveal the "truth" about CSR performance. Corporations should have hard data for evaluation purposes. They certainly rely on hard data to evaluate other aspects of business performance. But CSR initiatives may be labeled by some stakeholders or corporations as failures if they do not reach their specified targets. The corporation may be reluctant to report its CSR shortcomings. When evaluation data fail to support the value of a particular initiative, that initiative needs to be reviewed and perhaps reformulated. Why should a corporation continue to invest resources when desired outcomes are not achieved? The engagement process may help to identify alternatives or encourage reconsideration of ideas that were previously rejected. In addition, it may be the case that a short-term outcome objective has fallen short of expectations. But a long-term outcome objective might be reached if the corporation remains committed to pursuing the initiative. Failure to reach objectives can be demoralizing for those involved in the initiatives and engagement process. Regardless of what the data reveal, collecting and evaluating data on outcome objectives are good ideas. They contribute to transparency and can lead to a realistic appraisal of progress on CSR initiatives.

At http://www.starbucks.com/responsibility/learn-more/goals-and-progress, readers interested in Starbuck's "Global Responsibility" reports can download them in PDF format or view specific portions of them. In addition, readers can click on the "Global Responsibility Scorecard" to view an abbreviated version of the report. In 2009, the "Scorecard" presented the corporation's goals, progress, and specific statistics related to their Shared Planet goals. The scorecard also provided an evaluation of Starbuck's progress toward the goals. Each goal statement appears in a row followed by a description of the progress toward that goal using these labels: "achieved," "on track," or "needs improvement." A more precise description of the progress is offered along with statistics and graphic displays to help readers visualize the level of progress toward the goal. For long-term goals (e.g., goals that set a time frame for achievement, such as doubling farmer loans by 2015), the "on track" designation signaled that Starbucks' efforts are likely to meet that future-oriented goal. Another long-term goal, mobilizing employees and customers to contribute more than 1 million hours of community service per year by 2015, was evaluated as "needs improvement" because service hours actually decreased by 24% in 2009 compared to 2008. Some goals such as doubling purchases of FairTrade-certified coffee in 2009 were evaluated as "achieved" to indicate the specific outcome objective was reached because purchases increased from 19 million pounds in 2008 to 39 million pounds in 2009 (Starbucks, 2009a). Starbucks reports indicate transparency of outcome objectives and progress toward those objectives. They move beyond merely reporting process objectives and provide specific data and useful visuals to support their claims of progress in their CSR initiatives.

Assurance and CSR Evaluation

When corporations themselves present the data and information about objectives, it raises the question of assurance. *Assurance* is an established process in accounting. It involves having an outside, independent third party review and verify the information and communication that a corporation is providing to its stakeholders, including government officials. The assurance statement presents in writing the verification from the third-party source. There are a number of international requirements for the assurance of financial information. Clearly, CSR outcome evaluation data would benefit from assurance. However, there is no mandatory international code governing assurance of CSR. That does not mean you will not encounter CSR assurance statements. In fact, CSR assurance is considered a growth industry (Scott, 2008). The growth is much faster in Europe than in the United States. Around 30% of European reports contain assurance statements compared to only 7% in the United States. Assurance is discussed in connection with annual reports that provide data about the corporation's financial performance. In 2008, around 3,000 CSR reports were published globally and about 750 included an external assurance statement.

If there is no set standard, what guides CSR assurance? CSR assurance draws from two sources that address the principles of independence of assurance with a focus on CSR: AA100AS and the International Standard on Assurance Engagements (ISAE 100). The AA1000AS describes itself as

> unique as it requires the assurance provider to evaluate the extent of adherence to a set of principles rather than simply assessing the reliability of the data. AA1000AS (2008) requires the assurance provider to look at underlying management approaches, systems and processes and how stakeholders have participated. Using AA1000AS, the assurance provider evaluates the nature and extent to which an organisation adheres to the AccountAbility Principles. (AccountAbility, 2008)

ISAE 100 claims it

> was designed to provide a basic framework for large scale audits concerned with non-financial data process monitoring. These types of audits include environmental, social and sustainability reports; auditing of information systems, internal control, and corporate governance processes; and compliance audits for grant conditions, contracts and regulations. (IHS, 2008)

There is no one, accepted code, but there are some shared guidelines for CSR assurance.

Who conducts CSR assurance? A variety of actors supply CSR assurance. The dominant providers are major accounting firms, certification organizations, and specialized CSR consultancies (Scott, 2008). The belief is that the CSR assurance will increase the credibility of the CSR reports by verifying the data and, in some cases, the processes related to CSR. Assurance is a formalized third-party endorsement. In most countries, CSR reporting, including assessment of objectives, is still voluntary. Assurance adds an additional level of confidence to stakeholders who are reading and evaluating unregulated statements that corporations are making about the evaluation of their CSR efforts. Some verification from an independent, third-party source can enhance the believability of outcome evaluations provided in CSR or sustainability reports and other CSR messaging. Box 7.1 presents a sample assurance statement from the Musgrave Group's 2006 sustainability report.

Stakeholder Engagement in the Evaluation Process

Corporations and stakeholders should collaborate in deciding how to assess the objectives and report the results. Failure to engage stakeholders in the assessment and reporting process could taint the legitimacy of the CSR effort. Remember that stakeholders must remain relevant throughout the CSR process. Evaluation is very communication oriented because data must be collected, interpreted, and reported. Stakeholders can assist the collection and evaluation of data and/or help to verify the data collected by the corporation. Stakeholders must believe the evaluative data are credible, and continued stakeholder involvement in the data collection contributes to its credibility. To bolster confidence in the results, third-party sources can verify the results and/or conduct the evaluative research, and/or stakeholders can be involved in the evaluation process. Involving stakeholders in the evaluation process increases the transparency of the evaluation of objectives.

It is possible that stakeholders and corporations may differ in their interpretation of the meaning of objectives. For example, it may be the case that stakeholders are satisfied with the accomplishment of process objectives even though the corporation is disappointed with the initiative's failure to reach particular outcome objectives. For stakeholders, the fact that the corporation engaged in some action like giving employees time off from work to volunteer at a local food bank may be more important than the fact that the specific target number of employees who participated during the specified time frame did not reach the corporation's outcome objective. Along the same lines, stakeholders may be relatively uninterested in a corporation's return on investment (ROI). But the ROI does matter to

Box 7.1 Musgrave Group Assurance Statement 2006

Independent Assurance Statement

Scope and Objectives

Musgrave Group (Musgrave) commissioned csrnetwork to undertake a limited assurance engagement over the information and data within the printed version of the Musgrave 2006 Sustainability Report ('the Report'). The objectives of the assurance process were to check claims and the systems for collection of data, and to review the arrangements for the management and reporting of sustainability issues. The assurance process was conducted in accordance with the AA1000 Assurance Standard, and we have commented on the report against the principles of materiality, completeness and responsiveness. A review of Musgrave's performance against the UN Global Compact Principles was not included in the scope of our work. Any financial information contained within the reports is excluded from the scope of this assurance process.

Responsibilities of the Directors of Musgrave and the Assurance Providers

The directors of Musgrave have sole responsibility for the preparation of the Report. In performing our assurance activities, our responsibility is to the management of Musgrave, however our statement represents our independent opinion and is intended to inform all Musgrave stakeholders including the management of Musgrave. We were not involved in the preparation of any part of the Report. We have no other contract with Musgrave. This is the third time that we have acted as independent assurance providers for Musgrave. We adopt a balanced approach towards all Musgrave stakeholders and a Statement of Impartiality relating to our contract with Musgrave will be made available on request. The opinion expressed in this assurance statement should not be relied upon as the basis for any financial or investment decisions. The independent assurance team for this contract with Musgrave comprised Mark Line and Jon Woodhead. Further information, including a statement of competencies relating to the team can be found at: www.csrnetwork.com.

(*Continued*)

Basis of Our Opinion

Our work was designed to gather evidence to obtain a limited level of assurance on which to base our conclusions. We undertook the following activities:

- We conducted interviews with a selection of directors and senior managers responsible for areas of management and stakeholder relationships covered by the Report. The objective of these discussions was to understand Musgrave's governance arrangements and management priorities;
- We discussed Musgrave's approach to stakeholder engagement with relevant managers, although we undertook no direct engagement with stakeholders (other than employees and management) to test the findings from these discussions;
- We conducted a top level review of issues raised by external parties that could be relevant to Musgrave's policies to provide a check on the appropriateness of statements made in the report;
- Subject to the exclusions set out below, we reviewed data collated at the corporate level for accuracy and completeness, and against claims made in the Report. This process included a review of the systems and processes for data collection and analysis. Specific data were checked for consistency against these systems and processes. The scope of our work did not include visits to operational sites. Selected performance data at site and Divisional level were reviewed as part of our review of consolidated corporate data.
- We undertook an assessment of the company's reporting and management processes against the principles of materiality, completeness and responsiveness as described in the AA1000 Assurance Standard.
- We reviewed the Report against the Global Reporting Initiative (GRI) 2006 Sustainability Reporting Guidelines (Draft), including application of the principles and use of indicators.

Observations

Materiality – has Musgrave provided information on material issues to enable stakeholders to make informed judgements?

- With the exception of the issues noted below, the Report includes information on Musgrave's main sustainability performance issues and should enable stakeholders to make informed judgements. For the first time this year, the results of stakeholder engagement have been systematically analysed to assist in determining the contents or focus for reporting.

Source: Musgrave Group (2006).

Box 7.2 Basic ROI Formula

$$\text{Return on Investment} = \frac{(\text{Gain from Investment} - \text{Cost of Investment})}{\text{Cost of Investment}}$$

managers. The possibility of different perceptions of "success" and "failure" highlights the need for communication between stakeholders and the corporation. The objectives and progress toward those objectives should be documented and reported. But the meaning of the outcomes may differ for stakeholders and the corporation.

Considering Return on Investment

Return on investment is an important corporate concept for judging success. ROI is a way of assessing the value of corporate spending. Box 7.2 presents a commonly used ROI formula. ROI works well when all of the factors can be expressed in monetary amounts. Suppose a corporation invests $500,000 in a project over four years. The project results in returns of $3.5 million over the four years. The ROI over the four period years is 86%. The ROI calculation is heavily dependent on what counts as costs and what counts as returns. For CSR, costs and returns can be difficult to define and to assess.

Corporations treat CSR costs as the costs to the corporation for the CSR initiative. Should those costs include contributions from stakeholders? Stakeholders often supply their time and efforts. How do you quantify stakeholder costs? Would stakeholder costs be added to and subtracted from the corporate costs when calculating ROI? You could argue that the stakeholders are underwriting the corporate costs to a degree and therefore they should be subtracted. Or you could argue that the stakeholder costs are part of the total cost of the CSR initiative.

Costs are simple compared to returns. Corporations are looking at returns to assess the validity of the business argument for CSR. Returns are defined in terms of financial gains and reputational gains. Reputational gains are harder to quantify but corporations do recognize and attempt to assess this valuable symbolic asset. A common ROI for CSR includes the amount of money a corporation has saved from sustainability efforts. In spite of the fact that CSR initiatives are supposed to benefit society, the return for society is often neglected by corporations. What are the societal returns? Frequently a return is the end of some societal harm such as child labor. How do you quantify that return? We can list that child laborers have been removed from the corporation's supply chain but the societal value reaches beyond those numbers. It is difficult to place a price on having just one less child laborer in the supply chain. Is it enough to specify progress toward social improvement as a return? Can we really place a monetary value on that? As this discussion illustrates, determining ROI can be challenging.

Feedback

Feedback can be independent of evaluation. Feedback involves assessing stakeholder reactions to the CSR initiative as well as to the engagement process in which they participated. Managers need to hear both positive and negative feedback from stakeholders about their reactions to the corporation's efforts. Furthermore, employees should be among the stakeholders solicited for feedback. Stakeholders have an interest in all but the corporate objectives and perhaps the communication audit questions. Stakeholders want to make sure their views on the CSR initiative are heard and will be taken into account by management. Do stakeholders feel the CSR initiative is effective? How well do they believe it addresses the social concern? Do they feel it does enough? What additional information about the initiative would they like to see reported? What might be done in the future to improve the CSR initiative? Could additional elements be added to improve the implementation or assessment of the initiative? Were there any unintended consequences from the CSR initiative? What else could the corporation be doing to help society?

It is important to note that the corporation's efforts to solicit feedback from stakeholders return the CSR process to the scanning and monitoring stage discussed in chapter 3. CSR is a continuous process, much like quality improvement processes. There always will be more that a corporation can learn and could do. Stakeholder reactions to the CSR initiative provide valuable insights and connect directly to monitoring.

Feedback from Stakeholders on the CSR Process

The CSR process is designed to identify what a corporation can reasonably do by working with stakeholders on the development of CSR initiatives. We can separate CSR process evaluations into two cases: (1) when no action is taken by the corporation and (2) when a new CSR initiative is implemented. It is possible that through engagement, CSR ideas are discussed but are not translated into corporate action. In the first case, the corporation must gauge how stakeholders are reacting to the decision not to pursue the CSR issue. Engagement permits direct discussion with stakeholders about the lack of action. In addition, other data-gathering techniques such as surveys, statements in the news media, and statements posted online can be used to collect feedback from stakeholders. When corporations decide not to take action, they need to understand the overall sense of the reaction: will stakeholders be quiescent (accept it) or take action against the corporation (engage in stakeholder churn)? When stakeholders feel like the engagement process was genuinely two-way, they may be less likely to be surprised by any corporate decision. Important questions to consider include the following:

- Are stakeholders angry enough to take action against the corporation?
- Do stakeholders accept the corporation's justification for not taking action at this time?
- Do stakeholders want to restart engagement on the CSR concern?

Answers to these questions will dictate what actions the corporation must now pursue in relation to the particular CSR concern. Stakeholder reactions to CSR initiatives can provide information for refining the efforts. In essence, the feedback transitions the CSR process back to scanning and monitoring. It would be useful to know if stakeholders felt the CSR initiative was sufficient and effective, in addition to knowing what else stakeholders might like to see done to address the CSR concern.

In the second case where a CSR initiative is implemented, feedback about the process is needed as well. How satisfied are they with the engagement process? Corporations also can solicit feedback from stakeholders about the initiative itself. Important questions to consider include the following:

- How satisfied are they with the outcome?
- What additional issues remain unresolved with this CSR concern?
- What else might be done?

By improving the overall CSR process, the corporation can increase the effectiveness of its CSR initiatives and stakeholder satisfaction with those initiatives. A critical concern for feedback is that the CSR process as a whole is viewed as just. As discussed in chapter 5, perceptions of organizational justice are central to stakeholder satisfaction with the engagement process. Feedback may signal that future engagement efforts must be modified to enhance perceptions of justice.

The Communication Audit

Finally, corporations might want to execute a *communication audit* for the CSR initiative. Corporations could survey stakeholders concerning: (1) their knowledge of the CSR initiative, (2) how they learned about the CSR initiative (communication channels), and (3) their preferred channels for CSR information. The communication audit could be executed along with any surveys that assess reactions to the CSR initiative. The audit data would help improve future CSR communication. The corporation would be able to determine what information reached stakeholders and the utility of various channels that could be used for CSR communication. A CSR communication audit can indicate strengths and weaknesses in the CSR communication plan. For example, it may reveal that social media were highly effective for reaching stakeholders but failed to provide the specificity they wanted or that stakeholders preferred receiving CSR information from uncontrolled media compared to controlled media. Managers can build on the strengths and look to correct the weaknesses in future communication about CSR initiatives. The information obtained from a communication audit is likely to be of greater interest to the corporation than to stakeholders. However, there is no reason why the audit information cannot be shared with stakeholders who are interested in the results.

Conclusion and Critical Questions

After the CSR initiative is in full operation, it is time to assess whether or not it met the stated objectives. *Evaluation* refers to the formal process of assessing the success of the CSR initiative. In contrast, *feedback* involves soliciting stakeholder reactions to the CSR initiatives rather than the assessment of outcome objectives.

Critical Questions for Evaluation and Feedback	*Relevant Parties*	
	Corporation	*Stakeholders*
What evidence is there to support that the CSR initiative met stakeholder outcome objectives?	X	X
What evidence is there to support that the CSR initiative met the corporation's outcome objectives?	X	
What evidence is there to support that the CSR initiative met stakeholder process objectives?	X	X
What evidence is there to support that the CSR initiative met the corporation's process objectives?	X	
What type of assurance was provided for the outcome objective evaluation?	X	X
Is there a need for third-party verification of the CSR evaluation?	X	X
Which stakeholders should be involved in the evaluation process?	X	X
What role do stakeholders play in the evaluation process?	X	X
Do stakeholders feel the CSR initiative has sufficiently addressed the CSR concern?	X	X
Do stakeholders feel the CSR initiative is effective?	X	X
What might be done to improve the CSR initiative?	X	X
Do stakeholders feel the overall CSR process was just?	X	X
Do stakeholders accept the corporation's justification for not acting on a specific CSR concern?	X	X
Is a CSR communication audit warranted?	X	
Were there any unintended consequences from the CSR initiative?	X	X

Critical Questions for Evaluation and Feedback	*Relevant Parties*	
	Corporation	*Stakeholders*
Do stakeholders want to restart engagement on a neglected CSR concern?	X	X
Are stakeholders angry enough to take action against the corporation for neglecting a CSR concern?	X	X
What is the ROI on the CSR initiative for the corporation?	X	

A focal point in evaluation is whether or not the CSR initiative's objectives have been achieved. The objectives include those that concern the stakeholders and the corporation. Admittedly, some objectives may be more important to the corporation than to stakeholders, and vice versa. Managers must avoid the mistake of developing assessments that reflect only corporate concerns because doing so would only confirm stakeholders' fears about exclusion from the full CSR process. Sometimes corporations report only process objectives in an attempt to appear transparent and appease stakeholders. However, the more significant information about the results of CSR initiatives is provided by analyses of outcome objectives. Outcome objectives assess the specific results of the actions that were taken. What happened as a result of these CSR initiatives? Reporting outcome objectives can indicate the extent to which the CSR initiatives were effective and effective for whom. Although measurements of effectiveness can be difficult to conduct, they are a necessary component of evaluation. Reporting outcome objectives also helps the corporation determine its return on CSR investments. This could provide important information for financial stakeholders who were cautious about embracing CSR. In addition, managers should consider what the ROI is for society. Although return on investment can be difficult to assess, especially in the case of less tangible benefits for society, it is a necessary element in the evaluation process.

General feedback from stakeholders about the CSR initiative is valuable as well. Stakeholder reactions to CSR initiatives can provide information for refining to the efforts. In essence, the feedback transitions the CSR process back to scanning and monitoring. It would be useful to know if stakeholders felt the CSR initiative was sufficient and effective in addition to knowing what else stakeholders might like to see done to address the CSR concern. Future efforts might require changes to the process to increase perceptions of justice. Similarly, a CSR communication audit can indicate strengths and weaknesses in the CSR communication plan that can be addressed in the next iteration. Managers can build on the strengths and look to correcting the weaknesses in future CSR initiatives.

The potential negative effects of the CSR initiative must be considered. Carefully review the situation to determine if there were any unintended consequences from the CSR initiative. One serious unintended consequence could arise if certain stakeholders become angry enough to engage in churn. One reason for anger could be the corporation's failure to address the stakeholders' concerns. That is why it is helpful to assess reactions to the rationale the corporation provided for not taking action on a particular CSR concern. Stakeholders want to make sure their views on the CSR initiative are heard and will be taken into account by management.

8

CSR Issues

CSR can benefit both society and corporations. However, we must be aware of the word *can*. CSR initiatives also might result in no benefits to society, simply hide a social ill, or produce no benefits for the corporation. CSR is not a panacea for environmental and social problems, nor is it an investment with guaranteed returns for corporations. CSR has the potential to reduce harmful environmental and social concerns. Corporations may try to alleviate problems they have created or simply help to address broader social and environmental concerns that require attention. CSR efforts must be properly evaluated to determine whether or not they are helping to make the world a better place. We must know if the CSR initiative is simply some form of "washing" that gives the illusion of addressing a societal concern or if noneconomic stakeholders experience a tangible benefit from the efforts. We cannot assume that just because a CSR initiative is implemented it produces the promised societal benefits. Moreover, corporations cannot assume that engaging in CSR initiatives will produce the many business benefits often associated with CSR. The type of CSR effort undertaken, how it is enacted, and how it is communicated to stakeholders all have significant effects on whether or not a corporation realizes positive returns on its CSR investments.

It is easy to become cynical about CSR in general when some CSR initiatives are revealed as washing or serve to hide rather than to address a social problem. Managers also can become cynical if they believe that CSR may be just another fad that promises amazing returns on investments yet yields nothing. But cynicism should be resisted because it is equally easy to find

Managing Corporate Social Responsibility: A Communication Approach, First Edition.
W. Timothy Coombs, Sherry J. Holladay.

examples of where CSR initiatives are improving stakeholders' lives whilst benefiting the corporation engaging in the CSR efforts. Both stakeholders and managers should bring a healthy skepticism, not cynicism, to their involvement with CSR. But CSR should not be mindlessly embraced in a Pollyannaish fashion. Although CSR has an attractive public side, it can have a dark, seedy undercurrent as well. Stakeholders and managers should bring tempered optimism to CSR initiatives by maintaining a dose of skepticism and considering both the good and bad qualities of a CSR initiative. We have tried to raise awareness of CSR's positives and negatives for stakeholders and corporations throughout this book. We believe in the potential value of CSR but are not blind to the pitfalls it may entail.

Chapters 3 through 7 examined specific tasks and challenges related to each of the five phases in the CSR Process Model. In this chapter, we consider the bigger issues that managers need to consider. These issues are not confined to one phase of the CSR process but are salient to the CSR process as a whole. At various points in this book, we have touched upon these issues, but we include them here because of their importance to the overall CSR process. We have divided the issues into overarching concerns, responsibility for CSR, and limitations stemming from industry, law, and culture.

Overarching Concerns for CSR Initiatives

There are three overarching concerns that managers must consider when deciding to become involved in the CSR process. A failure to address these three issues is likely to doom a CSR program to failure. The first issue is the need to align stakeholder concerns with the strategic concerns of the corporation. To be effective, a CSR initiative must simultaneously be salient to stakeholders and support the corporation's business strategy. Admittedly, this is a pragmatic view of CSR. The effectiveness of a CSR initiative is defined in terms of benefits to both stakeholders and corporations. Some claim that corporations should "do the right thing" to improve society and not worry about the return on investment. A small number of CSR initiatives may fall into the purely altruistic category. However, the vast majority of CSR initiatives involve corporations reaping some benefit as well. As noted previously, those benefits might include improved employee morale, a more favorable reputation, increased sales, or reduced operating costs. CSR is more effective for corporations when it is integrated into their business strategies. Still, the CSR initiative must capture the concerns of stakeholders too. If a CSR initiative is not salient to stakeholders, it will be ignored by stakeholders and produce no benefit to the corporation.

The second issue is the need for tangible gains for stakeholders' concerns, not symbolic actions that simply appear to make the world a better place.

Throughout this book, we have repeatedly noted the danger of CSR-washing – giving the illusion of addressing environmental or social concerns when no substantive actions are taken or benefits are accrued. Any CSR initiative must demonstrate it actually makes a positive difference for stakeholders. If a CSR initiative claims to help protect indigenous rights, management should provide tangible evidence that it delivers on that promise. Corporations should report the outcomes produced through the CSR initiatives, even if those outcomes are less positive than anticipated. Ultimately, CSR initiatives need to be judged on their results, not their promises or appearances.

The third issue pertains to the importance of perceived justice in the CSR process. The term *perceived* is used because justice is perceptual rather than an absolute that is easy to measure. In essence, justice is about keeping the CSR process honest and transparent. Stakeholders should know how and why the corporation selected the CSR initiative and why other CSR concerns were not selected. Stakeholder engagement is a form of dialogue that offers significant contributions to perceptions of justice. Through engagement, stakeholders contribute to the decision-making process and understand how decisions are made. If that process is consistent and fair, stakeholders will perceive procedural justice surrounding the CSR process. Even formerly hostile stakeholders will accept decisions as just when they feel the decision-making process is fair (Jahansoozi, 2006, 2007). Moreover, how managers communicate with stakeholders during the engagement process helps to establish interactional justice. By treating stakeholders and their ideas with respect, management builds interactional justice. Perceptions of procedural and interactional justice make stakeholders more willing to accept and support rather than oppose decisions and the CSR initiatives born of those decisions.

Responsibility for CSR Initiatives

Who in a corporation is responsible for CSR initiatives? The short answer is *everyone* in the corporation. But effective CSR must begin at the top. Senior management must provide the leadership on CSR to prove its legitimacy and establish its importance to the corporation's strategy (Carter & Jennings, 2004). Without overt commitment from its leaders, a corporation's CSR efforts are unlikely to succeed. Top management becomes role models for CSR that others in the company emulate. With management buy-in, CSR is embraced as part of the core value system that influences the corporate culture (Mamic, 2005). Throughout this book, we have provided examples of companies that were born with CSR as part of their DNA. In those cases, CSR is viewed as a natural fit with the corporations.

Their worldviews are shaped by CSR. However, just as corporations learn, adapt, and develop new business-related competencies, corporations can adopt a CSR orientation and embrace values and practices consistent with a CSR orientation.

Along the same lines, the corporation must be willing to devote resources to CSR. Simply announcing that a company will undertake a CSR initiative is not enough to support a move toward a CSR orientation. The commitment needs to be more visible and tangible. Committing financial resources signals a determination to follow through on the announcement. To echo an earlier point, effective CSR is not a simple Band-Aid to be slapped on the corporation. Instead, CSR must be part of what a corporation does for CSR initiatives to be effective. This integration of CSR into business operations also makes financial sense and may appease opponents who contend that CSR initiatives drain resources. This is consistent with our strategic orientation to CSR.

But turf battles over the CSR process can develop, especially over communication responsibilities. The potential for conflict is rooted in resources and power. As CSR increases in importance and visibility, the units attached to CSR become more important, powerful, and resource attractive. When the issue of CSR was first emerging and struggling to gain traction in most corporations, departments considered it more of a burden than an asset. Almost by default, the public relations departments in many corporations oversaw CSR communication. CSR communication concentrates on external and internal communication to a variety of stakeholders; thus it was viewed as consistent with other public relations responsibilities. Unquestionably, it is important to spread the word about CSR initiatives. However, as we have described in this book, the stakeholder engagement process is central to effective CSR programs. This stakeholder orientation supports public relations' involvement in the overall CSR process. But we see a shift as marketing and other departments seek to claim CSR communication as their own. Some argue that CSR is "too important" to leave to public relations because the taint stemming from the association with public relations functions can undermine a corporation's CSR credibility (see Coombs & Holladay, 2010, for a discussion of this argument). Obviously those positions are debatable. Our point is that the appropriate "home" of CSR communication is a contentious issue and managers should prepare for turf disputes.

One viable solution to conflicts surrounding CSR communication is integrated communication. Some people talk about integrated marketing communication (IMC), but that orientation privileges the customer. We are using the term *integrated communication* to retain the focus on a variety of stakeholders, but the principles are similar. Integrated communication seeks consistency in messaging between the various communication tools and media used to reach stakeholders. The myriad communication functions in the corporation, primarily public relations and marketing, share information and coordinate their communication efforts (Harris, 1997). If CSR is to be the responsibility of everyone in the corporation, all communication units should be involved in CSR communication, as should all employees. The key is to find some way to coordinate the CSR communication to avoid contradictory messages and waste (e.g., messages overlapping in the same media).

Limitations from Industry, Culture, and Law

It is important to realize that the industries, cultures, and legal systems within which corporations operate can shape CSR. Industries differ in terms of their impacts on society and structures. The extraction industry and apparel and footwear industries face different CSR issues. While both can share concerns with worker safety and treatment, extraction faces significant environmental issues such as the amount and hazardous nature of byproducts from the process. It is estimated that 20 tons of often dangerous waste is created to produce just one gold ring (No Dirty Gold, n.d.). The diamond industry wrestles with issues related to "conflict diamonds," where funds from the sale of diamonds are used to fuel wars. The apparel and footwear industry is characterized by vast supply chains that have complex production networks and many layers of subcontractors. The complicated supply chain makes it difficult to monitor and to enforce codes of conduct designed to protect workers such as child labor bans, limits on working hours, and the safety of working conditions (Park-Poap & Rees, 2010).

Industry Standards

One source of information for guidance on CSR programs would be industry standards. Industries frequently develop their own standards for what is acceptable and unacceptable in the industry. Corporations should consider what CSR practices are common and practical within their industry. Managers can begin to think in terms of CSR due diligence. The concept of *due diligence* includes applying a certain standard of care as well as the more common definition of investigation before signing a contract. We can think of CSR due diligence as meeting certain standards of behavior. A corporation has met its industrial CSR due diligence by enacting CSR initiatives common in the industry. While these standards are voluntary, they can have a dampening effect on CSR. Individual companies within the industry may decide that the industry standards are "good enough" and do little to surpass them (Neef, 2004; Park-Poap & Rees, 2010). For instance, industry peers have a significant impact on corporate practices concerning environmental issues (Buysse & Verbeke, 2003).

Due diligence for CSR is becoming a topic of increasing interest. The UN holds that corporate responsibility includes due diligence to not infringe on the rights of others – what has been termed *human rights due diligence*. Human rights due diligence contains four elements: (1) development of a human rights policy statement, (2) periodic assessment of actual and potential human rights impacts of corporate activities and relationships, (3) integrating commitments and assessments into internal systems, and (4) tracking and reporting human rights performance. What constitutes human rights due diligence is a mixture of CSR-limiting factors including international law, local law, and societal expectations. In the end, human rights due diligence should result in a set of "best practices" that establishes expectations for compliance with these human rights concerns. Human rights due diligence becomes the process of investigating how well a corporation is meeting the best practices of protecting human rights. The challenge for CSR due diligence is to locate the best practices and standards for the various CSR concerns they encounter.

The Culture and Socioeconomic Context

A discussion of culture and CSR inevitably leads to comparing CSR expectations and practices in various countries. The argument is that CSR differences between countries are due in part to cultural factors. Of course, socioeconomic factors play a role as well. Culture and socioeconomic factors shape *which* CSR concerns are addressed in particular countries and *how* they are addressed. Some examples will illustrate these differences.

In Europe, the dominant CSR concerns vary from country to country (Doh & Guay, 2006). For example, one research study reports the dominant CSR concerns by country: Austria focuses on eco-efficiency and sustainable consumption; Belgium, on fair trade, nondiscrimination, and transparency; Czech Republic, on the environment and philanthropy; Germany, on ecological issues; the Netherlands, on water and climate change, biodiversity, and sustainable building; Italy, on climate change and safety in the workplace; Norway, on respect for human rights, environmental concerns, and combating corruption; Poland, on eco-efficiency and sustainable development; Spain, on transparency, and diversity management; and Sweden, on human rights and climate change (CSR Europe, 2009). Clearly, beliefs about the importance of various CSR issues are not easily condensable to a commonly shared set of concerns.

Recent research also has begun to explore the differences between CSR in developed and developing countries (e.g., Visser, 2008). While a Western concept, CSR does translate into many cultures. Developing countries frequently have a strong cultural tradition of philanthropy, concern for community, and business ethics embedded in their indigenous cultures. In Latin America, for example, there is a strong value placed on community self-help. In Asia, Buddhist tradition is a natural fit with CSR. In general, philanthropy dominates CSR in developing countries. In addition to culture, sociopolitical factors promote philanthropy. Corporations use financial contributions to address important local concerns such as health, education, and the environment. CSR concerns include addressing HIV/AIDS and poverty alleviation. Such CSR concerns can be viewed as an investment for the corporation because a strong community benefits the corporation located in that community (Visser, 2008).

Many developing countries have governments that are corrupt, weak, or underfunded. Whatever the reason, gaps exist in social services. Corporate CSR can become an alternative to government-provided social services (Blowfield & Frynas, 2005). Corporations assume more responsibility for housing, roads, utilities, education, and health care. Corporate CSR can be seen as part of the effort to support sociopolitical reform in a country (De Oliveira, 2006). However, we must recognize the counterpoint that turning to corporations to handle critical social concerns in developing countries is not enough. The CSR efforts amount to a number of bandages that create a piecemeal response to "problems" rather than a workable solution to "issues." Real solutions will be found through a mix of CSR, governmental, and international efforts.

Given our commitment to stakeholders in the CSR process, stakeholder activism is an important cultural variable to consider. Stakeholder activism can be a driver of CSR even in developing countries (Visser, 2008). Sriramesh and Vercic (2003) identified activism as a key infrastructure ingredient that influences international public relations. Activism is a reflection of their two other infrastructure ingredients, political system and level of development. Only pluralistic political systems tolerate activism, while people in developing nations do not view activism as a pressing concern. Activism exists in more oppressive regimes, but the risks to activists are very high. Private voluntary organizations (PVOs) can provide the lead in activism when the general populace is less interested in the CSR issue than basic survival issues. Activism in developing countries often is powered by international PVOs (Visser, 2008). Still, activism is of a different nature when it is driven by "outsiders." Sriramesh and Vercic's (2003) observations about activism have implications for CSR. CSR is intricately linked to activism. In part, CSR is a function of stakeholders becoming activists and pressing corporations for change. By demanding CSR and backing those demands with actions, stakeholders provide one mechanism for fostering CSR.

Activism is in part a function of culture (Katz, Swanson, & Nelson, 2001; Sriramesh & Vercic, 2003). Katz et al. (2001) used Hofstede's (1980) four cultural dimensions to identify the potential for various types of activism (consumer, environmental, employee, and community). Hofstede's (1980) original four cultural dimensions are (1) power distance, the degree to which those with less power accept the unequal distribution of power; (2) individualism, the degree to which people are interdependent in groups (collectivistic) or independent as individuals (individualistic); (3) masculinity, the degree to which aggression and traditional gender roles (masculinity) are valued over caring and less traditional gender roles (femininity); and (4) uncertainty avoidance, the degree to which people are willing to accept uncertainty and ambiguity.

Katz et al. (2001) argued that across all forms of activism, low power distance and low masculinity help to promote activism. People must question power issues with activism (low power distance), and most activist issues concern what may be considered "feminine" issues, especially in relation to CSR. Low uncertainty avoidance is best for all but environmental activism because activism generally creates uncertainty. Environmental activism, however, generally seeks to reduce risk, thus making high uncertainty avoidance a benefit. High individualism promotes consumer and employee activism as both are extensions of self-expression. Low individualism is best for environmental and community activism because these two forms of activism have strong collectivistic overtones because they focus on societal benefits. Box 8.1 summarizes Katz et al.'s (2001) position on cultural dimensions and activism.

There are implications in the work of Katz et al. (2001) for CSR because agitating for CSR can involve consumer activism, employee activism, environmental activism, community activism, or some mix thereof. These four types of activism are related to common social concerns found in CSR

Box 8.1 Culture and Activism

Type of Activism	*Power Distance*	*Uncertainty Avoidance*	*Individualism*	*Masculinity*
Consumer	Low	Low	High	Low
Environmental	Low	High	Low	Low
Community	Low	Low	Low	Low
Employee	Low	Low	High	Low

initiatives. Variations in cultural dimensions and activism can help to explain some of the differences found between CSR practices in various countries. Managers should expect greater pressure for CSR from native stakeholders when the national culture reflects a low power distance and is feminine, and when uncertainty avoidance is low. However, in our world, stakeholders represent a mix of cultures. In addition, national culture can vary throughout different regions of a country. Even if a specific culture does not have high standards for CSR and is unlikely to press for CSR, this does not mean a corporation can be lax in its CSR efforts. Noticeable disparities in CSR practices will bring charges of exploitation, such as those associated with the Bhopal tragedy discussed at the beginning of chapter 1.

The Legal Context

Many countries adopt laws or regulations that shape the conceptualizations and the practice of CSR. Some proponents of CSR feel that regulation is a positive step. The belief is that governments need to be an active part of developing CSR. At the end of 2008, Denmark enacted a law requiring 1,100 of its largest businesses, listed companies, and state-owned limited companies to include specific CSR information in their annual reports. The law does not mandate CSR in general or specific CSR initiatives; it only requires reporting by certain types of corporations. Although Danish corporations had been active in CSR, the government felt there was a lack of systematic CSR reporting by these corporations. By mandating the reporting of particular types of information, the government was insuring that the socially responsible corporations would receive the recognition they deserve and that stakeholders would have consistent information about CSR activities. The law was framed as a benefit to the vast majority of Danish corporations already engaged in CSR (Reporting, 2009).

In the United Kingdom, the Companies Act of 2006 is directly linked to CSR because directors were told their efforts to promote the success of the company must include a regard for community and environmental issues (Corporate, 2007). These are but two examples of the myriad of laws and regulations globally that touch on CSR directly or indirectly (Musikanski, n.d.). In general, Europe has stronger legal frameworks relevant to CSR than the United States (Matten & Moon, 2004).

Beyond Limitations

Industry standards, laws, and culture can be used to establish "good enough" standards for behavior. These standards can become limitations when they serve as the only targets for responsible behavior. But corporations can choose to exceed those standards. Corporations can innovate by pioneering new ground for CSR in an industry. Corporations can use the industry standards, cultural standards, and legal standards as a foundation and seek to raise expectations (Arnold & Hartman, 2004). Research suggests that raising expectations serves to alter the norms of what is "good enough." In time, these positive deviations by innovative corporations serve to elevate the standards for all companies in the industry (Park-Poap & Rees, 2010). Corporations should not be satisfied with simply meeting standards; they should devise ways to improve CSR standards if they are to maximize corporate benefits from CSR.

Although merely meeting industry standards or legal requirements may prevent charges of corporate irresponsibility, compliance with standards does little to generate the benefits associated with effective CSR. There is strategic value in raising expectations and behaviors. By positively deviating from the limitations of standards, a corporation can establish itself as a leader in CSR and differentiate itself from the competition. Given the voluntary aspect of CSR, simply meeting legal requirements does little to position a corporation as socially responsible. Meeting voluntary standards associated with the industry or culture is a step in the right direction, and exceeding voluntary standards serves as even stronger evidence of a corporation's sincere commitment to CSR.

Parting Thoughts

Throughout this book, we have resisted the temptation to provide a simple checklist of actions to be taken to implement an effective CSR initiative. To do so would be an oversimplification of a highly complex process that must be adapted to each company and the context in which it operates. An effective CSR initiative is one that benefits stakeholders and the corporation implementing it. The initiative should make "good business sense" because it reflects the corporation's fundamental business mission, processes, and values. Moreover, it should reflect concern with the web of stakeholder relationships in which it is embedded.

CSR is a complex process that is unique in each corporation that undertakes it. Simply prescribing a sequence of specific actions would be misleading and ultimately counterproductive to managers interested in creating effective CSR initiatives. We have outlined a communication-centered way of thinking about a corporation's potential relationships with CSR and with stakeholders. The CSR Process Model is designed to guide managers through a logical series of communication-based actions that acknowledges the importance of stakeholder engagement. Creating a meaningful dialogue and active partnership with stakeholders is not an easy undertaking. But committing to a process of stakeholder engagement is consistent with a CSR orientation in general. Managers begin with trying to determine if undertaking a CSR initiative is even a viable option for their corporation and stakeholders. Once the corporation has committed to pursue some form of CSR, a series of decisions must be made to create the CSR initiatives that are a good fit for that corporation and its stakeholders. We articulated the CSR process as a roadmap for the series of issues that managers, along with the corporation's stakeholders, must address on the path to an effective CSR initiative. We have identified the key issues that impact the CSR process and require managerial attention. This includes providing a series of questions that managers must ask and answer when developing a CSR initiative. Many of the questions are challenging – but so is the process of developing, implementing, and evaluating CSR initiatives.

We are under no delusions that the pursuit of CSR will create a utopian world. It is far too easy to find examples of CSR-washing. Some managers seek to leverage the benefits of CSR without committing to CSR by actually trying to improve society. It is easy for CSR to be "All talk and no show" or, as the British might say, "All mouth and no trousers." CSR communication risks becoming the providence of blowhards hyping the smallest action as saving the world. But if you look closely at current CSR initiatives, you will find many corporations and stakeholders working in concert to make at least some part of society better. CSR actions are helping to reduce child labor and poverty, improve human rights, pursue social justice, and help people live healthier lives. CSR is what we choose to make it. We hope this book can help provide a useful perspective and guidance on developing a workable process for those committed to bringing CSR initiatives to fruition in a meaningful way.

References

AccountAbility. (2008). AA1000 Assurance Standard. Retrieved March 16, 2011, from http://www.accountability.org/standards/aa1000as/index.html

Adidas. (2007). Corporate responsibility report. Retrieved March 31, 2011, from http://www.adidas-group.com/en/SER2007/pdf/adidas_SER2007_online.pdf

Alsop, R.J. (2004). *The 18 immutable laws of corporate reputation: Creating, protecting, and repairing your most valuable asset.* New York: Free Press.

Amnesty. (2009, October 16). Bhopal: End 25 years of injustice. Retrieved November 30, 2009, from http://www.amnesty.org/en/news-and-updates/bhopal-end-25-years-injustice-20091030

Armstrong World Industries. (2010). Connections: FloorScore. Retrieved March 22, 2011, from http://www.armstrong.com/corporate/connections.html#floor-score

Arnold, D.G., & Hartman, L.P. (2004, August). Beyond sweatshops: Positive deviancy and global labor practices. Paper presented at the annual meeting of the Society for Business Ethics, New Orleans, LA. Retrieved February 18, 2010, from http://www.positivedeviance.org/pdf/research/ArnoldHartmanPositiveDeviance[1].pdf

Bailly, O., Caudron, J.M., & Lambert, D. (2006). Sweden: Low prices, high social costs: The secrets of Ikea's closet. Retrieved August 28, 2010, from http://www.corpwatch.org/article.php?id=14272

Barilla. (2008). 2008 sustainability report. Retrieved March 31, 2011, from http://barillagroup.com/saveas/corporate/en/home/responsabilita/modello-di-sostenibilita/sidebar/01/items_files/file/Sustainability_Report_2008.pdf

Bartlett, C., & Ghoshal, S. (1989). *Managing across borders: The transnational solution.* Boston: Harvard Business School Press.

Bedford, C. (2009, December 3). Remembering Bhopal: A quarter-century later, lessons from the world's deadliest agrichemical disaster. Retrieved December

Managing Corporate Social Responsibility: A Communication Approach, First Edition.
W. Timothy Coombs, Sherry J. Holladay.

10, 2009 from http://www.grist.org/article/2009-12-03-remembering-bhopal-a-quarter-century-later/

Berens, G., & van Riel, C.B.M. (2004). Corporate associations in the academic literature: Three main streams of thought in the reputation measurement literature. *Corporate Reputation Review*, *7*(2), 161–178.

Bhattacharya, C.B., & Sen, S. (2004). Doing better at doing good: When, why, and how consumers respond to corporate social initiatives. *California Management Review*, *47*(1), 9–24.

Blowfield, M. (2007). Reasons to be cheerful? What we know about CSR's impact. *Third World Quarterly*, *28*, 683–695.

Blowfield, M., & Frynas, J.G. (2005). Setting new agendas: Critical perspectives on corporate social responsibility in the developing world. *International Affairs*, *81*(3), 499–513.

Bowen, S. (2005a). Ethics of public relations. In R.L. Heath (Ed.), *Encyclopedia of public relations* (Vol. 1, pp. 294–297). Thousand Oaks, CA: Sage.

Bowen, S. (2005b). Moral philosophy. In R.L. Heath (Ed.), *Encyclopedia of public relations* (Vol. 2, pp. 542–545). Thousand Oaks, CA: Sage.

Boyd, D.M., & Ellison, N.B. (2007). Social network sites: Definition, history, and scholarship. *Journal of Computer-Mediated Communication*, *13*(1), article 11. Retrieved March 16, 2011, from http://jcmc.indiana.edu/vol13/issue1/boyd.ellison.html

Brownlie, D. (1994). Organising for environmental scanning: Orthodoxies and reformations. *Journal of Marketing Management*, *10*, 703–723.

Bruno, K. (2000, December 14). BP: Beyond petroleum or beyond preposterous? Retrieved July 19, 2010, from http://www.corpwatch.org/article.php?id=219

Bruno, K., & Karliner, J. (2000, September). Corporate partnerships at the United Nations. Retrieved March 23, 2010, from http://www.corpwatch.org/article.php?id=996

Buchanan, D., & Dawson, P. (2007). Discourse and audience: Organizational change as multistory process. *Journal of Management Studies*, *44*(5), 669–686.

Bullert, B.J. (2000). Progressive public relations, sweatshops, and the net. *Political Communication*, *17*, 403–407.

Bullock, R.J., & Batten, D. (1985). It's just a phase we're going through: A review and synthesis of OD phase analysis. *Group and Organization Studies*, *10*, 383–412.

Buysse, K., & Verbeke, A. (2003). Proactive environmental strategies: A stakeholder management perspective. *Strategic Management Journal*, *24*(5), 453–470.

Cargill. (2009). Feeding America. Retrieved March 16, 2011, from http://www.cargill.com/connections/hunger-relief/index.jsp

Carmeli, A. (2004). The link between organizational elements, perceived external prestige and performance. *Corporate Reputation Review*, *6*, 314–331.

Carroll, A.B. (1979). A three-dimensional conceptual model of corporate performance. *Academy of Management Review*, *4*(4), 497–505.

Carroll, A.B. (1991, July–August). The pyramid of corporate social responsibility: Towards the moral management of organizational stakeholders. *Business Horizons*, 39–48.

Carter, C.R., & Jennings, M. (2004). The role of purchasing in corporate social responsibility: A structural equation analysis. *Journal of Business Logistics, 25*(1), 145–186.

Carty, V. (2002). Technology and counter-hegemonic movements: The case of Nike Corporation. *Social Movements, 1*(2), 129–146.

Colquitt, J.A. (2001). On the dimensionality of organizational justice: A construct validation of a measure. *Journal of Applied Psychology, 86*, 386–400.

Colquitt, J.A., Greenberg, J., & Zapata-Phelan, C.P. (2005). What is organizational justice? A historical overview of the Weld. In J. Greenberg & J.A. Colquitt (Eds.), *Handbook of organizational justice* (pp. 3–56). Mahwah, NJ: Lawrence Erlbaum.

Coombs, W.T. (2005). Objectives. In R.L. Heath (Ed.), *Encyclopedia of public relations* (Vol. 2, pp. 583–584). Thousand Oaks, CA: Sage.

Coombs, W.T. (2007). *Ongoing crisis communication: Planning, managing, and responding* (2nd ed.). Los Angeles, CA: Sage.

Coombs, W.T. (2010). Sustainability: A new and complex "challenge" for crisis managers. *International Journal of Sustainable Strategic Management*, 2, 4–16.

Coombs, W.T., & Holladay, S.J. (2007a). Consumer empowerment through the web: How internet contagions can increase stakeholder power. In S.C. Duhe (Ed.), *New media and public relations* (pp. 175–188). New York: Peter Lang.

Coombs, W.T., & Holladay, S.J. (2007b). *It's not just PR: Public relations in society*. Oxford: Wiley-Blackwell.

Coombs, W.T., & Holladay, S.J. (2009a). Cooperation, co-optation or capitulation: Factors shaping activist-corporate partnerships. *Ethical Space: The International Journal of Communication Ethics*, 6(2), 23–29.

Coombs, W.T., & Holladay, S.J. (2009b). Corporate social responsibility: Missed opportunity for institutionalizing communication practice? *International Journal of Strategic Communication*, *3*(2), 93–101.

Coombs W.T., & Holladay, S.J. (2010). *Public relations strategy and application: Managing influence*. Oxford: Wiley-Blackwell.

Co-operative Financial Services. (2006). Ethical banking. Retrieved March 16, 2011, from http://www.goodwithmoney.co.uk/ethical-banking/

Co-operative Financial Services. (n.d.). Why we have ethical policies. Retrieved March 16, 2011, from http://www.goodwithmoney.co.uk/why-do-we-need-ethical-policies/

Corporate social responsibility and the combined code on corporate covernance. (2007). Retrieved June 28, 2010, from http://www.out-law.com/page-8221

Covello, V. T. (2003). Message mapping, risk and crisis communication. Retrieved March 28, 2010, from http://dmh.mo.gov/ada/provider/sti/04/MessageMapping%20in%20High%20Risk%20Situations2.20.04.pdf

Crable, R.E., & Vibbert, S.L. (1985). Managing issues and influencing public policy. *Public Relations Review, 11*, 3–16.

CSR Europe. (2009). A guide to CSR in Europe: Country insights by CSR Europe's national partner organizations. Retrieved March 16, 2011, from http://www.csreurope.org/data/files/20091012_a_guide_to_csr_in_europe_final.pdf

CSRwire. (2010). About our corporate social responsibility professionals. March 16, 2011, from http://www.csrwire.com/about

Dawkins, J. (2004). Corporate responsibility: The communication challenge. *Journal of Communication Management*, *9*(2), 108–119.

Dean, D.H., & Biswas, A. (2001). Third-party organizational endorsement of products: An advertising cue affecting consumer prepurchase evaluation of goods and services. *Journal of Advertising*, *30*(4), 41–57.

De Oliveira, J.A.P. (2006). Corporate citizenship in Latin America: New challenges to business. *Journal of Corporate Citizenship*, *21*(2), 17–120.

Diamond, S. (1984, December 9). The pain of progress racks the third world. *New York Times*, sec. 4, p. 1.

Diamond, S. (1985, March, 21). Union Carbide's inquiry indicates errors led to India plant disaster. *New York Times*, sec. A, p. 1.

Doh, J.P., & Guay, T.R. (2006). Corporate social responsibility, public policy, and NGO activism in Europe and the United States: An institutional-stakeholders perspective. *Journal of Management Studies*, *43*, 47–73.

Dowling, G. (2002). *Creating corporate reputations: Identity, image, and performance*. New York: Oxford University Press.

E-Fluentials. (2010). Retrieved January 22, 2010, from http://www.burson-marsteller.com/Innovation_and_insights/E-Fluentials/Pages/default.aspx

Ellen, P.S., Webb, D.J., & Mohr, L.A. (2006). Building corporate associations: Consumer attributions for corporate socially responsible programs. *Journal of the Academy of Marketing Science*, *34*(2), 147–157.

Environmental Defense Fund. (1991). McDonald's Corporation–Environmental Defense waste reduction task force. Retrieved March 16, 2011, from http://www.edf.org/documents/927_McDonaldsfinalreport.htm

European Commission. (2010). Corporate social responsibility. Retrieved February 20, 2010, from http://ec.europa.eu/enterprise/policies/sustainable-business/corporate-social-responsibility/index_en.htm

Fediuk, T.A., Coombs, W.T., & Botero, I.C. (2010). Exploring crisis from a receiver perspective: Understanding stakeholder reactions during crisis events. In W.T. Coombs & S.J. Holladay (Eds.), *The handbook of crisis communication* (pp. 635–656). Oxford: Wiley-Blackwell.

Fisher, A. (2007, March 19). How to get a great reputation. *Fortune*, *155*(5), 88–94.

Fisher, W.R. (1987). *Human communication as a narration: Toward a philosophy of reason, value, and action*. Columbia: University of South Carolina Press.

Folger, R., & Cropanzano, R. (1998). *Organizational justice and human resource management*. Thousand Oaks, CA: Sage.

Fombrun, C.J. (2005). Building corporate reputation through CSR initiatives: Evolving standards. *Corporate Reputation Review*, *8*(1), 7–11.

Fombrun, C.J., & van Riel, C.B.M. (2004). *Fame and fortune: How successful companies build winning reputations*. New York: Prentice Hall Financial Times.

Forest Stewardship Council. (n.d.). Overview of the FSC principles and criteria. Retrieved March 6, 2011, from http://www.fsc.org/pc.html

Freeman, E. (1984). *Strategic management: A stakeholder approach*. Boston: Pitman.

Friedman, J. (2008, April 23). *The new PR*. Retrieved January 1, 2009, from http://www.sbnow.org/doc/the%20new%20pr.pdf

Friedman, M. (1962). *Capitalism and freedom*. Chicago: University of Chicago Press.

Friedman. M. (1970, September 13). The responsibility of business is to increase its profits. *New York Times Magazine*. Retrieved March 15, 2010, from http://www.colorado.edu/studentgroups/libertarians/issues/friedman-soc-resp-business.html

Gap Inc. (2007, October 28). Gap Inc. issues statement on media reports on child labor. Retrieved March 16, 2011, from http://www.gapinc.com/public/Media/Press_Releases/med_pr_vendorlabor102807.shtml

Gladwell, M. (2002). *The tipping point: How little things can make a big difference*. New York: Little, Brown.

Global March against Child Labor. (2007, November 14). Gap addresses child labor abuses. Retrieved March 16, 2011, from http://www.globalmarch.org/gap/other_statements_across_the_world.php

Global Reporting Initiative. (2006). RG: Sustainability reporting guidelines. Retrieved March 15, 2010, from http://www.globalreporting.org/NR/rdonlyres/ED9E9B36-AB54-4DE1-BFF2-5F735235CA44/0/G3_GuidelinesENU.pdf

Greenberg, J. (1990). Organizational justice: Yesterday, today, and tomorrow. *Journal of Management*, *16*, 399–432.

Greenberg, J., & Colquitt, J.A. (Eds). (2005). *Handbook of organizational justice: Fundamental questions about fairness in the workplace*. Mahwah, NJ: Lawrence Erlbaum.

GreenBiz.com. (2009, December 4). Coca-Cola puts HFC vending machines on ice, full phaseout set for 2015. Retrieved March 16, 2011, from http://www.greenbiz.com/news/2009/12/04/coca-cola-puts-hfc-vending-machines-ice-full-phase-out-set-2015

Greenpeace. (2009a, October 21). Apple first to eliminate toxic PVC. Retrieved March 16, 2011, from http://weblog.greenpeace.org/makingwaves/archives/2009/10/apple_first_to_eliminate_toxic.html

Greenpeace. (2009b). Victory for the boreal forest! Kimberly-Clark announces new paper policy. Retrieved March 16, 2011, from http://www.greenpeace.org/international/news/victory-for-the-boreal-forest

Greenpeace. (2010). How the companies line up. Retrieved April 14, 2010, from http://www.greenpeace.org/international/campaigns/toxics/electronics/how-the-companies-line-up

Greenpeace. (n.d.). Greenpeace greenwashing criteria. Retrieved March 16, 2011, from http://stopgreenwash.org/criteria

Harris, T.L. (1997). Integrated marketing public relations. In C.L. Caywood (Ed.), *The handbook of strategic public relations and integrated communications* (pp. 90–105). New York: McGraw-Hill.

Hatch, M.J., & Schultz, M. (2000). Scaling the tower of Babel: Relational differences between identity, image, and culture in organizations. In M. Schultz, M.J.

Hatch, & M.H. Larsen (Eds.), *The expressive organization: Linking identity, reputation, and the corporate brand* (pp. 11–35). New York: Oxford University Press.

Heath, R.L. (1990). Corporate issues management: Theoretical underpinnings and research foundations. In L.A. Grunig & J.E. Grunig (Eds.), *Public relations research annual* (Vol. 2, pp. 29–66). Hillsdale, NJ: Lawrence Erlbaum.

Heath, R.L. (1994). *Management of corporate communication: From interpersonal contacts to external affairs*. Hillsdale, NJ: Lawrence Erlbaum.

Heath, R.L., & Coombs, W.T. (2006). *Today's public relations: An introduction*. Thousand Oaks, CA: Sage.

Heinz. (2009). Stakeholder engagement. Retrieved April 3, 2010, from http://www.heinz.com/CSR2009/about/stakeholder_engagement.aspx

Hess, D. (2008). The three pillars of corporate social reporting as new governance regulation: Disclosure, dialogue and development. *Business Ethics Quarterly, 18*(4), 447–482.

Hofstede, G. (1980). *Culture's consequences*. London: Sage.

Huitt, W., & Hummel, J. (1997). An introduction to operant (instrumental) conditioning. *Educational Psychology Interactive*. Valdosta, GA: Valdosta State University. Retrieved November 30, 2009, from http://www.edpsycinteractive.org/topics/behsys/operant.html

Husted, B.W., & Salazar, J.d.J. (2006). Taking Friedman seriously: Maximizing profits and social performance. *Journal of Management Studies*, *43*, 75–91.

IHS. (2008). ISAE 3000: International Standard on Assurance Engagements. Retrieved March 16, 2011, from http://www.ess-home.com/regs/isae-3000.aspx

IKEA. (2010a). Forestry and wood. Retrieved March 16, 2011, from http://www.ikea.com/ms/en_US/about_ikea/our_responsibility/forestry_and_wood/index.html

IKEA. (2010b). Preventing child labor. Retrieved March 16, 2011, from http://www.ikea.com/ms/en_US/about_ikea/our_responsibility/working_conditions/preventing_child_labour.html

ING. (2010). ING in society: Corporate responsibility report 2009. Retrieved March 16, 2011, from http://www.ingforsomethingbetter.com/files/pdf_downloads/ING_CR_Report_2009.pdf

International Institute for Sustainable Development. (2004). ISO social responsibility standardization: An outline of the issues. Retrieved April 5, 2010, from http://www.iisd.org/pdf/2004/standards_iso_srs.pdf

International Organization for Standardization (ISO). (2009). Guidance on social responsibility. Retrieved March 16, 2011, from http://www.unit.org.uy/misc/responsabilidadsocial/ISO_DIS_26000.pdf

International Organization for Standardization (ISO). (2010a). Background. Retrieved March 16, 2011, from http://isotc.iso.org/livelink/livelink/fetch/2000/2122/830949/3934883/3935096/07_gen_info/timefr.html

International Organization for Standardization (ISO). (2010b). Social responsibility. Retrieved April 5, 2010, from http://isotc.iso.org/livelink/livelink/fetch/2000/2122/830949/3934883/3935096/home.html?nodeid=4451259&vernum=0

ISO social responsibility standardization: An outline of the issues. (2004, May). Retrieved January 7, 2010, from http://www.iisd.org/pdf/2004/standards_iso_srs.pdf

Jahansoozi, J. (2006). Organization-stakeholder relationships: Exploring trust and transparency. *Journal of Management Development*, *25*, 942–955.

Jahansoozi, J. (2007). Organization-public relationships: An exploration of the Sundre Petroleum Operators Group. *Public Relations Review*, *33*, 398–406.

Jones, B.L., & Chase, W.H. (1979). Managing public policy issues. *Public Relations Review*, *5*(2), 3–23.

Katz, E., & Lazarsfeld, P. (1955). *Personal influence*. New York: Free Press.

Katz, J.P., Swanson, D.L., & Nelson, L.K. (2001). Culture-based expectations of corporate citizenship: A propositional framework and comparison of four cultures. *International Journal of Organizational Analysis*, *19*(2), 149–171.

Keller, E., and Berry, J. (2003). *The influentials*. New York: Free Press.

Kleercut. (2009, August 5). Kimberly-Clark and Greenpeace agree to historic measures to protect forests. Retrieved March 16, 2011, from http://www.kleercut.net/en/

Kotler, P., & Lee, N. (2005). *Corporate social responsibility: Doing the most good for your company and your cause*. Hoboken, NJ: John Wiley & Sons.

Kreps, G. (1991). *Organizational communication: Theory and practice* (2nd ed.). New York: Longman.

Kruckeberg, D. (1996). Transnational corporate ethical responsibilities. In H. Culbertson & N. Chen (Eds.), *International public relations: A comparative analysis* (pp. 81–92). Hillsdale, NJ: Lawrence Erlbaum.

Landman, A. (2008, June 12). Can shopping cure breast cancer? Pinkwashing. Retrieved March 3, 2010, from http://www.counterpunch.org/landman06122008.html

Learning Technology Center. (n.d.). Behavioral theory: Part 2: Operant conditioning. Retrieved March 16, 2011, from http://teachnet.edb.utexas.edu/~lynda_abbott/Behavioral2.html

Leon H. Sullivan Foundation. (n.d.). The Global Sullivan principles of social responsibility. Retrieved March 16, 2011, from http://www.thesullivanfoundation.org/about/global_sullivan_principles

Lerbinger, O. (1997). *The crisis manager: Facing risk and responsibility*. Mahwah, NJ: Lawrence Erlbaum.

L'Etang, J. (2006). Corporate responsibility and public relations ethics. In J. L'Etang & M. Pieczka (Eds.), *Public relations: Critical debates and contemporary practice* (pp. 405–422). Mahwah, NJ: Lawrence Erlbaum.

Levine, M.A. (2008). The benefits of corporate social responsibility. Retrieved January 18, 2010, from http://www.law.com/jsp/cc/PubArticleCC.jsp?id=1202423730339

Li, L. (2008). Starbucks green ideas: Consumers vote for an eco-friendly Starbucks. Retrieved March 16, 2011, from http://bub.blicio.us/starbucks-green-ideas-consumers-vote-for-an-eco-friendly-starbucks/

Maignan, I., & Ferrell, O.C. (2004). Corporate social responsibility and marketing: An integrative framework. *Journal of the Academy of Marketing Science*, *32*, 3–19.

Mamic, I. (2005). Managing global supply chain: The sports footwear, apparel and retail sectors. *Journal of Business Ethics*, *59*, 81–100.

Marks and Spencer. (2006, January 30). M&S launches new "Look behind the label" campaign and unveils plans to sell Fairtrade clothing. Retrieved March 16, 2011, from http://corporate.marksandspencer.com/investors/press_releases/30012006_mslaunchesnewlookbehindthelabelcampaignandunveilsplanstosellfairtradeclothing

Marks and Spencer. (2010). Plan A: Doing the right thing: About Plan A. Retrieved March 16, 2011, from http://plana.marksandspencer.com/about

Marlin, A., & Marlin, J.T. (2003). A brief history of social reporting. Retrieved March 16, 2011, from http://www.mallenbaker.net/csr/page.php?Story_ID=857

Marquez, A., & Fombrun, C.J. (2005). Measuring corporate social responsibility. *Corporate Reputation Review*, *7*, 304–308.

Matten, D., & Moon, J. (2004). "Implicit" and "explicit" CSR: A conceptual framework for understanding CSR in Europe. Retrieved June 25, 2010, from http://www.basisboekmvo.nl/files/implicit.pdf

McMillan, J.J. (2007). Why corporate social responsibility: Why now? How? In S. May, G. Cheney, & J. Roper (Eds.), *The debate over corporate social responsibility* (pp. 15–29). Oxford: Oxford University Press.

McWilliams, A., Siegel, D.S., & Wright, P.M. (2006). Corporate social responsibility: Strategic implications. *Journal of Management Studies*, *43*, 1–18.

Meijer, M.M. (2004). *Does success breed success? Effects of news and advertising on corporate reputation*. Amsterdam: Aksant Academic.

MerriamWebster.com. (n.d.). Noblesse oblige. Retrieved March 16, 2011, from http://www.merriamwebster.com/dictionary/noblesse+oblige

Miller, K. (2002). *Communication theories: Perspectives, processes, and contexts*. New York: McGraw-Hill.

MillerCoors. (2009, November 19). MillerCoors launches corporate responsibility web site. Retrieved March 16, 2011, from http://www.millercoors.com/news/press-releases/release/millercoors-launches-new-web-site.aspx

MillerCoors. (n.d.). Our commitment to volunteerism. Retrieved March 16, 2011, from http://www.greatbeergreatresponsibility.com/SocialResponsibility/Volunteerism.aspx

Miner, T. (2010, August 26). Sony Ericsson has mobile phone sustainability dialed. Retrieved August 27, 2010, from http://www.sustainablelifemedia.com/content/story/brands/sony_ericsson_mobile_phone_sustainability_dialed

Mitchell, R.K., Agle, R.A., & Wood, S.J. (1997). Toward a theory of stakeholder identification and salience: Defining the principle of who and what really counts. *Academy of Management Review*, *22*(4), 853–886.

Morsing, M., Schultz, M., & Nielsen, K.U. (2008). The catch 22 of communicating CSR. *Journal of Marketing Communications*, *14*(3), 97–111.

Motion, J., & Leitch, S. (2009). On Foucault: A toolbox for public relations. In O. Ihlen, B. van Ruler, & M. Fredriksson (Eds.), *Public relations and social theory: Key figures and concepts*. New York: Routledge.

Mucha, J. (2009, September 12). Dissecting a Facebook fan page. Retrieved July 29, 2010, from http://sproutinc.com/2009/09/dissecting-a-facebook-fan-page/

Muralidharan, R. (2004). A framework for designing strategy content controls. *International Journal of Productivity and Performance Management*, *53*(7), 590–601.

Musgrave Group. (2006). Independent assurance statement. Retrieved March 16, 2011, from http://www.musgrave.ie/sustainability/assurance_statement.html

Musikanski, L. (n.d). CSR and the triple bottom line: Tool for issuing a CSR report. Retrieved March 7, 2010, from http://www.zipcon.net/~laura/laws.htm

Neef, D. (2004). *The supply chain imperative: How to ensure ethical behavior in your global suppliers*. New York: American Management Association.

Nielsen, A., & Thomsen, C. (2007). Reporting CSR: What and how to say it? *Corporate Communications: An International Journal*, *12*(1), 25–40.

Nike. (2009, July 22). Nike, Inc. commits to helping halt Amazon deforestation. Retrieved August 2, 2009, from http://www.nikebiz.com/media/pr/2009/07/22_AmazonLeatherPolicy.html

No Dirty Gold. (n.d.). Why a campaign focused on gold? Retrieved March 16, 2011, from http://www.nodirtygold.org/about_us.cfm

Okada, N. (1986). The process of mass communication: A review of studies of the two-step flow of communication hypothesis. *Studies of Broadcasting*, *22*, 57–78.

O'Keefe, D.J. (2002). *Persuasion: Theory and research* (2nd ed.). Thousand Oaks, CA: Sage.

O'Rourke, D. (2005). Market movements: Nongovernmental strategies to influence global production and consumption. *Journal of Industrial Ecology*, *9*(1–2), 115–128.

O2. (2010). O2 launches UK's first eco mobile phone rating scheme. Retrieved August 27, 2010, from http://www.o2.co.uk/thinkbig

Park-Poap, H., & Rees, K. (2010). Stakeholder forces of socially responsible supply chain management orientation. *Journal of Business Ethics*, *92*, 305–322.

Pasternack, A. (2008, September 4). Coke's new green vending machines: "Like taking 218,000 cars off the road for a week." Retrieved February 18, 2010, from http://www.treehugger.com/files/2008/09/coca-cola-green-coolers-vending-machines-hfc-free.php

Patagonia. (2009a). Our history. Retrieved March 16, 2011, from http://www.patagonia.com/web/us/patagonia.go?assetid=3351&ln=79

Patagonia. (2009b). Our reason for being. Retrieved March 16, 2011, from http://www.patagonia.com/web/us/patagonia.go?slc=en_US&sct=US&assetid=2047

Patagonia. (2010). Our mission. Retrieved March 21, 2010, from http://www.onepercentfortheplanet.org/en/aboutus/mission.php

Patagonia. (n.d.). Corporate social responsibility. Retrieved March 16, 2011, from http://www.patagonia.com/web/us/patagonia.go?assetid=37492&ln=65

Pfau, M. (1992). The potential of inoculation in promoting resistance to the effectiveness of comparative advertising messages. *Communication Quarterly*, *40*(1), 26–44.

Pinkston, T.S., & Carroll, A.B. (1994). Corporate citizenship perspectives and foreign direct investment in the US. *Journal of Business Ethics*, *13*, 157–169.

Pomering, A., & Dolnicar, S. (2008). Assessing the prerequisite of successful CSR implementation: Are consumers aware of CSR initiatives? *Journal of Business Ethics*, *85*, 285–301.

Porter, M.E., & Kramer, M.R. (2006, December 1). Strategy and society: The link between competitive advantage and corporate social responsibility. *Harvard Business Review*, 78–92.

Prahalad, C.K., & Doz, Y. (1987) *The multinational mission*. New York: Free Press.

Prieto-Carron, M., Lund-Thomsen, P., Chan, A., Muro, A., & Bhushan, C. (2006). Critical perspectives on CSR and development: What we know, what we don't know, and what we need to know. *International Affairs*, *82*(5), 977–987.

Reinchart, J. (2003). A theoretical exploration of expectational gaps in the corporate issue construct. *Corporate Reputation Review*, *6*, 58–69.

Reporting on corporate social responsibility: An introduction for supervisory and executive boards. (2009). Retrieved June 27, 2010, from www.samfundsansvar.dk

Reuben, T. (2009, August 3). Why does PND use EWG's cosmetic database? Retrieved March 16, 2011, from http://www.purenaturaldiva.com/2009/08/why-does-pnd-use-ewgs-cosmetics-database/

Roddick, A. (1991). *Body and soul*. New York: Crown Trade.

Safko, L., & Brake, D. K. (2009). *The social media bible: Tactics, tools & strategies for business success*. Hoboken, NJ: John Wiley & Sons, Inc.

Scientific Certification Systems. (2010). FloorScore: Indoor air quality. Retrieved March 16, 2011, from http://www.scscertified.com/gbc/floorscore.php

Scott. P. (2008, October 9). CSR assurance: Growth industry. Retrieved March 16, 2011, from http://www.accountancyage.com/accountancyage/features/2227795/csr-assurance-growth-industry

Sen, S., & Bhattacharya, C.B. (2001). Does doing good always lead to doing better? Consumer reactions to corporate social responsibility. *Journal of Marketing Research*, *38*, 225–243.

Sen, S., Bhattacharya, C.B., & Korschun, D. (2006). The role of corporate social responsibility in strengthening multiple stakeholder relationships: A field experiment. *Journal of the Academy of Marketing Science*, *34*(2), 158–166.

Sephora. (n.d.). Naturally gorgeous. Retrieved February 25, 2010, from http://sephora.com/browse/article.jhtml?id=720901

Sethi, S.P. (1975). Dimensions of corporate social performance: An analytic framework. *California Management Review*, *17*, 58–64.

Sethi, S.P. (1977). *Advocacy advertising and large corporations: Social conflict, big business image, the news media, and public policy*. Lexington, MA: Heath.

Sethi, S.P. (1979). A conceptual framework for environmental analysis of social issues and evaluation of business response patterns. *Academy of Management Review*, *41*, 63–74.

Shabecoff, P. (1984, December 13). Officials tell a House hearing that plant in West Virginia is safe. *New York Times*, sec. A, p. 10.

Smeltzer, L.R. (1991). An analysis of strategies for announcing organization-wide change. *Group and Organization Studies*, *16*, 5–24.

Smith, N.C. (2003). Corporate social responsibility: Whether or how? *California Management Review*, *45*, 52–76.

Sriramesh, K., & Vercic, D. (2003). A theoretical framework for global public relations research and practice. In K. Sriramest & D. Vercic (Eds.), *The global public relations handbook* (pp. 1–19). Mahwah, NJ: Erlbaum.

Stacks, D. W. (2002). *Primer of public relations research*. New York: Guilford.

Starbucks. (2009a). Starbucks Shared Planet: Global Responsibility Report 2009. Retrieved March 31, 201s1, from http://assets.starbucks.com/assets/ssp-g-p-full-report.pdf

Starbucks. (2009b). Starbucks Shared Planet: Goals and progress 2009. Retrieved March 16, 2011, from http://www.starbucks.com/responsibility/learn-more/goals-and-progress

Starbucks. (2010a). My Starbucks Idea. Retrieved March 22, 2011, from http://mystarbucksidea.force.com

Starbucks. (2010b). My Starbucks Idea: FAQ's. Retrieved March 22, 2011, from http://mystarbucksidea.force.com/ideafaq

Stoker, K. (2005). Utilitarianism. In R.L. Heath (Ed.), *Encyclopedia of public relations* (Vol. 2, pp. 883–885). Thousand Oaks, CA: Sage.

StumbleUpon. (2011). About StumbleUpon. Retrieved March 22, 2011, from http://www.stumbleupon.com/aboutus/

SustainabilityForum.com. (n.d.). Welcome to SustainabilityForum.com! Retrieved March 16, 2011, from http://www.sustainabilityforum.com/page/about-us

Svoboda, S. (1995). Case A: McDonald's environmental strategy. Retrieved February 20, 2010, from http://www.umich.edu/~nppcpub/resources/compendia/CORPpdfs/CORPcaseA.pdf

Team Sweat. (2008. September 21). Short history of the fight against Nike's sweatshops. Retrieved March 16, 2011, from http://www.teamsweat.org/?p=74

Tench, R., Bowd, R., & Jones, B. (2007). Perceptions and perspectives: Corporate social responsibility and the media. *Journal of Communication Management*, *11*(4), 348–369.

Tennery, A. (2009, April 20). The four biggest enviro-scams: Green claims that make us see red. Retrieved February 25, 2010, from http://www.thebigmoney.com/articles/greenwash/2009/04/20/four-biggest-enviro-scams?page=full

Think before You Pink. (n.d.). [Postcards]. Retrieved March 16, 2011, from http://thinkbeforeyoupink.org/wp-content/uploads/2009/09/TBYPPostcard2.pdf

Thompson, C. (2008, February 1). Is the tipping point toast? *Fast Company*. Retrieved January 16, 2010, from http://www.fastcompany.com/magazine/122/is-the-tipping-point-toast.html?page=0%2C5

Thompson, J.K., & Smith, H. L. (1991, January). Social responsibility and small business: Suggestions for research. *Journal of Small Business Management*, 30–44.

Timmerman, C.E. (2003). Media selection during the implementation of planned organizational change: A predictive framework based on implementation approach and phase. *Management Communication Quarterly*, *16*(3), 301–340.

Trade Environmental Database. (1997). TED case studies: Bhopal disaster. Retrieved March 16, 2011, from http://www1.american.edu/TED/bhopal.htm

2Sustain. (2009, December 4). All Coca-Cola's new vending machines will be HFC-free by 2015. Retrieved March 16, 2011, from http://2sustain.com/2009/12/all-coca-cola%E2%80%99s-new-vending-machines-will-be-hfc-free-by-2015.html

UNICEF. (n.d.). IKEA social initiative. Retrieved March 16, 2011, from http://www.unicef.org/corporate_partners/index_25092.html

Visser, W. (2008). Corporate social responsibility in developing countries. In A. Crane, A. McWilliams, D. Matten, J. Moon, & D. Siegel (Eds.), *The Oxford handbook of corporate social responsibility* (pp. 473–479). Oxford: Oxford University Press.

Vodafone. (n.d.-a). Clear pricing. Retrieved March 16, 2011, from http://www.vodafone.com/content/index/about/sustainability/customers/earning_customertrust/clear_pricing.html

Vodafone. (n.d.-b). Dialogue: Privacy and mobiles. Retrieved March 16, 2011, from http://www.vodafone.com/start/responsibility/cr_dialogues/privacy_and_mobile.html

Vodafone. (n.d.-c). Dialogue: Stakeholder engagement. Retrieved March 16, 2011, from http://www.vodafone.com/start/responsibility/cr_dialogues/dialogue_1_-_stakeholder.html

Vodafone. (n.d.-d). Mobile theft. Retrieved March 16, 2011, from http://www.vodafone.com/content/index/about/sustainability/customers/earning_customertrust/mobile_theft.html

Vodafone. (n.d.-e). Sustainability. Retrieved March 16, 2011, from http://www.vodafone.com/start/responsibility.html

Vodafone. (n.d.-f). The Vodafone CR dialogues. Retrieved March 16, 2011, from http://www.globalchallengenetwork.com/PDF%20files/VF_CR_Dialogue_3_Economic_Empowerment.pdf

Vogel, D. (2005). *The market for virtue*. Washington, DC: Brookings Institution Press.

Waddock, S. (2007). Corporate citizenship: The dark-side paradox of success. In S. May, G. Cheney, & J. Roper (Eds.), *The debate over corporate social responsibility* (pp. 74–86). Oxford: Oxford University Press.

Wakefield, R.I. (2001). Effective public relations in the multinational organization. In R.L. Heath (Ed.), *Handbook of public relations* (pp. 639–647). Thousand Oaks, CA: Sage.

Wartick, S.L. (1992). The relationship between intense media exposure and change in corporate reputation. *Business & Society*, *31*, 33–42.

Wasilewski, N. (n.d.). The pursuit of transnational strategies. Retrieved November 10, 2009, from http://www.sba.muohio.edu/abas/2001/brussels/Wasilewski_TransnationalStrategies.pdf

Watts, D.J., & Peretti, J. (2007, May). Viral marketing for the real world. *Harvard Business Review*. Retrieved January 16, 2010, from http://www.fastcompany.com/magazine/122/is-the-tipping-point-toast.html?page=0%2C5

Werther, W.B., Jr., & Chandler, D. (2006). *Strategic corporate social responsibility: Stakeholders in a global environment*. Thousand Oaks, CA: Sage.

Werther, W.B., Jr., & Chandler, D. (2011). *Strategic corporate social responsibility: Stakeholders in a global environment* (2nd ed.). Thousand Oaks, CA: Sage.

WKBN.com. (2009, March 18). City of Warren, KFC and PETA discuss potholes. Retrieved March 16, 2011, from http://www.wkbn.com/mostpopular/story/City-of-Warren-KFC-and-PETA-Discuss-Potholes/THE6anUuhUGiBZmHUdiWYA.cspx

Index

activism: culture's effect, 159–61
alignment approach, 80–5
alignment process for CSR and reputation, 38, 80
apartheid, 1
Apple, 114
Armstrong World Industries:FloorScore, 112

Ben & Jerry's, 18, 37, 115
Bhopal, 2–3, 5, 26
bluewashing, 75–6
Body Shop, 37, 40
Bowen, Howard, 17
BP: Deepwater Horizon, 52, 57

Cargill: Feeding America, 42
certifying bodies:
  FairTrade, 18
  Forest Stewardship Council, 18, 19
  International Federation of Organic Agriculture Movement, 18
  International Social and Environmental Accreditation and Labeling, 18
challenge crisis, 76
Chouinard, Yvon, 39
Clorox, 114–15
Coca-Cola: HFCS, 81–2
communicating the CSR initiative:
  awareness, 111
  big seed, 126
  certification, 114–15
  communication channels, 116–20
  control, 117, 120
  corporate responsibility/sustainability report, 128–33
  cost, 112, 113, 115–16
  critical questions, 133–5
  CSR promotional communication dilemma, 110–11
  CSR promotional communication strategy, 128–33
  e-fluentials, 125
  employees as channels, 122–3
  external stakeholders as channels, 123
  influentials, 125
  Internet, 118
  message tone, 112
  partnerships (with activists), 115–16
  public relations, 115–16
  social media, 115–16, 117, 118–20, 123, 126–7, 128
  source, 115–6
  stakeholder engagement, 113–4, 123–4
  third-party endorsement direct, 114

Managing Corporate Social Responsibility: A Communication Approach, First Edition.
W. Timothy Coombs, Sherry J. Holladay.

third-party endorsement indirect, 114–15
tipping point, 125
transparency, 113–14
two-step flow, 124–5
uncontrolled channels, 117
Watts, Duncan, 125–6, 127
websites, 121–2
Companies Act, 161
contestable nature of CSR:
collaboration, 94–5
company competence, 93
differing stakeholder expectations, 90–2
empowerment, 94–6
involvement, 94–5
right amount of CSR, 98–9
stakeholder participation in decision making, 94–6
what constitutes CSR, 92–7
Co-operative Group/Bank, 96
corporate reputation, 13
corporate social performance, 19–20
corporate social responsibility (CSR):
benefits and costs, 9–14
benefits for corporation, 13–14, 30, 32
benefits for society, 14
complexity, 4
costs for corporation, 10–12
costs for society, 12–13
definition, 6–8
European Commission, 7
fit, 42
forms of CSR, 20–2
irresponsible corporate behaviour, 4
modern or historic, 16–20
perceived motives, 38–44
public scrutiny, 4
pyramid (Carroll), 20
reputation benefits, 35–8
should CSR be localized or globalized, 24–7
triple bottomline, 8
voluntary, 7
washing, 30, 163
where is CSR's home, 22–4
winning and sustaining support, 14–16
CSR challenges:
expose, 73–7
organic, 73, 76–7
villain, 73, 76–7
CSR Initiative (Creating):
balance costs, 94
contestable nature of CSR, 90
critical questions, 105–7
definition, 90
developing CSR objective, 101–3
message mapping, 101–2
outcome objectives, 103–5
process objectives, 102–3, 104, 105
stakeholder concerns, 94
stakeholder rating system, 93
strategic planning, 94
CSR issues:
align stakeholder and corporate concerns, 154
beyond limitations, 161–2
culture and socioeconomic limitations, 158–61
due diligence, 157–8
industry standards limitations, 157–8
legal limitations, 161
perceived justice, 155
responsibility for CSR concerns, 155–7
tangible gains for stakeholders, 154–5
CSR process as change management:
administrative change, 44
buy-in, 44–5
communication, 45
narrative fidelity, 46–7
narrative probability, 46
narratives, 45–7
phases of change, 44
CSR process model, 47–9, 80
CSR International, 117, 127
CSRwire.com, 120, 127

engagement:
informational justice, 97
interactional justice, 97
organizational justice, 96–7
procedural justice, 97

Engagementdb, 65, 67
evaluation and feedback:
  assurance, 141–2, 143–5
  communication audit, 148
  critical questions, 148–51
  evaluation, 138–46
  feedback, 146–48
  objectives, 138–9
  return on investment (ROI), 142, 145–6
  stakeholder engagement, 142, 145, 146–8

FairTrade, 37, 57, 103, 114–5, 140; *see also* certifying bodies
Forestry Stewardship Council, 114, 115; *see also* certifying bodies
formative research:
  alignment, 67, 80–5
  corporate concerns, 85
  critical questions, 85–7
  expectation gaps, 67, 69–77
  opportunity, 64
  perception gap, 69–70
  problem, 64
  reality gap, 70
  stakeholder expectations, 67
Freeman, R. Edward, 5
Friedman, Milton, 6, 10

GAP, 113
Global Exchange, 3
Global Reporting Index (GRI), 18, 59, 110, 129–30, 133
  stakeholder engagement, 59
  UN, 129, 130
Green Mountain Roasters, 37
Greenpeace:
  Green Freeze, 81–2
  Green My Apple, 114
  greenwashing, 74
  Kleercut, 93
  Nike, 53
greenwashing, 17, 74

Heinz, 65
Home Depot, 114

identification, 111
IKEA, 42, 70–3
integration-responsiveness grid, 24–5
Intel: CSR@Intel, 121
ISO 26000, 110, 129, 131–3
issues management, 53–4, 80

KFC, 76
Kimberly-Clark: Boreal Forest, 43
Kreps, Theodore, 17

Marks and Spencer:
  Plan A, 37, 57
  Look Behind the Label, 57
Mattel, 52
McDonald's, 37, 96
Methodists, 17
MillerCoors: GreatBeerGreatResponsibility.com, 121–2
mobile phone sustainability:
  Ecorating, 55–6
  O2, 55–6
  Sony Ericsson Elm, 55
My Starbucks Idea, 67–8

Nike, 3–4
  Amazon leather policy, 53
non-government organizations (NGOs), 3, 14, 76, 81

operant conditioning and stakeholder challenges:
  boycotts, 79
  buy-cotts, 79
  defined, 77
  negative punishment, 78, 79
  negative reinforcers, 78, 79
  positive punishment, 78, 79
  positive reinforcers, 78, 79
  punishment, 78–80
  reinforcers, 78

Patagonia, 37, 39–40
People for the Ethical Treatment of Animals (PETA), 76
pinkwashing, 74–5

power, 78
private voluntary organization (PVO), 159

Quakers, 17

Rain Forest Alliance, 115
RC2, 52
reputation:
  connection to CSR, 35–8, 111
  defined, 35
  Most Admired Companies, 35–6
  RepTrak, 35–6
Roddick, Anita, 31, 37
rule utilitarianism, 40

scanning and monitoring:
  critical questions, 60–1
  CSR scanning, 47–8, 54
  impact, 55
  likelihood, 55
  monitoring and CSR, 57–8
  monitoring defined, 53
  potential CSR concerns, 52
  prioritizing CSR concerns, 54–6
  scanning defined, 51–2
  stakeholder engagement, 58–60
Sephora: Naturally Sephora, 74
Sierra Club: Green Works, 114–15
social audit, 17–18
social media, 65–7, 99–100
social reporting (social accounting, social audit), 17–18
socially responsible investing, 17
stakeholder analysis/map, 64–6
stakeholder challenges and operant conditioning, 77–80
stakeholder empowerment, 95
stakeholder engagement, 58–60, 83
stakeholder panel, 59
stakeholder salience, 91–2
stakeholders:
  churn, 13, 56, 77, 79
  defined, 5
  expectations and CSR, 32, 41–3, 52, 57, 67, 69–77
  identification, 32–5
  stake, 5
  stakeseeker, 78
Starbucks, 67–9, 114, 120-1, 128, 130–1, 140
strategic CSR, 29–35, 49
Sullivan Principles, 1–2
Sustainability Forum.com, 117–20
Sweatshop, 3–4
Sweatshop Watch, 3

transparency, 113–14

Union Carbide, 2–3, 5
UN Global Compact, 75–6, 130

Vodafone:
  CR Dialogues, 82–3
  stakeholder engagement, 83–5
  website, 121